GLOBAL GREEN SHIFT

GLOBAL GREEN SHIFT

WHEN CERES MEETS GAIA

JOHN A. MATHEWS

ANTHEM PRESS

Anthem Press
An imprint of Wimbledon Publishing Company
www.anthempress.com

This edition first published in UK and USA 2017
by ANTHEM PRESS
75–76 Blackfriars Road, London SE1 8HA, UK
or PO Box 9779, London SW19 7ZG, UK
and
244 Madison Ave #116, New York, NY 10016, USA

© John A. Mathews 2017

British Library Cataloguing-in-Publication Data
A catalogue record for this book is available from the British Library.

Library of Congress Cataloging-in-Publication Data
A catalog record for this book has been requested.

ISBN-13: 978-1-78308-640-5 (Hbk)
ISBN-10: 1-78308-640-8 (Hbk)

ISBN-13: 978-1-78308-641-2 (Pbk)
ISBN-10: 1-78308-641-6 (Pbk)

This title is also available as an e-book.

CONTENTS

FIGURES

FOREWORD

DR SHI ZHENGRONG

Founder, former Chairman and CEO, Suntech Power, China

I first met John Mathews when he invited me to give a business breakfast address in Sydney in February 2015 on the theme of the greening of the global economy, drawing on my experience with Suntech Power in China. We hit it off and found commonality of views on many aspects of what we agreed was the dominant trend of our time. Now I am delighted to provide this Foreword to his new book, which elaborates on the theme of the greening that is driving China's transformation and is now diffusing around the world. His argument is compelling.

When I started Suntech Power back in 2001, and particularly after our IPO on the New York Stock Exchange in December 2005, I felt that we were helping to fashion a new world that would be independent of fossil fuels and supplant them as the dominant energy source. These were exciting times as we created the world's first mass production system for solar cells. Despite the setback of Suntech's financial stumble (which saw me part company with the firm), the Chinese build-up of solar and wind power and renewables generally has been inexorable, and is clearly the dominant energy trend in our time given the fact that the electricity price for solar and wind is now well below 10 cents/kWh in many countries in the world. I can endorse John Mathews's interpretation of this trend as providing China with real energy security, based on the fact that all renewables devices are the products of manufacturing. There would appear to be no argument superior to this in accounting for the global green shift, with China as its driver.

I agree with John Mathews that we are living through a great transformation of our energy systems, one that is going to see the supersession of the fossil fuel systems that underpinned the rise of the West and subsequently shaped the rise of East Asia in the twentieth century. Now it is a greening that is shaping the rise of China and India in the twenty-first century. The global stagnation created by the twilight years of the fossil fuel sector, and the dynamism associated with the renewables sector, is striking.

Three quarters of a century ago, the Austrian economist Joseph Schumpeter outlined a radical view of the workings of the capitalist economy in his *Capitalism, Socialism and Democracy*, where he outlined the influential view that capitalism proceeds through the rise of new industries that creatively destroy the old. John Mathews picks up this Schumpeterian theme in his new book, arguing that the global green shift is driven by creative destruction of the fossil fuels status quo. He is persuasive in his account of this dynamic process, presenting it as a major sociotechnical transition – indeed the sixth such transition since the Industrial Revolution. He paints a convincing picture of the scale of this sixth transition, following on the previous five transitions, and capturing how it is disrupting industrial processes in the worlds of energy, resource flows, water and food production and ultimately in the creation of new eco-cities. This transition is generating the business opportunities of tomorrow that can be seized by smart entrepreneurs in China and around the world.

I am proud of the role that I have played in this global green transition, and am happy to endorse the analysis of this transition that John Mathews provides, with his emphasis on the driving role played by China and Chinese firms. I wish his book great success.

Shanghai and Sydney
November 2016

PREFACE

In this book I present an argument that is grounded in recent and emerging developments and framed to make sense of the evidence. My argument starts with the enormous transformation that is under way in the global economy as manufacturing activities shift East – to China as well as to India and other Asian countries. Behind the shift in manufacturing lies an energy revolution needed to power the new world factories. And as China and other countries seek to build their energy systems in the same way that powered the West – with fossil fuels and unlimited resource flows – they come up against the inconvenient truth that the Western model will not scale. It will not scale to the level needed by China and India and certainly not to the global scale needed by the 'rest' as they embark on their industrialization. My argument then proceeds to identify the source of this inconvenient truth. It is not so much that there are physical limits to the powering of economies by fossil fuels (of the kind made famous by the 'limits to growth' arguments) as that there are immediate environmental limits in the form of unbreathable air and undrinkable water, and equally important near-term geopolitical limits. As China scours the planet in search of fossil fuels and expanding resource flows, so it meets limits in the form of civil wars, revolutions and terror – the real 'limits to growth' faced by an industrializing giant in the twenty-first century.

This is where greening enters the picture. My argument is that China is greening its energy system and its resources system (by closing industrial loops and building a circular economy) not so much because of fears of global warming, but because greening represents the only feasible way of resolving the geopolitical limits to growth that would otherwise halt in its tracks the country's industrialization. It is not that China sees global warming as unimportant – far from it. But China and to some extent India as rising industrial powers have to find ways to feed their huge energy and resource appetite in a way that enables them to evade the geopolitical limits to growth. Such a source of energy is available, based not on drilling or mining but on manufacturing; feeding that appetite would similarly require a source of commodities that is based not on mining or extraction but on closing industrial loops. How convenient it is then, that China has stumbled on just such a solution – renewable energies and the circular economy – and is framing a feasible path forward that can be emulated by India and by many others. For renewables are always the products of manufacturing – and as such can be renewed virtually without limit – and without costing the earth. Renewables benefit from the exercise of manufacturing capabilities and reduction in costs associated with the learning or experience curve. And the circular economy (or urban mining) adapts manufacturing to the capture of resources not as virgin commodities but from circular flows under manufacturing control. Greening thus represents a way forward towards industrialization in a form that goes a long way in reconciling economy with ecology – and at the same time provides China, India et al. with their only hope of a prosperous and industrious future.

My account starts with the significant shifts taking place in the east in manufacturing, and it frames the demonstrated rapid rise of renewables in China (a green energy revolution that is overtaking the black coal–fired economy) and the emergence of a circular economy based on urban mining as strategic responses taken to support these shifts. My analysis accounts for these great transformations *not* so much as an effort to reduce carbon emissions as a means of mitigating climate change (important as this may be, albeit more as a serendipitous side-effect) but rather as a fierce drive for energy and resource security. Successful industrialization depends on enhancing these sources of security.

Most discussions of renewables and the circular economy tend to start with climate change; they then proceed to frame the need to decarbonize industrial systems as a moral imperative to mitigate climate change. This book takes a different tack. It emphasizes the drive by China et al. for energy and resource security as primarily a geopolitical and domestic legitimacy imperative that leads them inevitably to promote renewables and the circular economy. For these countries it is not so much a moral choice as an economic imperative to green their economy. Reduced carbon emissions are a fortunate side-effect (Weber's 'unintended consequences') that these strategic choices generate. Emerging industrial giants are more readily attracted to renewables and circular flows precisely because renewables devices are always the products of manufacturing, as are closed resource loops – creating pathways that enable resource-hungry industrializers to find ways around the geopolitical hurdles that would block their way forward were they to attempt to follow the conventional fossil-fuelled pathway.

The broader framework for my story is one that grounds it in technological and industrial dynamics and successive waves of industrial epochs, as captured in Schumpeterian analysis. In the Schumpeterian world it is waves of creative destruction that unleash the new against the old, mediated through changes in cost structures that destroy the status quo and allow the insurgents to access the finance that drives their new investments. In the world of neoclassical economics, by contrast, there is only a limited sense of how firms and consumers react to shocks that disturb the prevailing equilibrium and induce substitutions – facilitated by market-based instruments like carbon taxes. Such a limited picture of the world has never been able to account for major technoeconomic shifts in the past – like the rise of steam power, or railroads, or electrical power grids or the IT revolution – and certainly cannot account for the major transformations that are now under way with the greening of industrial economies.

A proto-version of this argument was outlined in my 2014 book *Greening of Capitalism*. It was elaborated succinctly by Hao Tan and myself in our two articles published in *Nature*, in 2014 and 2016. As one of the world's two leading science journals, *Nature* requires that articles selected for publication be radically compressed – every word counts. This book grows out of the need to amplify and elaborate the argument that we made in these articles.

DEBTS INCURRED

My first debt then is to my long-time collaborator Dr Hao Tan, with whom I have co-authored many articles on China's greening strategies, culminating in our publishing two articles in *Nature*, on manufacturing as a means of providing energy security and on China's circular economy initiatives as a means of providing resource security. As I sketch above, this book is conceived as an elaboration of the argument of these two articles. The next debt is then to the editor of the Commentary section of *Nature*, Dr Joanne Baker, who showed confidence in our argument and provided us with superb editorial guidance in bringing the articles to fruition. Likewise our editor at *Asia-Pacific Journal*, Professor Mark Selden from Cornell University, who has critically engaged with many of our joint articles on China and its greening strategies, has proven to be an insightful collaborator.

My next debt is to Dr Shi Zhengrong, who has written the Foreword for this book. He is an inspiring pioneer of the green shift and one who sets a positive example for young Chinese and Australian business people who wish to contribute to the global green shift.

I am indebted to the editors of the Anthem Press series in which this book appears. My thanks in particular to Erik Reinert, chair of technology governance and development strategies at the Tallinn University of Technology, for his valued collaboration over the reasons why manufacturing is so important; and to Rainer Kattel, chair of innovation policy and technology governance at the Ragnar Nurkse School of Innovation and Governance at the Tallinn University of Technology, who invited me to speak to his colleagues at a time when my ideas were just taking shape. I would like to acknowledge as well my publisher, Tej Sood, for taking on this project, and not least the able advice of the editors who have guided the work through the press – Katy Miller, Abi Pandey and Vincent Rajan.

In the course of presenting my perspectives in various forums, I have incurred many other debts. For the opportunity to try out the ideas presented in this book, I especially wish to thank Federico Bonaglia and Annalisa Primi at the OECD in Paris; Kevin Tu at the International Energy Agency in Paris; Dimitri Zenghelis at the Grantham Institute at the LSE in London; Jan Fagerberg at the Center for Technology, Innovation and Culture at the University of Oslo; Nicola Armaroli at the Bologna CRS; Franco Malerba at Bocconi University in Milan; Tancrede Voituriez at IDDRI in Paris; Jean-Francois Huchet at INALCO and Florence Biot at the Asia Centre in Paris; Poul Andersen at the School of Business at Aalborg University; John Zysman at BRIE, UC Berkeley; Martin Kenney at UC Davis; Paolo Figueiredo at the FGV in Rio de Janeiro; and Martin Green and Mark Keevers at the School of Photovoltaic and Renewable Energy Engineering, UNSW in Sydney.

In China I would like to acknowledge the invitations by leading scholars including Li Jinhui at the School of Environment, Tsinghua University, and his colleague Xianlai Zeng; and Zheng Yong Nian, head of the Institute for Public Policy at South China University, Guangzhou, and his colleagues Lijun Yang and Caixia Li; and Hu Angang and Wang Hongchuan at the School of Public Policy & Management, Tsinghua University.

For their assistance, hospitality or collaborative endeavours, I am most grateful to: Leonardo Burlamaqui of the Federal University of Rio de Janeiro; Bill Lazonick at the University of Massachusetts; Mika Ohbayashi and Tomas Kåberger at the Japan Renewable Energy Foundation; Myung-Kyoon Lee and Darius Nassiry as well as Ivo de Boer at GGGI, Seoul; Soogil Young at the KAIST School of Business, Seoul; Keun Lee at Seoul National University; Jason Tay at the SSGKC; Rasmus Lena at Aalborg School of Business; Keith Lovegrove at IT Power, Canberra; Oliver Yates, former head of the Clean Energy Finance Corporation; Sean Kidney, CEO of Climate Bonds Initiative,

London; Vincenzo Balzani, Bologna; Hans-Joerg Naumer, at Allianz Global; Petronela Sandulache at PwC; Rajah Rasiah at the University of Malaya; Ana Celia Castro at the Federal University of Rio de Janeiro; Gabriel Zlamparet at Tsinghua University; Andy Zhu at SANY, Beijing; Clas-Otto Wene in Sweden; and my Macquarie University colleagues and former colleagues, David Baker and Keith Williams.

For their special understanding and assistance, I wish to thank my editor at *Taipei Times*, Noah Buchan; the indefatigable editor-in-chief at *Energy Post* Karel Beckman; and the editor at *RenewEconomy*, Giles Parkinson.

I have been fortunate in having a number of younger colleagues who have worked closely with me in developing the greening perspective. In particular Elizabeth Thurbon and Sung-Young Kim have given unstinting advice and valuable comments on earlier drafts of this manuscript. My former doctoral students Mei-Chih Hu at NTHU and Ching-Yan Wu in Taiwan have also been wonderful collaborators. I am indebted to my current doctoral students Dan Prud'homme in Beijing and Simran Talwar in Sydney.

Finally, my thanks as always to my wife and partner, Linda Weiss, whose guidance and unfailing good sense made sure that this project never strayed too far from the bounds of academic rigour and respectability.

ACRONYMS

6W	Sixth wave
ADs & CVDs	Anti-Dumping and Countervailing Duties
BAU	Business as Usual
BICS	Brazil, India, China, South Africa
BRICS	Brazil, Russia, India, China, South Africa
C&CC	Circular and cumulative causation
CE	Circular Economy
CEA	Closed Environment Agriculture
CERES	Circular Economy and Renewable Energy System
CLF	Contingent loan facility
CSP	Concentrated solar power
EEW	Electrical and electronic waste
FDI	Foreign Direct Investment
FYP	Five Year Plan (China)
GEI	Global Energy Interconnection
GG	Green growth
INDCs	Intended Nationally Determined Contributions
IoT	Internet of Things
IPO	Initial Public Offering
IPRs	Intellectual Property Rights
LCR	Local content requirement
LED	Light emitting diode
MED	Multiple Effect Distillation

PCB	Printed circuit board
PV	Photovoltaic
REs	Renewable energies
SSGKC	Sino-Singapore Guangzhou Knowledge City
WWS	Water, wind and sun (hydro, wind and solar power)

PART I

DYNAMICS OF THE GREEN TRANSITION

CHAPTER 1

INTRODUCTION

We are now in the middle of a long process of transition in the nature of the image which man has of himself and his environment [...]. There was almost always somewhere beyond the known limits of human habitation [...] a frontier. That is, there was always someplace else to go when things got too difficult [...] The image of the frontier is probably one of the oldest images of mankind, and it is not surprising that we find it hard to get rid of. Gradually, however, man has been accustoming himself to the notion of the spherical earth and a closed sphere of human activity.

K. E. BOULDING, THE ECONOMICS OF THE
COMING SPACESHIP EARTH (1966)

Fifty years ago, Kenneth Boulding argued in his predictive essay on the economics of the coming Spaceship Earth that the world would eventually have to move to a more responsible mode of economic interaction with our planet – from a Cowboy economy (reckless, wasteful) to a self-contained 'Spaceship economy' (regenerative, contained). Now we are at last catching up with Boulding's vision, as the prospect of an economy centred on accessing renewable energy resources from the sun and the wind, and tapping regenerated resources from a circular flow, becomes a realistic option. We are living through a profound industrial transformation, a 'green shift' that is being driven by global demographic, economic and technological forces.

We do indeed live in a period of profound change, particularly in terms of energy and resources utilized. The upheavals in the patterns of energy production and consumption – with dramatic swings away from established systems of fossil fuel usage and linear resource throughput – are occurring so fast that it is difficult to keep up with them. Innovations like the Tesla electric vehicles now transforming the global automobile industry, new sources of electric power, new smart grids and new ways of producing food in urban settings (e.g., vertical farms) all appear so dramatic partly because they are, well, dramatic. But they also invite contrast with decades of stasis in the energy, electrical and transport worlds, that have long been held in a 'frozen' state by patterns of corporate power established earlier. Now it is all being shaken up. There is a green ferment in the air.

The difference in this case is that it is a ferment that is touching not just a handful of countries or a small fraction of the world's population, but it is instead mobilizing the great populous countries of China and India in a world-historic transformation. These two countries (more civilizations than nations) are now reclaiming their traditional place as leaders of the world economy in a profound transformation that may be characterized as the Great Convergence. This term itself is carefully chosen to depict a contrast with the Great Divergence that separated Europe, North America and then Japan – the (not strictly geographical) 'West' – from 'the Rest'.

The relevance to the story of 'greening' is immediate and profound. China started on its quest to join the advanced world three decades ago, with its famed 'opening up' that ushered in sustained economic growth fluctuating around ten per cent per year. This process has now brought Chinese firms to quasi-parity with advanced firms, and in the process lifted hundreds of millions of people out of poverty. India is following the same astonishing pathway with perhaps a lag of a decade or so. As with all previous industrial powers before them, China and India have been following the Western route of utilizing fossil fuels – above all, coal – as their primary source of power, as well as extensive supplies of resources as material inputs. But as they do so, they come across the inconvenient truth that this Western fossil-fuelled model will not scale to global dimensions. There is the issue of carbon emissions and global warming, of course. But the real barrier that China and India face is not so much climate change (a problem that they feel, rightly, they inherited from the West) as immediate pollution from the burning of fossil fuels with their particulate emissions, and the geopolitical entanglements that result from global sourcing of such fuels and resources. This globalization of resource extraction impinges on established patterns of trade and production and sparks trade wars, if not civil wars, revolutions and terrorism. These are the real 'limits to growth' faced by China and India.

The resolution of the problem can be found not in terms of manipulating global political and trade-based economic relations, nor in simplistic calls for a shift to 'zero growth' even before China, India and the other industrializing countries have enjoyed their time in the sun. Rather, the resolution is to be found in a new pattern of economic growth that is coming to be termed 'green growth', where growth is complemented by changes in energy and resource flows that are more sustainable. Countries embark on a revolution in their energy system, displacing the established fossil fuel supplies and centralized electric power systems, and reduce their resource vulnerability by shifting from linear patterns of resource throughput to circular resource flows. The unanticipated aspect of this global green shift is that it is actually being led by China and (to some extent) by India. These are the countries where the problems are felt acutely and where the solutions present themselves most forcefully.

As the green shift involves new energy and resource and food production technologies, and new companies to drive their adoption, we see Chinese and Indian players emerging in newfound positions of leadership. These players are utilizing strategies of convergence (catch-up) that were perfected by East Asian countries like Korea and Taiwan in their catch-up with the West – initially, in a surge of fossil-fuelled industrialization. We also see Western companies striking out in new entrepreneurial ventures that break with the deadening hand of 100 years of stasis in the oil industry (the period of the 'seven sisters'), the coal industry with the prolonged dominance of firms like Peabody and the commodity giants. As they do so they are imposing Schumpeterian 'creative destruction' on the established order – and Chinese and Indian firms are only too willing to pick up the pieces and scale up the new, insurgent technologies to create new global businesses. These new firms are founded on wind power, solar power, and imminently, water regeneration, urban food production and other constituents of the worldwide green shift.

IT'S NOT ALL ABOUT CLIMATE CHANGE

The conventional argument on these matters of renewables and low-carbon energy and resource systems is that they are all about preventing – or mitigating – climate change. I present in this book a fresh alternative approach to the question of renewables. Yes, climate change is a large and important issue – but to focus on this question alone is to exclude other important aspects of renewables, such as their contribution to enhancing energy security and their cleaning up immediate particulate pollution problems. These are the aspects of renewables that are of most relevance to the emerging industrial giants like China and India.

The major trends I wish to focus on are those that *decouple* economies and economic processes from natural constraints. Now a qualification is in order at the outset of this discussion. The whole rationale of greening is, ultimately, one that locates our industrial systems within their ecological setting rather than pretending that they lie 'outside' ecological processes and cycles. This is my main objection to the story as told by mainstream neoclassical economics – it makes no reference to natural cycles, and works only with abstractions like wealth and income without ever grounding them in real flows of energy and resources. By contrast, 'greening' initiatives like those involved in introducing green taxes that tie economic activities to their origins and degree of pollution – and penalize polluting behaviour – make sense because they make producers of goods (like manufactured products) and services (like intercontinental transport) take greater cognizance of their impact on the earth. And this impact is frequently negative, as we are now realizing – and getting worse as 'business as usual' industrialization proceeds.

So far, so good – this account does not differ from numerous treatments that view the climate changes resulting from our 'unthinking' carbon-based industrialization as the primary issue, and decarbonization (clean energy and dematerialization) as the necessary way forward. But in the way this is posed it frequently comes across as the West forcefully imposing its view of how industrial evolution needs to proceed. As Pascal Bruckner (2013a; 2013b) put it in well-argued texts, even as the West's influence is diminishing, its arrogance in dictating to others on the planet how they should adjust their processes to make them climate-friendly is rising in its insistence.

A quite different argument is presented in these pages. The argument is that China (and to some extent India) are already feeling the pressures of pollution and geopolitical tensions created by their wholesale replication of a Western industrialization strategy, and are now seeking a green alternative with serious intent, on a global industrial scale. The driver is not so much a concern to save the world from climate change. It is rather a very real concern that the industrialization process being mounted by emerging giants like Brazil, India and China will be stalled by increasing local pollution and by geopolitical complications, and that a green alternative represents the only option available that can guarantee energy and resource security. And the key to this security lies in a feature of renewables that is seldom highlighted, namely, the fact that the devices used in power systems based on renewable resources are in all cases products of manufacturing. If manufacturing is what produces the devices needed to generate power and drive a circular flow, then it can be performed – in principle – anywhere. This is why manufacturing is central to resolving the issues of energy and resource security, as discovered by countries like China and India.

Manufacturing the devices needed to produce power is a completely different process from drilling for oil in more and more hostile locations, shipping the oil across the world in giant tankers, and then building a vast infrastructure for the processing, distribution and sale of the oil-based products. Manufacturing wind turbines and solar cells is governed by quite different 'laws' and places a country that pursues this alternative green strategy on a quite different footing, free from concerns over 'energy security' (meaning access to fossil fuels at a reasonable price) and able to frame energy and resource strategy as a part of its manufacturing and industrial development strategy.[1]

Manufacturing is a special process that creates increasing returns, by virtue of declining costs as markets expand and new niches for specialization are created. This is the process of intensive economic growth driven by circular and cumulative causation described so clearly by Allyn Young (1876–1929) in his account of how mass production industries work. We are now grappling with the same issues as industrializing countries like China and India build new green industries based on mass production and falling costs that promise to oust industrial products based on fossil fuels, resource extraction and open-air food production. If we apply this reasoning to the rise of new green industries, where China and now India are the countries taking a leading role, then we have a new and arresting twist to the story of our industrial evolution.

The story told here is one where China and India are able to enhance their energy and resource security – mitigating the domestic pollution created by their earlier coal-based industrialization strategies, and ensuring a reliable source for raw materials through the 'mining' of urban resource flows. This is not a shift dictated by any technological demand or geopolitical constraint – as has been the case for fast followers on the path of industrialization like Japan, then Korea and Taiwan in the fossil fuel era. In this story, the real driver is the shift to green growth, undertaken as a strategic and entrepreneurial initiative that turns out to have far-reaching implications. The driver is the strategic goal of enhancing energy and resource security – with decarbonization resulting as a fortunate side-effect. I propose in this book to leave climate change to one side and to focus instead on the strategic issues – the choices that are being made by the converging countries, and their material and energetic implications.

As my collaborator Hao Tan and I have argued in successive articles in *Nature*, there is a profound aspect to this shift and a reason why Chinese and

1. Erik Reinert and I developed this argument in an article published in *Futures* in 2014.

Indian firms are emerging as leaders of the transition.[2] It is manufacturing that lies at the core of the shift. What is being disrupted is not just a way of producing concentrated power, but a way of producing power via the extraction of fuels in a global system of drilling, mining, processing and transport. This system is now being disrupted by a new emergent global system based on the different principles of manufacturing. New power devices like wind turbines and solar cells can operate anywhere on the planet and produce power and store it any time.

The fact that some Western companies like Tesla are surging to world leadership in the new green era only serves to underline the point that they too are doing so by basing their strategies on manufacturing. They are the exceptions that prove the rule that the new, green era that is opening up is one that will be based on secure foundations of manufacturing. This green shift offers emerging countries an optimal way forward both in terms of industrialization through manufacturing (with all its labour enhancement and employment aspects) as well as clean and green energy that does not tie them up in geopolitical knots.

The fact that the green growth strategy is also one that delivers low-carbon emissions is a convenient side-effect that runs counter to the inertia displayed by Western oil, coal and gas and electric power and transport industries. We need to be clear about what is driving the disruptions in these industries. The driver is lower costs induced by expansion of markets as China and India enter world production and distribution systems for renewable power and circulation of resources.

This is the fascinating world of upheaval that I tackle in this book. Kenneth Boulding would no doubt have been fascinated as well – if a little disappointed that we had taken so long to heed his words.[3]

---

2. See 'Manufacture renewables to build energy security', *Nature*, 11 September 2014, at: http://www.nature.com/news/economics-manufacture-renewables-to-build-energy-security-1.15847; and 'Circular economy: Lessons from China', *Nature*, 23 March 2016, at: http://www.nature.com/news/circular-economy-lessons-from-china-1.19593.

3. Boulding is one of the core group of Western scholars who made decisive contributions to an understanding of the green shift, well before it had become global and well before it attained its present significance. Others would be Barry Commoner, Herman Daly, Allen Kneese, Robert Costanza and Robert Ayres. Their contributions will be reflected in the arguments presented in this book.

GEOPOLITICAL AND ENVIRONMENTAL LIMITS
TO FOSSIL FUELS

Fossil fuels conferred enormous benefits on the Western world as it industrialized over the past 200 years. The transition to a carbon-based economy liberated countries from age-old Malthusian constraints. For a select group of countries representing a small slice of the global population, burning fossil fuels enabled an era of explosive growth, ushering in dramatic improvements in productivity, income, wealth and standards of living.

Now the 'peripheral' countries that missed out on this initial industrial revolution are clamouring to have their time in the sun. For much of the past 20 years, China and India have led the charge in claiming the benefits of fossil fuels for the rest of the world, mainly through the use of coal. Recently, however, they have begun to moderate their approach. As their use of fossil fuels brushes up against geopolitical and environmental limits, they have been forced to invest seriously in alternatives. In doing so, they have put themselves at the vanguard of a planetary transition that in a few short decades could eliminate the use of fossil fuels altogether and transform the global industrial system.

In the United States and Europe, the benefits of renewable energy are predominantly seen as environmental. Energy from the wind and sun can indeed offset the need to burn fossil fuels, helping to mitigate climate change. In China and India, however, renewable energy is viewed as serving multiple purposes. The relatively rapid transition away from fossil fuels that is under way in both countries is driven not so much by concerns about climate change as by the economic benefits renewable energy sources are perceived as conveying.

Indeed, while the economic benefits of renewables can be attractive to advanced economies such as Germany or Japan (both of which are starting to move away from fossil fuels), the advantages for emerging industrial giants are overwhelming. For India and China, an economic trajectory based on fossil fuels could spell catastrophe, as efforts to secure enough for their immense populations ratchet up geopolitical tensions. By contrast, an economy based on renewables and the circulation of resources would promote domestic manufacturing and improve local environmental quality by, for example, reducing urban smog, as well as enhancing resource and energy security. The greening economy would offer supplies of energy and resources that would renew themselves, at costs that diminish because of the manufacturing learning curves involved.

The arguments advanced against renewable sources of energy – that they can be expensive, intermittent, or not sufficiently concentrated – are easily rebutted. And while renewables' opponents are legion, they are motivated more by interest in preserving the *status quo* of fossil fuels and nuclear energy than by worries that wind turbines or solar farms will blot the landscape. We will deal with – and demolish – these objections as the argument unfolds.

In any case, those wishing to halt the expansion of renewables are unlikely to triumph over simple economics. The renewable energy revolution is not being driven by a tax on carbon emissions or subsidies for clean energy; it is in fact being driven by reductions in the costs of manufacturing that will soon make it more cost-effective to generate power from water, wind and the sun than from burning coal. Likewise the costs of battery energy storage are falling, as are costs of operating electric vehicles – all part of the current disruption to the power, energy distribution, transport and other industries associated with the green shift. Already in 2013 these trends were so striking that the investment bank UBS was advising its clients to become active in what it called 'the unsubsidised solar revolution' – meaning that the renewables revolution was passing the point where subsidies were needed, and would henceforth be driven by cost reductions making it more competitive than power generated from fossil fuels. The trends have only grown stronger since this report appeared.[4]

Countries like China and India are discovering that they can build their way to energy security by investing in the industrial capacity needed to produce wind turbines, solar cells and other sources of renewable energy – at scale. As China and India throw their economic weight into the renewables industrial revolution, they are triggering a global chain reaction (via a process known as 'circular and cumulative causation') that promises to drive diffusion of the alternatives until they have completely superseded their fossil fuel antecedents. With solar in the lead, we can anticipate a wholesale transformation of energy by 2030 or sooner. Likewise we can anticipate that the dependence on extracting resources from the earth, and the build-up of industrial wastes, will give way to a circular flow of resources in countries that take the necessary measures (as China is demonstrating). These are the directions in which our global industrial system is now evolving.

---

4. See UBS Investment Research, 'The unsubsidised solar revolution', 15 January 2013. For a full copy of the report, see: http://www.qualenergia.it/sites/default/files/articolo-doc/UBS.pdf.

The evolutionary dynamics of this shift are driven not by simple product or technology substitution, as conceived by mainstream economics with its focus on costs, taxes and substitution, but by processes of technoeconomic supersession as captured in Schumpeterian analysis. What is really driving the change is the creative destruction wrought by one group of firms at the expense of an established group as industrial infrastructures are transformed and new business models oust the old. The green shift is the latest episode of this process of Schumpeterian industrial evolution.[5]

There is indeed a wave of initiatives emerging that is transforming our industrial system, disrupting the established patterns in one industry after another – in power generation, in resources regeneration, in food production, in transport (e.g., electric vehicles, high speed rail) and in the finance that is driving all these disruptions. Established companies in the fossil fuel industries, the power generation business, the transport business and agribusiness are all reeling from the new challenges that come one on top of another. And what is so striking is that it is manufacturing companies that are leading the disruption – placing manufacturing once again at the centre of industrial expansion and wealth generation, this time as the driver of the green shift.

Unlike mining, drilling or extraction, manufacturing activities benefit from learning curves that make production increasingly efficient – and cheaper. Investments in renewable energy drive down the cost of their production, expanding the market for their adoption and making further investment more attractive. The cost reductions are significant. From 2009 to 2014, these mechanisms drove down the cost of solar photovoltaic energy by 80 per cent and reduced the cost of land-based wind power by 60 per cent, according to Lazard's Power, Energy and Infrastructure Group.[6]

The impact of the rapid uptake in renewable energy and the shift to a Circular Economy can be expected to have consequences as profound as those unleashed by the Industrial Revolution. In the eighteenth century, the economies of Europe and

---

5. See the classic descriptions of capitalist industrial dynamics provided by Schumpeter starting with his *Theory of Economic Development* (1912) or in its academic exposition (Schumpeter 1928) and proceeding through *Capitalism, Socialism and Democracy* (1947) which introduced the concept of creative destruction, and culminating in his numerous contributions to understanding processes of entrepreneurship. The challenge is to link these classic descriptions of capitalist industrial dynamics to the green shift that is currently under way.

6. See the regular reports from New York bank Lazard on levelized costs of energy, available at: https://www.lazard.com/perspective/levelized-cost-of-energy-analysis-90/.

the United States initiated the transition to an energy system based on fossil fuels as well as an extensive resource acquisition system based on colonies without fully understanding what was happening and what the consequences might be. This time, we can see the way things are changing and prepare for the implications.

Despite prognoses of ecological catastrophe, the outlook is not all gloom and doom. On the contrary the current initiatives to green the industrial system are creating the biggest business opportunities of the twenty-first century. Efforts to reduce carbon dioxide emissions may not after all be the prime driver of the renewable energy revolution. It is very possible that without the green shift that is occurring in China and India, efforts to minimize the impact of climate change would never succeed. If the world is to avoid the worst dangers of a warming planet, we may have China and India to thank for it.

CHINA'S ENERGY STRATEGIES

There are many ways of demonstrating how China is leaping ahead in renewables and circular economy initiatives. One of the simplest and most graphic of the visualizations is the comparative build-up of capacity in renewables, emphasizing the role being played by generating sources from water (hydro), wind and sun – or WWS sources. This is shown in Figure 1.1.[7]

When we focus just on solar photovoltaic power, the impact that China is having is even more striking. Figure 1.2 shows how China has rapidly moved to world leadership in PV cell manufacturing, starting from virtually nothing in the year 2000. This is evidence of a healthy industry and one where Chinese firms now exercise considerable influence on technological trends.[8]

It is striking to consider the direct comparison between China and an advanced set of countries such as the EU, in terms of investment in clean energy systems, where it is clear that China has now caught up with and overtaken the EU. Drawing on data from BNEF and Xinhuanet, the London-based consultancy *E3G* reveals the widening gap in the chart (see Figure 1.3) that shows just how far China has come in consolidating its position in the lead in the shift to a green economy. China invested over $100 billion in clean energy in 2015, compared with just $40 billion for the EU – outranking the EU 2.5 times.

---

7. See my updated analysis of trends in China's renewable energy revolution at: http://apjjf.org/2016/17/Mathews.html.

8. See Green (2016) for a discussion of the state of the PV industry and the influence of China, and Zhang and White (2016) for further details of China's rise to become the world leader in solar PV manufacturing.

FIGURE 1.1. China's generation capacity from WWS sources compared with other leading industrial countries, 2015.

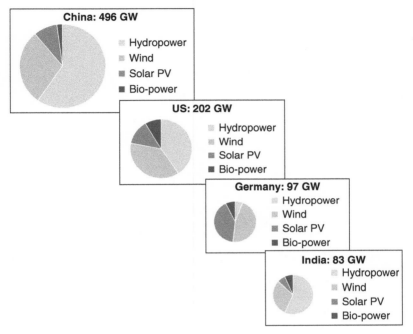

SOURCE: Mathews and Tan 2015.

The tipping point, where China's investment overtook that of the EU, came in 2013, and has strengthened each year since then – while EU investment has actually declined. Per capita investment by China also overtook that of the EU in 2015, while China's investment in clean energy as a proportion of its GDP has already reached 1 per cent, compared with less than 0.3 per cent for the EU.[9]

The *E3G* authors comment that this is a poor way for the EU to approach the biggest business challenge of the twenty-first century, by cutting back on its expenditure and handing China clear leadership. This in turn can be expected to translate into dominance of next generation product development,

---

9. See the *E3G* report 'Pulling ahead on clean technology: China's 13th Five Year Plan challenges Europe's low carbon competitiveness', by Shinwei Ng, Nick Mabey and Jonathan Gaventa (March 2016), available at: https://www.e3g.org/docs/E3G_Report_on_Chinas_13th_5_Year_Plan.pdf.

FIGURE 1.2. Transformation of PV cell manufacturing over the past 20 years.

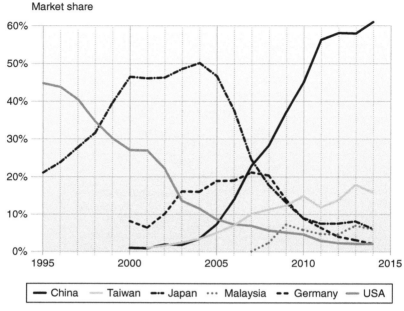

SOURCE: *PV Magazine,* June 2016.

FIGURE 1.3. Clean energy investment, China vs. EU, 2005–2015.

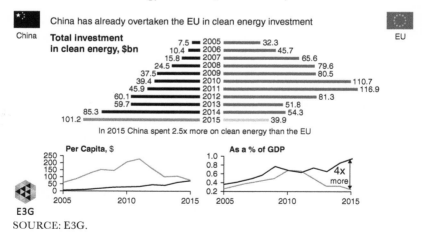

SOURCE: E3G.

FIGURE 1.4. Global investment in power capacity, 2008–2015.

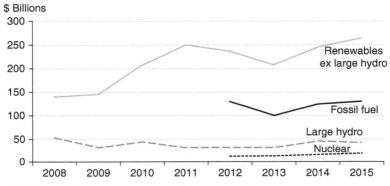

SOURCE: UNEP/Frankfurt School of Finance and Management.

next generation patenting and next generation standards setting, all fruits of expanded R&D spending.

The dominance of wind and solar power in this global green transition is also striking. Figure 1.4 makes the point strongly, revealing how investment in wind and solar is racing ahead of all other investments in electric power capacity, exceeding $250 billion per year. By contrast, investment in thermal (coal burning) power generation languishes at around $130 billion per year, large hydro at around $50 billion, and nuclear is still a long way behind, at around $10 billion. Investment data tell us where a complex system is headed in the future – and these data could not be clearer about the direction of evolution of the world's electric power system.

ANTHROPOCENE CHOICES: MORAL VS. ECONOMIC

We live in the era of the *Anthropocene* – the geological era where human activity is viewed as the most significant force shaping the planetary environment. Paul Crutzen, the joint founder of the idea, dates the Anthropocene from the beginnings of the industrial era in the early eighteenth century; others date it from the end of World War II, and specifically from the detonation of the world's first atomic explosion, at Alamogordo in New Mexico in 1945.[10]

10. See Crutzen's article in *Nature* (2002), 'The geology of mankind'; for the later dating of the onset of the Anthropocene, see Steffen et al. (2015).

Depending on the date chosen, we are witnessing either an epoch of fossil fuel usage or an acceleration of the use of fossil fuels and human-sourced power such as nuclear power since the 1950s.

This world that we (our species, *Homo sapiens*) have created is a dynamic entity that is subject to constant change and evolutionary pressures. I build on the arguments of Yuval N. Harari that what drives our evolution now is not so much biological processes as technological and economic choices that are occurring much faster – hundreds of times faster.[11] And the biggest set of changes under way are those associated with the greening of the technoeconomic system we have created called capitalism.

There are two quite distinct approaches to comprehending the changes under way in the global industrial system that is now encompassing the planet as a whole. There is the approach that takes the achievements for granted and looks to the means available for curbing carbon emissions that are widely understood to be responsible for triggering climate change. This is the approach that is embodied in the UN-sponsored Kyoto process that looks to convince countries that it is in their long-term interests to decarbonize their economies – a process that culminated in the series of 'intended nationally determined contributions' (INDCs) for reducing carbon emissions proposed and adopted by countries at the Paris Conference of the Parties meeting in December 2015. In the end this is viewed as a decision point in our industrial civilization that is framed as a *moral choice*. It is not 'Socialism or barbarism' this time but 'Decarbonization or heat death' that appears to define the choice.

But there is a quite different approach that looks at the real trends away from the Western-centric industrial manufacturing system and the shift towards a Sinocentric system (China as the world's factory) as the dominant trend, with China's (followed by India's) ramping up of energy and resource systems needed to power these immense manufacturing engines being created. As they scale up their systems, China (and India) are discovering limits, not so much in terms of energy (oil, coal) or resource limits but in terms of geopolitical limits. Put bluntly, this is to view the world in terms of their concern over triggering wars, revolutions or terror in response to their striding across the world in search of energy and material resources and securing them through their own companies' activities.

As they discover the limits to scaling up the traditional Western 'business as usual' system, these emerging countries are discovering the advantages of greening – in the sense of switching away from fossil fuels towards renewable

---

11. See Harari (2014). I discuss his approach to our species' history further in Chapter 2.

energies, and away from linear resource flows to resource regeneration via circular flows. China in particular has embraced these green growth strategies with determination, in terms of greening its energy system, its resource regeneration system and the financial system that is feeding both – even as it continues with its black systems based on fossil fuels and linear resource throughput. This approach sees greening not so much as a moral imperative but instead as an *economic imperative* – as the only feasible means for China and India to maintain their vast industrialization efforts without triggering wars, revolutions or terror that would undo all their aspirations for modernization.

The really interesting feature of this dichotomy, of two quite different sets of choices, is that as China and India green their industry and financial systems, they effectively decarbonize their systems as well and achieve the goals that have been sought by those pursuing the moral imperative of change. China (and India) discover that in order to make their industrial initiatives manageable from a geopolitical standpoint, they must bring them under control from an environmental and ecological standpoint. They discover through green growth that economy and ecology become compatible.

ECOMODERNIZATION STRATEGIES

Ecomodernization is the generic term for the processes that are under way. The term refers to a way of reducing the impact that our industrializing processes have on our planet, by decoupling economic processes from their 'natural' moorings. Ecomodernization refers to a strategy, a shift in direction. It is not a 'model' where a given input produces a given output. In the ecomodernization story the production of food, of water, of resources and of energy are all seen to be processes that are placing increasing strain on the earth, but as they become progressively decoupled from their natural settings, they allow us (*Homo sapiens*) to eliminate or reduce the negative impact imposed by our industrial processes.[12]

There is under way a series of technoeconomic transitions that all share the feature that they involve in one way or another the disruption of existing patterns in the production of food, water, energy and resource regeneration in favour of IT-enhanced 'smart systems' that are driving down costs and facilitating

---

12. On ecomodernization see contributions such as Spaargaren and Mol 1992; or Mol 2006. The most recent and comprehensive contribution to this genre is *The Ecomodernist Manifesto*, produced by the Breakthrough Institute (2015). I will be engaging with this text throughout the chapters to come.

widespread diffusion of these eco-modern systems. We are not dealing here with an autonomous process with a technological dynamic of its own so much as a process driven by the expansion of markets and consequent cost reductions that typically characterize the rise of new mass production industries ousting the old. The difference this time is that it is the industrialization of China and India that is driving the cost reductions as they diffuse around the world through capitalist competition.

Ecomodernists such as the authors of the *Ecomodernist Manifesto* are correct in pointing to these processes as being associated with the dominance of cities (urbanization) and their more rapid greening than other parts of the world. But what they fail to point out is that China and India are emerging as the drivers of the process, based on their quest for green modernization. Processes for producing food, water, energy and resources can all be discerned as reducing the human footprint, concentrating activities into smaller areas (or where large land areas are required, in ways that do not interfere with ongoing activities), and generally decoupling human settlements from their natural moorings. It is in China and India that these processes are manifested most clearly.

So – we are on the cusp of the greatest transformation of our global industrial system, a transformation that will enable us to live with natural processes and ecological balance in a way that has not been possible in previous (fossil-fuelled) phases of our industrial evolution. The goal of returning over half of the earth to rewilding processes (as enunciated by Harvard biologist E.O. Wilson in his new book *Half Earth*) is in sight of being achieved; the bigger and more ambitious the goal, the more likelihood of its being achieved. [13]

Are China and India aiming for such lofty goals? We do not know. They are hardly going to reveal explicitly their deep strategic goals. But we do know that in pursuit of their eminently sensible goals of integrating themselves into the capitalist-industrialist world system, they are having to do so through managing their industrial processes – their energy systems, resource regeneration systems, food production systems – in ways that were never an issue for the Western powers as they industrialized. We have moved into a completely new era in our species' industrial evolution – an evolution that involves cultural and economic initiatives rather than the genetic/biological changes that dictated our earlier evolution. And the latest of these strategic shifts is the shift towards

---

13. On rewilding, see Wilson (2016). Goals of nature conservation and biodiversity protection now loom large; see F. Mathews (2016) for a philosophical investigation.

greener industries, products and manufacturing processes, where China and India are no longer spectators but key players helping to drive the process. What we see emerging is a completely new sociotechnical industrial system that promises to reconcile the economy with its ecological setting.

WHEN CERES MEETS GAIA

In Greek mythology the goddess *Gaia* is the great mother of all: the primal Greek Mother Goddess; creator and giver of birth to the Earth. She has famously been adopted by James Lovelock as the name for his biological Earth stabilizing system, elaborated on by Lovelock and Margulis in numerous books and influential articles.[14] Gaia is both a dynamic entity and one that pre-exists: there was a Gaia before the species *Homo sapiens* rose to prominence, and there is sure to be a Gaia after we have lived our span as a civilization on the earth. As an industrial civilization we are seeking to adapt to Gaia and finding a way to accommodate to her demands. In the first two to three hundred years of our industrial era we have learnt how hard this is going to be. But we take heart from the fact that our early excursions into energy and resource systems have not as yet actually killed off Gaia, and we are finding ways through renewable energy and the recirculation and regeneration of resources to minimize our impact.

In the interests of keeping our eyes focused on the goal, let us agree to call the technoeconomic system that we as a species are constructing as CERES (denoting a Circular Economy and Renewable Energy System), as counterpart to the wildness of Gaia.[15] *Ceres*, who in the Roman pantheon is the goddess of agriculture and fertility, is an appropriate reference point for our goal of creating a self-sustaining technoeconomic system that can leave Gaia to get on with things, without our trying to replace her. Ceres is the Roman counterpart to the Greek goddess Demeter. Ceres is ideal as a name for our emerging

---

14. See Lovelock's early exposition, *The Ages of Gaia: A Biography of Our Living Planet* (1995) and more recent pessimistic accounts *The Vanishing Face of Gaia: A Final Warning* (2010) and most recently *A Hard Ride to the Future* (2015); for the original scientific statement in the journal *Tellus*, see Lovelock and Margulis (1974).

15. In my 2015 book on *Greening of Capitalism* I coined the acronym CERES for a Circular Economy and Renewable Energy System – and I would like to elaborate on this in the present text, and defend it as a meaningful contribution to the debate over the transition that is under way.

sustainable technoeconomy because of her linkage with notions of fertility, childbearing and nurturance.[16] These female attributes are more appropriate to a sustainable technology than the male attributes of strength, heat, perseverance and hardness, associated with the male god *Hephaestus* (metallurgy, fire, and craftsmen – along with volcanoes), or his Latin equivalent, *Vulcan.*

Vulcan and Hephaestus are the gods that have led the fossil-fuelled world close to the abyss. We now need a more caring, motherly and fertile character to depict our emergent technoeconomy, and Ceres is the appropriate figure (along with her acronym that captures both Circular Economy and Renewable Energy). Of course there is a wild side to these mythologies of fertility; many of the pantheons depict goddesses like Ceres as having a dangerous element, aroused to fury if not treated properly. The Hindu female Matrikas ('seven mothers') certainly capture this wild side of the mythologies of fertility.[17]

The British scientist James Lovelock has done the world an enormous service in his formulating the theory of a 'living earth' named Gaia, that is, one where life self-regulates itself and the planet by keeping the atmospheric environment more or less constant, and likewise the oceans. But Lovelock in his most recent writings (he is now in his 90s) comes across as decidedly pessimistic. What I am proposing in this book is a way in which Gaia (a product of the processes of the earth) can be complemented by Ceres (our own creation of a renewable energy and Circular Economy system). Can these two concepts of how the earth works, represented by two powerful deities, be reconciled? Lovelock has become very pessimistic, asserting that Gaia will look after herself, and that if we survive at all it is likely to be as a greatly diminished industrial civilization, numbering no more than 1 billion people. In this book I argue why I believe this prognosis to be mistaken. As industrialization proceeds at a global scale, I maintain that the changes

---

16. I first came across CERES as the inspired name for an eco-park in inner Melbourne, where it stands for Centre for Education and Research in Environmental Strategies (CERES); its website can be found here: https://en.wikipedia.org/wiki/CERES_Community_Environment_Park. I would hope that the people who now run Ceres in Melbourne would approve of my use of the name for a broader purpose, namely as a technoeconomic system (involving a Circular Economy and Renewable Energies) that is compatible with Gaia.

17. In most early references, the Matrikas are described as having inauspicious qualities and often described as dangerous. They come to play a protective role in later mythology, although some of their inauspicious and wild characteristics still persist in these accounts. Thus, they represent the prodigiously fecund aspect of nature as well as its destructive force aspect.

that 'we' are driving, as a species, and now encompassing moves to green the economy in China and to some extent in India, in the form of green growth strategies, represent a viable way forward.[18] They give us a chance of reconciling economy with ecology – or Ceres with Gaia.

OUTLINE OF CHAPTERS

The book is structured as follows. Part I canvasses the issues involved in the global green shift, starting with an overview of the major transitions that have occurred since a group of countries industrialized by discovering how they could extract power from fossil fuels. Chapter 2 traces this story through the original Industrial Revolution, which sparked the Great Divergence between West and East; its Great Acceleration during the post-world war II era; and now the Great Convergence as China, India and other countries look to catch up with the erstwhile leaders. For the reasons canvassed above, they find they cannot do so by emulating the Western model, and are perforce having to invent a new green growth model, and one that promises to be the most fundamental transition of all – the next Great Transformation. Chapter 3 introduces the main theoretical frameworks to be used, focusing on the concept of ecomodernization and how it depends for its success on a decoupling between growth in physical activities and growth in income. Chapter 4 brings the focus back to technoeconomic transitions, of which the current Green Shift may be characterized as a sixth wave fulfilling the most recent IT-driven fifth wave but as applied to energy and resources and food production. The story progresses in Chapter 5 with an outline of how China, India et al. are benefiting from their adoption of green growth strategies, and how they are blazing a trail to be followed by other industrializing countries Chapter 6 discusses the role of finance – serious finance, created by banks and financial institutions in the form of green bonds targeted at institutional investors, and capable of raising the trillions of dollars that are going to be needed for the Green Shift to be successful. Chapter 7 then returns to the issue of developing countries and whether they can energize their development by becoming early protagonists of the green shift, emulating the China model.

---

18. In his most recent musings, on a future with robotics, Lovelock is more relaxed about climate change; see his interview with *The Guardian*, at: https://www.theguardian.com/environment/2016/sep/30/james-lovelock-interview-by-end-of-century-robots-will-have-taken-over. I am dealing with his arguments as they have been articulated over the past two decades.

This theme is extended in Chapter 8, which introduces the important concept of local content requirements as being key to building of new green industries, and how this brings the world climate system into potential conflict with the world trade system – and offers a means of reconciliation. The final chapter in Part I rounds out the set of issues by bringing in the decline of fossil fuels. Much of the book is devoted to the rise of new energy and resources industries – but the counterpart is the decline of the old fossil fuel based industries. They are now facing a prolonged phase-out – and one that needs to be executed in a socially responsible manner.

Part II canvasses the processes of the green shift in greater detail, starting in Chapter 10 with the fundamental driver of population, which is widely expected to peak at around 9 billion people before mid-century, as foreseen by the all-important theory of the demographic transition. This peaking is argued to be the key to success of all the other greening strategies. In successive chapters we then discuss the major determinants of the green shift, namely energy, resources, water and food and the character of the sixth wave innovations that are emerging in each of these sectors. Chapter 11 canvasses the most important features of the green shift involved in the energy transition, with a focus on the likely choice of renewables over fossil fuels and nuclear power. The discussion moves to a detailed examination of the role of renewables in enhancing energy security, which as argued in Chapter 12 should be viewed as their major feature (rather than their contingent contribution to reducing carbon levels), while Chapter 13 provides a detailed rebuttal of many of the myths raised to discredit renewables, particularly the myth of vast areas of land needed by wind and solar power (the myth of 'Renewistan').

Chapter 14 then takes the story forward to resources, where a parallel argument is developed that sees countries like China and India enhancing their resource security by building circular flows of materials based on closing industrial loops, in the pattern of the Circular Economy. Chapter 15 extends these arguments to encompass water and food production, where ecomodernizing trends are viewed as making major breakthroughs in regeneration and production of water and food in urban settings – encompassing vegetables as well as artificial meat and dairy products that are cultured. This discussion is capped in Chapter 16 with the concept of hydrosolar gardening, which draws together food, water and energy production in a positive triple nexus of synergistic interactions. Chapter 17 brings all these sixth wave initiatives together to discuss their integration in the creation of new eco-cities, where again we find China in the lead with Sino–Singapore joint ventures creating new eco-cities in Suzhou, in Tianjin and in Guangzhou. Others are likely to follow – sparking emulation around the world. The final chapter returns to the themes of ecomodernization and asks whether we as a civilization can create a circular economy and renewables-focused industrial system, named after the Latin goddess Ceres, to provide a fitting complement to the mother goddess who rules our living planet, Gaia. The book closes by asking: is there a way to reconcile ecology with economics, or Gaia with Ceres?

CHAPTER 2

EVOLUTIONARY DYNAMICS OF OUR INDUSTRIAL CIVILIZATION

The story of our species, *Homo sapiens*, is one of extraordinary conquest – with our rising, as Yuval N. Harari has put it so eloquently, from an insignificant primate just like any other animal 70,000 years ago to become the masters of the planet today.[1] As a species we have passed through three major revolutions on our way to mastery – the cognitive revolution, that enabled us to cooperate in large numbers in hunting and foraging (and causing our first ecological catastrophes in doing so); followed by the agricultural revolution, where we learned to tame a selection of plants and animals for our own ends (or as Harari puts it mischievously, the plants like wheat tamed us) and thereby released dramatic new growth in population, cities, techniques and culture; and a scientific revolution, occurring around 500 years ago, where the key was our discovery of the power of systematic investigation from an explicit position of accepted ignorance (as opposed to assumed dogmatic knowledge, not tested by empirical observation). Harari has a chapter on the industrial revolution that he traces directly to the effects of the scientific revolution and its bias towards systematic observation. Western capitalism was able to spawn the industrial revolution, he argues, because of its propensity to view the future as potentially better than the past, and its preparedness to invest profits in production in order to bring about this imagined future. The growth that resulted, which is unprecedented in our species' long history, called for massive new inputs of energy and materials.[2] It is at this point, where Harari breaks off his narrative (more or less), that I start mine.

---

1. See Harari, *Sapiens: A Brief History of Humankind*, Vintage Books, 2014.

2. The Stanford historian and archaeologist Ian Morris (2015) has advanced an alternative evolutionary account, moving through the phases of foraging, followed by farming and then moving to the industrial revolution and the use of fossil fuels. Both

INDUSTRIAL TRANSFORMATIONS

We can trace this industrial revolution and the new world it created through three main transformations of the global technoeconomic system. There was first the introduction of fossil fuels themselves, initially coal, which in one country after another (starting with Britain) ousted previous organic and natural energy sources based on wood (from forests) and water. The impact that these new sources had on raising productivity levels and through this to rising incomes through trade leading to rising wealth, has been dramatic.[3] This was followed by utilization of materials at a new 'industrial scale' – starting with cotton, grown in vast quantities in the American South and feeding the new textile mills in Yorkshire, and then moving on to other materials such as iron, steel and a multitude of synthetic materials resulting from the application of science to production. Geopolitically these upheavals created the *Great Divergence*, as the west started to pull away from the traditional leaders of the global economy, China and India. This is seen graphically when data on per capita incomes for the Western industrializing countries are plotted over a time interval spanning hundreds of years (Figure 2.1).

The 'Great Divergence' created a new divide between West and East, and laid the foundations for Western supremacy, based as it was on superior access to fossil energy sources and raw materials.[4] A flourishing line of scholarship has arisen which examines the 'coal question' linking the rise of incomes and wealth in the UK to its rapid diffusion of coal power, through the invention of the steam engine and its application to the first railroads. This was one of the first examples of how humans collectively were able to lift constraints on activity by introducing new sources of energy and materials. Railroads, for example, made transport of both people and goods vastly more reliable than on canals, on the open sea (sailing vessels) and of course on terrible roads.

There followed in the period in the twentieth century and particularly after World War II a new flowering of industry and transport, this time based on

---

accounts emphasize the fundamental character of these shifts and their wider economic and cultural impact.

3. See Wrigley (2013) for a recent discussion of the role of coal in the English Industrial Revolution – thereby countering the long-practised ignoring of the role of energy in previous accounts of this fundamental transformation.

4. See Pomeranz (2000) for the original exposition of the case for a 'Great Divergence' and Goldstone (2002) for an informed discussion. The themes of different kinds of growth being developed by China are canvassed in Goldstone (2002).

FIGURE 2.1. Diverging national incomes per capita, 1500–1950.

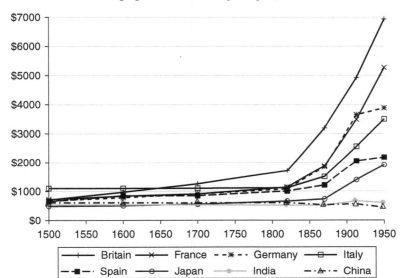

SOURCE: Data excerpted from *Contours of the World Economy, 1–2030 AD: Essays in Macro-Economic History* by Angus Maddison, Oxford University Press, 2007, ISBN 978-0-19-922721-1, p. 382, Table A.7; available at Wikipedia: https://upload.wikimedia.org/wikipedia/commons/4/44/Maddison_GDP_per_capita_1500-1950.svg

oil rather than coal and further cementing the new Western power, the United States, as world leader. This has been called the *Great Acceleration* (by Steffen et al.), and is captured by a series of charts documenting the rapid spread of modern technologies like refrigeration, telecommunications, antibiotics, and other conveniences of modern life. Will Steffen and his colleagues have documented the changes in the years post-1950.[5] In fact they propose the date 16 July 1945 as the start of the Anthropocene – when the first atomic bomb was tested at Alamogordo in New Mexico, signalling that humankind would now shape its planetary environment, and not be shaped by it as in all previous epochs (Figure 2.2).

---

5. Steffen et al. provide a planetary 'dashboard' of charts to demonstrate how everything has accelerated since the advent of the industrial era – with a marked upturn around 1950: http://www.igbp.net/news/pressreleases/pressreleases/planetarydashboardshows greataccelerationinhumanactivitysince1950.5.950c2fa1495db7081eb42.html.

FIGURE 2.2. The Great Acceleration – socio-economic trends, 1750–2010.

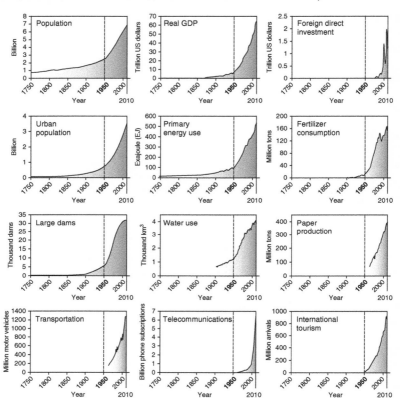

SOURCE: http://www.igbp.net/news/pressreleases/pressreleases/planetarydashboardsho
wsgreataccelerationinhumanactivitysince1950.5.950c2fa1495db7081eb42.html

These trends are underpinned by ease of access to a convenient fossil fuel, namely oil. But so far the transition had been confined to the one billion (or so) people living in the West – in North America, Western Europe and Japan. Increasingly the countries of the East have been clamouring for their turn as well. They have been able to tap into the store of technology and scientific knowledge that has been accumulated by the West, in a time-honoured process of Convergence, or catch-up, utilizing fast follower strategies. This process has led to a third industrial transformation, which may be called the *Great Convergence*, as the Eastern countries, now led by China, are pursuing catch-up strategies and are converging on the prior Western leaders. This process where influence is

FIGURE 2.3. Share of manufacturing value-added, OECD vs. non-OECD countries, 1995–2013.

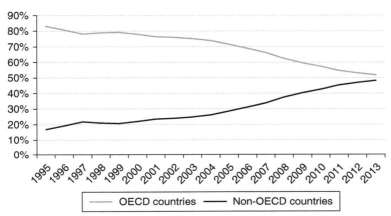

SOURCE: OECD Development Centre.

shifting back to China and the East (where it always was for most of the past 2000 years) is best captured by the chart that the OECD calls 'Shifting wealth' (see Figure 2.3), which shows how manufacturing value-added (manufacturing revenues net of costs) is shifting East, to non-OECD countries such as China and India. These countries are accounting for a rising proportion, and will almost certainly reach a point exceeding 50 per cent of manufacturing value added before the year 2020. This is a tipping point of immense significance. [6]

SHIFTING WEALTH

The OECD Development Centre has been tracking the shift, under the term 'Shifting Wealth'. Their statistical team has now extended their analysis (at my request) up to the year 2013 – with the clearest possible results: the 'non-OECD' countries are rapidly catching up with the OECD countries, and look set to overtake them well before the year 2020 (and have probably already done so).

Indeed, China's significance has been increasing rapidly over the past three decades. China was fourth in the world table in 1993, rising to third

---

6. The *Financial Times* journalist Gideon Rachman captures the significance of this shift in another phrase: Easternization (Rachman 2016).

in 2003 and first by 2010, consolidating this position in 2013. China is now recognized as the world's premier manufacturing nation. According to UN data analysed by the US-based Manufacturers' Alliance for Productivity and Innovation (MAPI), China accounted for no less than 23 per cent of world manufacturing value-added in 2013, as compared with just 17 per cent for the US and 8 per cent for Japan. India accounts for 2 per cent of the world total, and is also rapidly catching up, replicating China's rise of two decades earlier.[7] Note that the BRICS countries were responsible for just under 30 per cent of the world total in 2013, revealing again the significance of this non-OECD grouping of countries.

These three transformations – the Great Divergence, the Great Acceleration and the Great Convergence – have all been driven successively by the remarkable growth in the world's access to and utilization of fossil fuelled energy and material resources.[8] Now, at the beginning of the twenty-first century, we find new constraints on this process of endless growth in the scale of industrial activity, leading to rising productivity and through this, to rising incomes and wealth. These constraints are being felt initially and most severely by the rising 'catch-up' countries, led by China and India, as they harness fossil fuels and deploy resources in vast amounts – and run into constraints in the form of extreme pollution and geopolitical tensions. It is the latter constraints that are felt acutely in the convergent countries but are not so much appreciated in the West. The geopolitical constraints are felt through exposure, for example, to a global price of oil manipulated by the OPEC cartel; or by efforts to find new sources of oil such as South Sudan that become embroiled in civil war; or by attempts to utilize sources of oil and gas like the Gulf states where war and revolution are never far off the agenda.

Out of these tensions and constraints has emerged a new agenda for dealing with energy and materials – where the energy is tapped from renewable sources like the sun and the wind, and the materials are tapped from circular flows within the industrial system itself. These paradigm-breaking initiatives started as efforts undertaken at the margins in the West, but as they proved themselves to be economically and technologically sound they have been adopted and scaled up by the convergent powers, led by China and India.

---

7. See the MAPI website, at: https://www.mapi.net/.

8. Andrey Korotayev, Jack Goldstone and Julia Zinkina (2015) have published an account of the Great Divergence and Great Convergence that sees the demographic and economic shifts as being tightly correlated; indeed they view the Divergence and Convergence as two sides of the same 'Global Modernization' process.

This new set of transformations – the fourth of the industrial era – is what I am calling the *Green Shift*; it is a global, fundamental and world-historic transition that we are currently immersed in, and which can be expected to continue until there has been a complete transition to a world of renewables and the circular economy. This is what I called the next 'Great Transformation' in my 2015 Stanford book on *Greening of Capitalism* – a name which continues to have great resonance in its building on Polanyi's term the Great Transformation for the rise of industrial capitalism itself. The focus of this next, fourth transformation is likewise fourfold: there is a focus on energy (renewables in place of fossil fuels), materials (circular flow in place of linear throughput), and food production (enclosed activities in place of open, irrigated agriculture), and the finance that drives investment in these new directions. We shall deal with each of these aspects of the transformation in coming chapters.

In terms of the story of humankind as told by Harari, there is no more significant transformation than this, which promises to end the war between ecology and economics. Harari is certainly correct in pointing to the ecological serial murders that we as a species are responsible for, and now with our mastery of the earth, our casual destruction of wildlife, natural habitat and the living hell we create for our tamed livestock. But he is less willing to acknowledge that there is underway a transformation that is actually the only feasible path forward to 'healing' these gross blunders and crimes that we have committed and which is potentially setting us on a path to a genuinely sustainable future. It may of course be too late, and we may be doomed already. This is something that we cannot know. But it seems clear that if China, India and the other 'converging' countries are looking to bridge the gap between themselves and the West, then it will have to be through an alternative process of 'green growth' or what is more generally described as ecological modernization (or ecomodernism), or what the Chinese call 'ecological civilization'. No other pathway can possibly succeed.

THE FEASIBLE ECOMODERNIZATION STRATEGIES OF CHINA AND INDIA

What I outline in this book is the ecomodernization strategy that China and India are pursuing, plus reasons for viewing this strategy as being feasible – indeed, this is the only feasible strategy available to these industrializing giants. It is a strategic choice that underpins the new direction being taken by China, India et al. in their pursuit of green growth. This strategy works – it sets a feasible direction for the evolutionary processes that drive our industrial civilization – for a number of reasons. First, it works because it is based on manufacturing, and on its capacity to overcome constraints that are imposed by the natural world rather than on resource extraction and its vulnerability to such constraints. The prime example is energy, where the original breakthroughs associated with use of fossil fuels have now turned to constraints which can be overcome only by delinking power production from extraction of raw materials, that is, through a turn to renewables. The task is to demonstrate that renewables can indeed power the planet.

Resources in vast quantities have been the fuel of industrialization, and now the traditional approach to their extraction, via a linear throughput economy, is running into limits of resource availability and pollution. The resolution can be found in urban mining, whereby 'waste' outputs of one industrial process are taken up by another process, in a process known as closing the loop (circular economy). The task here is to demonstrate that the world can work on a circular flow basis. Likewise food production constraints as experienced by open field agriculture with all its chemical inputs and its huge consumption of water can be overcome by manufacturing principles of contained production in a closed environment. The task in this case is to demonstrate that such strategies can feed nine billion people comfortably.

Second, the strategy works because the underlying population that drives the whole process is capped; it will peak at around nine billion and will thenceforth stabilize or decline. We can make this prediction with a degree of assuredness because of the theory of the demographic transition. If population were to keep expanding indefinitely there would be no assurance that a closed system of resource flows could ever work. The alternative to our capping our own population through a civilized process of social reduction via a demographic transition is a nasty process of culling population through war, famine or disease. This is the real alternative to green growth.

Third, the strategy works because it is framed by an overarching process of urbanization. It is in cities that these contained processes as well as processes of resource extraction make sense; it is a further chapter in the story of cooperation at large scale as told by Harari. In this case the cooperation is between firms in an urban environment, as recognized in the long history of clusters, industrial districts and industrial parks. In China, for example, over 50 per cent of manufacturing value-added is conducted in industrial parks, which provide an optimal base for current greening initiatives in the creation of a circular economy.

Finally, the strategy works because ecomodernization can be framed as a series of technoeconomic choices that are ours to make rather than being imposed by some external force. Cities, firms, countries that make the choices best aligned with an ecomodernizing dynamic are the ones that can be expected to flourish; the ones that fail to do so can be expected to fall by the wayside. They will make no contribution to our further evolution as an urbanized, industrialized species that is greening its nest. This is an essentially Schumpeterian view of our evolving industrial system, driven not by simple product substitutions but by one technoeconomic formation succeeding another. Framing choices in these terms as investment choices (as done by China through its successive five year plans) is superior to imposing choices retroactively via taxes. The strategy works because it brings finance in as crucial player in the transition.

Strategic Choices – and Objections

The ecomodernizing choices described in this book are the fruits of what Harari has called the scientific revolution; they are the culmination of this half-millennium of experimental validation of ways of overcoming our admitted ignorance. Through our newfound techniques of reliable knowledge generation we created new fuels that overcame original natural constraints; we overcame constraints imposed by local materials production and use; we overcame constraints of traditional food production by chemical inputs and mechanization. But we are running into the limits of all these powerful innovations. It is taking a new twist in this evolutionary story, one that is operating at a scientific, technical and cultural level rather than a biological level – a twist that favours a green shift in all four spheres of energy, resources, water and food production, to resolve our current dilemmas. These dilemmas are not irresolvable.

The technoeconomic choices that we face are indeed epochal – these choices will determine whether or not we enjoy a 'good Anthropocene' (to use the clever, pithy phrase of the Breakthrough Institute and its *Ecomodernist Manifesto*). To the evident dislike of many, it turns out to be China that is leading the world into this next transition, this next phase of our industrialized species. No one would have predicted that the most astute practitioner of the strategies of Greenpeace and Friends of the Earth would turn out to be the Chinese Communist Party in its management of the vast country/civilization that is China. No one would have predicted that China would turn out to be the strategist par excellence of green growth.

The advantages of green choices turn out to be overwhelming for emerging industrial giants like China and India. Their dependence on imported fossil fuels and resources diminish as they ramp up renewable power sources and regenerated resources via the Circular Economy. These shifts in turn reduce pollution and traditional extraction disasters while building manufacturing capabilities and export platforms for the future. The fluctuating costs of utilizing fossil fuels are displaced by the one-way diminishing costs of resorting increasingly to manufactured devices like solar PV cells and wind turbines. The costs of 'fuels' decline as the marginal costs of generation from solar and wind continue to approach zero.

Yet the objections raised to the green growth strategy, clear and simple as it is, are legion. There is of course the anti-Chinese factor, where objections are raised on the basis that green products are emanating from China, with its alleged lax labour laws and environmental shortcuts that make for unfair competition (something I will deal with below). There is of course the suite of objections coming from vested interests and in particular the fossil fuel lobby – objections that take on criminal dimensions, if we can judge by the cases likely to be brought by the District Attorney of the state of New York against companies like Exxon-Mobil.[9] There are objections raised against the clean, cheap, abundant, and safe renewables on various economic grounds, mostly using out-of-date arguments concerning their alleged high costs and the issues created by their fluctuating character.

There are objections based on 'technical' grounds, such as the alleged limits to their contributions to the grid of the future. One of the most common of these technoeconomic objections is the claimed lack of power density of solar and wind power; this is seen by many scholars as their failure to continue the hypothesized process of decarbonization and increasing power density that is found in the sequence from wood, to coal, to oil, and then to nuclear. Dispersed solar and wind power upsets this neat sequence, and raises the ire of scholars such as Ausubel as well as the authors of the *Ecomodernist Manifesto* – as evidenced in their call for energy sources that are not just clean, cheap, abundant and safe but also 'dense' (an emotive

9. In March 2016 the Attorneys-General of six US states, including the states of New York, California and Massachusetts, met to discuss ways in which they could bring charges against fossil fuel firms like Exxon-Mobil on grounds of fraud in their dealing with issues of climate change http://www.insidesources.com/gore-schneiderman-defend-exxon-investigation-this-is-certainly-not-a-publicity-stunt/.

word, as I shall argue below).[10] Then there are objections based on environmental grounds, such as their alleged over-use of resources (particularly land resources); their alleged blotting out of vast swathes of virgin bush or desert, or their dependence on materials like rare earths.

Any visitor from Mars would be excused for thinking, after reading this long list of objections, that the sources of energy from water, wind and sun that China and India are utilizing in their Green Shift (their pursuit of a green growth strategy) are the source of more problems than the fossil fuels and nuclear power that they are successfully displacing. A good part of the text to come will be devoted to demonstrating that this is far from the case; the arguments for renewables are as clear and strong as the sun and wind themselves.

As a civilization whose evolution is now conducted in technoeconomic terms, and where choices and turning points are framed primarily as technoeconomic strategic choices, these issues as to which is the optimal way forward in terms of food production, energy production, resources production and water production are the critical choices of our time. There is an overarching ecomodernist narrative that helps us make the right choices – and of course the very spirit of the ecomodernist turn is itself the subject of widespread debate. What I offer here is a contribution to that debate, shorn of any sense that there is a technically determined path forward. The future is, as ever, open to strategic choice. This is the genius of our industrial civilization.

---

10. See for example Ausubel (2007) and similar writings. I deal with these in my *Futures* paper (2016).

CHAPTER 3

ECOMODERNIZATION – WITH 'CHINESE CHARACTERISTICS'

Intensifying many human activities – particularly farming, energy extraction, forestry, and settlement – so that they use less land and interfere less with the natural world is the key to decoupling human development from environmental impacts. These socioeconomic and technological processes are central to economic modernization and environmental protection.

AN ECOMODERNIST MANIFESTO, 2015

The process that dominates our world today is the rise of China and India as serious industrial powers. Whereas the Rise of the West enhanced the wealth and income of around 1 billion of the world's population, leaving the rest in poverty, the current Rise of the Rest that we are living through promises to raise several billion more into the ranks of the middle class, making industrialization and modernization the property of the world as a whole. This is indeed a *Great Transformation* of our global industrial system.

As the scale of global industrial production increases, and with it the scale of our civilization's burning of fossil fuels and plundering of resources, so we come up against the limits of that burning and plundering mode of economic behaviour. The limits are not just felt in terms of resource limits (will the world depart the oil age for want of oil?) but in terms of more immediate geopolitical limits, with nations contesting the increasingly precious fuels and resources needed to sustain their industrial systems. If the twentieth century was a century of oil wars, the twenty-first century promises to be even worse – unless something is done to change the 'Business as usual' paradigm.[1]

---

1. On oil wars and the 'race for resources' see Klare (2012). An earlier treatment was provided by Rutledge (2006).

That change is indeed coming – but not from the West itself, given its 'carbon lock-in' that ensures priority is given to coal, oil and gas as well as to behaviour based on assumptions of unlimited resource throughput and waste generation.[2] Instead it is coming from the 'Rest' – in this case led by China – because it is in the Rest that pollution is felt most acutely and geopolitical pressures are experienced most severely. It is China and India that are experiencing pressures from resource-import dependence, and so are transforming their industrial models most radically, leading them to become renewable energy superpowers and progenitors of a new Circular Economy in place of the conventional Western linear economy. They are doing so by exploiting their latecomer status and converging on the West, emulating companies like Tesla that are leading the field as exemplars and sources of ideas and technology.[3]

It is the combination of industrialization (rise of manufacturing as principal source of wealth and income) with a green economy, made imperative through considerations of energy security and resource security, that we may call *Ecomodernization*. It may be viewed as the world's leading ideology that makes sense of the Great Transformation under way. And because the change is led by China, we may truly call this a process of 'Ecomodernization with Chinese Characteristics'.

ECOLOGICAL MODERNIZATION

Ecological modernization is a body of ideas that goes back to debates in Western sociology of the 1980s, when scholars advanced the proposition that economy and ecology could be reconciled.[4] This was a radical departure at a time when the twin worlds of economic development and ecological sustainability had little to do with each other.

While the ideas of ecological modernization (ecomodernism) continued to exercise influence in the West, it is in the East that they have become dominant and transformative. China, experiencing the fastest and most profound industrial transformation in history, and also experiencing the worst levels of

---

2. See Unruh (2002) for the original exposition of carbon lock-in, which refers to the battery of techno-institutional systems that bias Western economic activity towards continued use of fossil fuels.

3. Tesla took the radical step in 2015 of releasing its patents, inviting small and medium sized companies to make use of its patented technology in order to grow the EV industry.

4. There is a broad literature on ecological modernization; for a representative sample of writing, see the collection edited by Mol and Sonnenfeld (2000).

pollution ever encountered, as well as rising levels of dependence on resource and fossil fuel imports, reacted by adopting a national goal of an 'ecological civilization'. While a clumsy phrase, this was interpreted in sharp terms as placing ecological goals on a par with those of economic growth. In the Chinese system this meant that career paths of provincial officials would be determined not just by their contribution to economic growth but also by their achievements in cleaning up the environment.

The Chinese have as yet produced no commanding literature underpinning their conversion to the tenets of 'ecological civilization'. Instead it is a group of largely Western scholars, for example those grouped around the Breakthrough Institute in California, who have produced a document that succinctly captures the essential features of ecological modernization.[5] Just as Martin Luther defined the terms of the Protestant Reformation in 1517 when he nailed his 95 Theses to the door of the All Saints Church in Wittenberg (directed largely at condemning papal indulgences) so we find something comparable happening today. The Breakthrough Institute has nailed its Manifesto with 71 Theses arranged in 7 chapters to the 'door' of the Internet, promising to launch a revolution within environmentalism and capitalism. Its fundamental (unspoken) thesis is that the two are compatible.

DECOUPLING

The idea of *decoupling* is what drives the whole enterprise. Thesis 18 of the Manifesto introduces decoupling as implying that 'human environmental impacts rise at a slower rate than overall economic growth. Thus, for each unit of economic output that is added, less environmental impact (e.g., deforestation, defaunation, pollution) results. Overall impacts may still increase, just at a slower rate than would otherwise be the case' (p. 11). This concept of decoupling is then clarified as 'relative decoupling'; an alternative, more profound notion of 'absolute decoupling' is introduced to imply that resource usage/consumption is actually declining in absolute terms.

It is with this notion of decoupling that I wish to begin my own reflections on this topic, because it is clearly the driver of ecological modernization and the key to understanding China's (and following China, India's) next Great Transformation. We are interested fundamentally in how an economy's resource consumption/

---

5. See the *Ecomodernist Manifesto* (Asafu-Adjaye et al. 2015) with 14 authors, available at: http://www.ecomodernism.org/manifesto-english/.

usage changes with the economy's growth. The more tightly the resource consumption follows economic growth, the more the economy is said to be coupled to its resource throughput. The goal is to become decoupled.

We can be precise about this. Let us define a *Decoupling Index* as the rate of change of resources used per unit rate of change in the economy. Normally this index will have a value exceeding 1 – meaning that the resources consumed will increase faster than the economy grows. This is otherwise known as 'Business as usual' – and it is what spells ruin for an economy like China's because of the increasing geopolitical pressures experienced as it tries to keep running on the resource throughput treadmill. It also spells ruin for the planet if that resource footprint keeps on getting larger. If an economy's resource usage/consumption increases just as fast as the economy is growing, then it is said to have a Decoupling Index equal to 1 – an important tipping point. When the Decoupling Index falls below 1 (but is still positive) this is a situation known as relative decoupling. This is the situation reached in many OECD countries, where falling resource intensities mean that the countries consume less and less resources to achieve a given level of economic growth. For China the achievement of relative decoupling is a pre-eminent goal, measured assiduously in its Five Year Plans (FYPs) with their national targets for resource intensity reduction and energy intensity reduction. Finally, if the Decoupling Index actually falls into negative territory, then this means that the economy consumes fewer resources as it grows – a situation known as absolute decoupling. No major country has reached this situation as yet. But it is the end goal of any green growth strategy.

The Decoupling Index is introduced in the important UNEP/IRP report of 2011 on *Decoupling Natural Resource Use and Environmental Impacts from Economic Growth.* The report provides a useful chart that explicates the shift in the Decoupling Index very clearly (Figure 3.1).

Although they are rarely mentioned in the same breath in the literature, the Circular Economy as promoted by China is in fact an excellent example of a state-driven material decoupling without sacrificing economic growth.[6]

---

6. An important exception is the 2014 report from the International Resource Panel/ UNEP, on *Decoupling Natural Resource Use and Environmental Impacts from Economic Growth*, which has a chapter on China and the Circular Economy. This report's lead author is Professor Marina Fischer-Kowalski, from the Institute of Social Ecology at Alpen-Adria University, Austria, and with contributing authors including Ernst Ulrich von Weizsäcker (chair of the Decoupling Working group), Yuichi Moriguchi, Fridolin Krausmann and others. See: http://www.unep.org/resourcepanel/decoupling/files/pdf/Decoupling_ Report_English.pdf.

FIGURE 3.1. The Decoupling Index and economic growth.

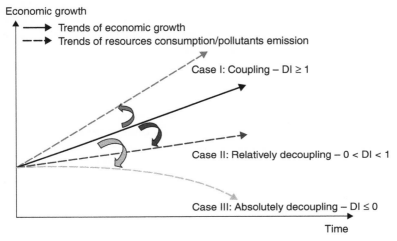

SOURCE: UNEP/IRP report *Decoupling Natural Resource Use and Environmental Impacts from Economic Growth*, Fig. 8-2.

The Circular Economy thus qualifies as a case of relative decoupling. The drive indicated by China's strong commitment to the Circular Economy is precisely the drive to reduce its resource intensity – and this is indeed a central measure in its newly introduced Circular Economy Index, introduced by China's National Bureau of Statistics (NBS) in 2015. Hao Tan and I argued in our article published in *Nature* in March 2016 that China is seeking through its Circular Economy initiatives to reduce its resource intensity, without sacrificing economic growth. This is what is arguably enhancing the resource security of a huge country like China.

My contribution in this text is to insist on the close links between the notion of decoupling and that of the Circular Economy. Usually these are discussed separately – and yet in reality they are tightly linked – or 'coupled' (to make a poor pun). Analysts like Walter Stahel, who published the first papers on the Circular Economy (then called the closed-loop economy) emphasize dematerialization and the extended use of artefacts, stretching to the hiring of products by the hour or the day rather than their purchase and ownership. This is one line of development of the concept. Another emphasizes decoupling and dematerialization, in an effort to reduce the global material intensity of economies like China.

In the spirit of decoupling, ecomodernization is concerned with raising resource productivity (getting more out of resource consumption per unit economic activity) and energy productivity – or equally so in the converse, in reducing resource intensity and energy intensity. The OECD countries have already made considerable progress in these endeavours – but the real issue for the world is whether China and India can make comparable progress at their vastly greater scales of activity.

The good news is that they are indeed making progress. I shall be focusing in this text on the fundamental processes that are driving everything else – the transformations in the energy system, resources regeneration (circular economy), and food production and water. In each case, we can identify the technoeconomic processes that are providing a substitute 'decoupled' process. The chapters on energy and materials circular flow and new enclosed methods of food production will provide the details. In the next chapter I wish to outline what these processes have in common, and what makes them so interesting as drivers of change.

CHAPTER 4

SOCIOTECHNICAL TRANSITIONS: A SIXTH WAVE

Before tackling the details of the green shift insofar as it affects energy transformations, resources, food production and water, we want to ask what is the character of the transition overall. Is it simply a process of substitution of one material or technology for another, as maintained by the models and policy prescriptions of neoclassical economists? Or do we need to dig deeper, to engage with the Schumpeterian dynamics of one industrial system or paradigm superseding another?

Focusing on the technoeconomic drivers of change in our industrial system, we can draw from a Schumpeterian literature to identify five transitions in the period since the Industrial Revolution – with a sixth putatively under way in the current period. The point is that each transition involves major social, technical and business upheavals that go well beyond mere economic substitutions effected by relative price movements. In my 2015 book *Greening of Capitalism*, the five transitions were outlined as follows.

FIVE WAVES OF SOCIOTECHNICAL TRANSITION

A first wave was created by the diffusion of the improved steam engine, which for the first time created a universal power source independent of natural constraints like river courses, wind or horse power. This wave went through an upswing from the 1780s to around 1810 and then into a downswing into the 1840s. It is what is conventionally known as the Industrial Revolution.[1] A second wave was initiated by the railway investment craze, with thousands of kilometres of track being laid in the emerging industrial powers – and creating

---

1. The timing and sources and impact of the Industrial revolution are of course all contested. For a comprehensive overview, see Allen (2009).

a second upswing from the 1840s to the 1870s, followed by a downswing into the 1890s. A third wave was launched by the new applications of electricity, in electric motors fed by new power grids, combined with the advances in steel and chemical technologies, culminating in the 'modernist' wave from the 1890s to the period of the First World War and a downswing lasting through the Great Depression and the Second World War. The post war period then saw a fourth upswing, driven by oil and the internal combustion engine, with all the features of suburbanization, with new consumer products and services that characterized this new wave, in upswing from the close of the war to the late 1960s and downswing up to the early 1980s. The fifth wave, driven by microelectronics and IT with its numerous applications across the economy (except in energy and transport), saw an upswing from the 1980s to the early 2000s followed by a downswing expected to last until the 2020s. The great debates of the 1980s over how well the world was accommodating to the imminent arrival of a fifth wave are now giving way to debates over the world's accommodation to a sixth such transition.

This periodization of five Schumpeterian upswings and downswings since the Industrial Revolution is relatively widely accepted.[2] The real issue is whether there is a sixth wave now appearing earlier than anticipated, and being driven by renewable energies and the application of IT to energy and transport where it had been prevented from exercising its revolutionary effects during the period of tight oligopolistic control during the fourth and emerging fifth wave periods.[3] If it is real (and I have no doubt of its reality) this sixth wave would be based on the revolutionary impact of a shift in the underlying energy foundations, from fossil fuels to renewables, with all the associated applications of IT, microelectronics and the Internet. It can be expected to create the dominant technological wave of the twenty-first century.

SIXTH WAVE TRANSITIONS: FOOD, WATER, RESOURCES, ENERGY

We may characterize a series of transitions as being 'sixth wave' (6W) processes where they share the feature that they promise to substitute traditional open-air

---

2. See the successive works by Freeman, by Perez (e.g., Perez 2010) and by Freeman and Perez (1988) as exemplary. Freeman and Louçã (2001) provide another perspective on the same theme. In their discussion of energy, climate change and sustainable development, Grubb et al. (2014) emphasize the role of strategic investment and innovation as shaping emerging markets for renewables.

3. See the exposition in my *Greening of Capitalism* (Table 7-1) based on Korotayev and Tsirel (2010), Tables 1, 2, p. 2.

operations dependent on natural cycles or on natural resources with closed-environment operations or operations involving manufactured products utilizing technologies that are clean, cheap, abundant – and safe. In the most general terms possible I agree with the authors of the *Ecomodernist Manifesto* that this is a shift from processes that are coupled to nature to ones that are not so coupled (i.e., they are decoupled). Let us follow through how this works.

Food production

The production of food has remained more or less tied to the great innovations that we associate with the Agricultural Revolution of 10–12,000 years ago such as, domestication of plants, breeding of superior varieties, regular planting, watering, fertilizing and harvesting. It is a process that in its open-air form is subjecting larger and larger areas of the planet to intensifying agriculture, with all the negative impacts like soil degradation and overuse of water resources, leading to overreliance on fertilizers, herbicides, pesticides, use of antibiotics in farmed animals and all the runoff involved, resulting in the 'silent spring' effects in killing off biodiversity.

Take vegetables production first. The ecomodernizing approach is to decouple agriculture from its open air form with all its sources of insecurity such as being subject to variations in factors like rainfall, soil salinity and fertility, and to produce food instead in what can aptly be described as 'plant factories' or 'vegetable factories' or more generally 'controlled environment agriculture' (CEA). [I will not use this term because 'ager' as the root word for agriculture refers to open fields. It is better to coin a term like 'controlled environment food production'.] This alternative means of producing food is one that brings principles of manufacturing to food production, controlling all the parameters such as water flow, air flow, acid–base balance and gaseous mix (including carbon dioxide levels) in a controlled environment generally known as a greenhouse. But 'plant factories' extend the notion of greenhouse so far as to become unrecognizable – including stacking rows of plants in vertical frames, rotating them to receive light and water mist, dispensing with sunlight altogether through use of energy-efficient LED lamps with their wavelength outputs tuned to the needs of growing plants, and dispensing with soil altogether in what is called aeroponics.

Such plant factories are ultra-clean, thus eliminating pests and microbes from the growing environment and producing leafy vegetables such as lettuce that are so clean that they do not need to be washed by the consumer. Such an approach to 'farming' (better, food production) is obviously associated more with cities than with the countryside, and hence has given rise to terms like 'urban farming', or 'vertical farming' and other descriptors that seek to capture the artificial or decoupled aspect of the process. The key driver of such systems (which already exist in Japan, Taiwan and China and are penetrating elsewhere) is that they are vastly more productive than traditional farming (in terms of yield per hectare); their costs are coming down to attain parity with costs of traditionally farmed vegetables (a convergence that we might term 'food market parity', by analogy with the term 'grid parity' used in the energy sector). Since the inputs are minimal we can expect the costs to continue to fall, as per the experience curve that is characteristic of manufacturing processes.[4]

Likewise we can envisage an ecomodernizing alternative to traditional livestock production of meat, utilizing tissue culturing methods scaled up to huge vats and reactors that resemble nothing so much as a brewery. The vats would be producing real cultured meat as well as other traditional animal products like the proteins found in milk and eggs. Already the world has witnessed a cultured meat hamburger cooked and eaten at a public demonstration in London in August 2013 – to widespread acclaim. Again, costs can be expected to plummet as the market expands.

Water production

Likewise in the production of clean water, we see a trend associated with urbanization and industrialization where increasingly intolerable pressures on 'natural' water usage are being countered by artificial water production via new techniques of desalination and water recycling. Methods of water extraction that are coupled to natural phenomena like seasonal rainfall and exploitation of ground water are being stressed beyond their limits, through intensification of agriculture and its dependence on irrigation and ground water. There are also water-dependent industrial processes such as oil refining and other water-hungry processes that have been conducted without regard to natural water limits and now pose severe threats as water shortages loom.

Again, a solution presents itself in the form of decoupling the water usage from its natural setting – as in water extraction from dirty water recirculation and desalination via new technologies such as 'multiple effect distillation'

---

4. It must be conceded that 6W methods of food production so far are limited to vegetables and horticultural production plus aquaculture – but no successful cases as yet of broad-acre production of grains have been demonstrated. This remains a major technical 'reverse salient' to be resolved.

or new forms of membrane-based desalination via forced osmosis. These innovations liberate cities from traditional water supply sources and open up new possibilities of recycling water, decoupling the process from dependence on natural water cycles. Sources of power to drive the requisite desalination processes can increasingly be derived from renewable sources including sun and wind, so reducing the costs of desalination and facilitating its wider adoption through the power of the learning curve.

Resources reproduction – circular economy

Industrialization has been associated with intensive use of resources – extracting them from the earth (mining, drilling) and then dumping them in the earth again (waste disposal). This traditional, linear approach to resource extraction and disposal is even older than agriculture – and just as unchanged. As the scale increases to encompass the planet as a whole, the disasters associated with more intense and larger-scale mining are getting worse – such as coal mining disasters that are reported every year in China and collapses of tailings dams as occurred in 2015 in Brazil. Now of course some resources have to be burned and as such are not recyclable – and so we call them 'fuels' and discuss them separately, under the rubric of energy. But all other resources are subject to conditions of increased scale of use, increasing intensity, increasing pollution, and increasing insecurity as nations and companies fight for access to the dwindling resource supplies. China as the latest arrival in this industrializing process and the world's largest manufacturer is also the world's largest exploiter of resources in this 'take, make, dump' mode and the world's largest producer of waste. But it is also developing the world's most radical and successful approach to solving the problem – a solution consistent with other ecomodernizing trends that taken together are called the *Circular Economy*.

The Circular Economy (CE) decouples resource use from its natural setting and aims to recirculate resources, allowing them to be regenerated by extraction from waste flows. This is what is aptly called 'urban mining' which may be characterized as (re)production of resources by artificial means, through closing industrial loops and turning outputs into inputs for other processes – emulating the cycles of nature where waste is made into food. The CE as a national goal is most advanced in China, where successive Five Year Plans (FYPs) devote major sections to achievement of CE targets to bring China's material intensity levels closer to those of OECD countries overall. What is driving its uptake in China is mainly legislative and planning requirements, including the channelling of investment into CE initiatives via use of state development banks that follow FYP targets in making their loans contingent on meeting green targets. But what ultimately will drive the supersession of the linear economy by the circular economy – a process that can already be seen – will be the reducing costs of regenerated resources (urban mined resources) as opposed to 'open air' traditional mining and associated waste disposal costs. I have suggested that this process could be accelerated if commodities futures markets were to introduce traded contracts that differentiated between virgin resources and regenerated resources – allowing the traders to create a price differential between the two.[5] There are also clear productivity gains as resource intensity is reduced and waste disposal is almost completely eliminated. There is an urgent need for econometric estimates of these cost and productivity advantages to be anticipated from CE initiatives.

Energy production/generation

When we look at energy issues, we see the same processes at work. Taking the burning of high carbon containing resources (termed fossil fuels) as the prevailing 'business as usual', with its tight coupling between power generation and natural resources of these fuels (mined, drilled), with price fluctuations depending on availability of accessed deposits, we can see that a sixth wave remedy again presents itself. The remedy is to divorce energy generation from these natural moorings, and to generate power utilizing devices manufactured for the purpose. These machines would include wind turbines or solar photovoltaic cells or arrays of mirrors and lenses as in concentrated solar power systems, together with energy storage systems to accumulate the energy generated and release it as needed. This is best described as energy generation using artificial or manufactured systems as a sixth wave transition.

The *Ecomodernist Manifesto (EM)* complicates its otherwise clear discussion of these matters by calling it 'energy extraction', which retains a link back to fossil fuels. A clean terminological break – energy generation from renewable sources – is what is called for. I surmise that the *EM* authors use the nebulous term 'energy extraction' because they want the focus to be on 'extracting' energy from nuclear processes like fission and fusion. But I have no such constraint: the best term is clearly 'energy generation utilizing artificial measures', as opposed to remaining tied to natural deposits of fuels and being subjected to all the geopolitical uncertainties as nations and corporations fight

---

5. See Mathews (2008b). This contribution is framed in terms of a putative sustainable biofuels contract, but is easily extended across to commodities futures contracts in general.

for access to these fuels (including uranium) and their pricing. By contrast, manufacturing their way to energy security by shifting to renewables is a promising way forward, consistent with the other ecomodernizing trends discussed so far.[6] Again it is China that is in the lead in this endeavour, driven no doubt by concerns over energy security which can be mitigated by manufacturing the (means to produce) the energy needed – rather than depending on 'natural' supplies.

What drives this shift in energy systems is cost reduction – down to and beyond 'grid parity'. Some energy scholars depict the driver as decarbonization, which runs through the sequence: wood, to coal, to oil, to gas – and then to hydrogen (derived from fossil fuels) and nuclear.[7] But in my argument the driver is not decarbonization; it is cost reduction, which derives from the learning curve that is in turn linked to manufacturing. Some scholars seem to emphasize decarbonization at the expense of cost reductions – perhaps because they view the decarbonization process as one that moves directly from one fossil fuel to another and then to the hydrogen economy, with nuclear reactors being deployed to split water to produce the hydrogen at colossal scale. This is a very different vision of energy systems evolution from the one that I discuss in this text.

REVERSE SALIENTS

Thomas Hughes is the source for much of our understanding of how large-scale technoeconomic systems evolve. His paradigm case was the electric power networks that were developed at the end of the nineteenth century and into the twentieth century, as analysed in his magisterial work *Networks of Power* (1983). This study tackled the first of the technological innovations that constituted a whole system – even more so than the railways and the gas and water utilities of the earlier nineteenth century. The electric power networks involved innovation at the level of units and installations – such as electric motors, generators, and dynamos – but even more significantly at the level of the distribution system with its famous 'battle of the systems' between AC and DC power. The DC power system was developed and championed by Edison

---

6. The reference is to the article in *Nature* published by Hao Tan and myself in 2014.

7. See for example the arguments mounted by Jesse Ausubel (e.g., Ausubel 2007), which draw from a long tradition developed by others such as Marchetti. I provide a critique of this school of thought in Mathews (2016a).

and his General Electric company – but its fatal flaw was that it was very limited in its range of distribution. The solution to this was provided by the Serbian genius Nikola Tesla with his invention of AC power and the polyphase generator that provided it, working in alliance with the Westinghouse company – the eventual victor in the war of the systems.

In taking a systemic approach to the issue, Hughes worked with the concept of *reverse salient*. He introduced this concept as a means of accounting for the concentration of effort on certain technological problems and less on others.[8] The term is a military one, depicting 'that section of an advancing battle line, or military front, but which has fallen behind or been bowed back' (1983: 79). The term had been a household word during the First World War when it was used to describe the German efforts to eliminate what was for them the reverse salient at Verdun. Hughes explained that the term is preferable to others like 'disequilibrium' or 'bottleneck' because of its connotations of complexity involving individuals, groups, material forces, historical influences and other factors. Ultimately the reverse salient is a subsystem that is underperforming and holding back the advance or development of the system as a whole. Hughes argued that the idea of a reverse salient 'suggests the need for concentrated action (invention and development) if expansion is to proceed' (1983: 79) – that is, concentrated attention devoted to solving the issues raised by the underperforming subsystem.

The DC power system developed by Edison and GE had many reverse salients all of which were solved – except the overwhelming problem of its rising cost of transmission as the distance from the power station increased. Likewise the AC system had its own reverse salients which were also solved, making the AC system in the end overwhelmingly superior to the original DC system. Edison had early on identified the issue of the rising cost of transmission of the DC system as its major reverse salient. To his frustration he and his engineers could not find a solution within the DC paradigm.[9]

Now the point of introducing this discussion of 'reverse salient' is to deploy the concept in our discussion of the diffusion of new, green technological systems – with renewable energy systems and smart grids taking over from

---

8. I would like to acknowledge discussions on this point with my colleague Dr Mei-Chih Hu, a professor at National Taiwan University.

9. As described by Hughes, the solution was found eventually by Gaulard and Gibbs in the form of an alternative AC paradigm, involving polyphase generators, with high-voltage utilized for distribution (achieved via transformers) and low voltage for local distribution. See Hughes 1983: 86.

fossil fuelled, centralized, non-intelligent grids, and circular economy networks (closed loops) taking over from the linear economy, and new food production systems taking over from traditional, open-air, irrigated systems. How does the concept work in these cases?

For the case of renewable energy, there is a clear reverse salient in the form of energy storage subsystems. Until recently there was no sense of there being a strong technological process of innovation bringing costs and prices of batteries and storage systems to the level where mass production could take over. This situation is now changing and the one remaining reverse salient standing in the way of rapid diffusion of renewable energy systems is now closing.

In the case of the shift to a circular economy, the reverse salient is doubtless that of companies in a supply chain failing (or refusing) to act on their common interests in sharing resources such as energy, heat and power and waste disposal. But the case of China is different since CE initiatives are targeted on existing industrial parks and export processing zones where there is already a governing body or representative council that embodies the interests of all participants, and is better able to recognize where firms might have common interests. It also helps that these representative bodies also carry local authority and have the means to require firms to act where their interests are seen to coincide.

In the case of water regeneration and food production in enclosed spaces, the reverse salient has been heavy use of energy and high costs of power, particularly for lighting in enclosed-space horticulture using greenhouses. This situation is neutralized by the use of solar sources for power and seawater, as in the Sundrop farms concept discussed below, and by use of LEDs for lighting that offer cost-effective solutions that can improve yield through tuning the wavelengths of their outputs. Reverse salients thus slow down diffusion of innovations, but do not block them forever.

Interconnections

The four dominant processes that may be viewed as constituting the core of ecomodernization (or what I call 6W processes) are expounded here, together with their reverse salients. But of course they are interconnected – and we shall explore such interconnections when we discuss the concept of the 'triple nexus' between water, energy and food production below. No doubt we could extend the list of 6W processes. Transport is increasingly being decoupled from natural moorings as the urbanizing world moves towards electric vehicles (both pure battery powered and hybrid vehicles), high-speed rail, metro subway systems, air transport as well as electric powered sea transport. In fact the case can be made that the invention and commercialization of the automobile at the end of the nineteenth and beginning of the twentieth century was the original version of 'decoupling' (leaving aside the issue of fossil fuel dependence) that provides the template for all the subsequent cases being discussed under the rubric of ecomodernization. The automobile (as the name implies) liberated humans from natural constraints on mobility, measured in terms of range or speed or acceleration. Likewise steam-powered vessels liberated sea craft from the natural constraints of wind, and aircraft set a new standard of naturally unconstrained transport that had no known antecedents. Of course the analogy breaks down when one introduces constraints associated with fossil fuels – which are themselves being mitigated as private transport moves towards electric vehicles and fuel cell vehicles with battery charging networks as the new infrastructure.

What is demonstrated here is that these 6W changes are both feasible and real, and the reverse salients that have been holding back their diffusion are being resolved. The new systems are already being implemented, albeit sometimes at small scale, but in a way that lends itself to scaling up to global level. This is the challenge being met by China and India, with powerful benefits for themselves and powerful repercussions for the rest of the world.

* * *

Where I differ from the authors of the *Ecomodernist Manifesto* is that I see the diffusion of 6W technologies as being likely to be driven by their reducing costs – which are ensured by the fact that products embodying these technologies are all manufactured. As such they benefit from increasing returns and reducing costs because of the learning curve effect. Their diffusion will also be driven by the wide applicability of these technologies – taking over from traditional operations in such diverse areas as food production, water production and resource (commodity) production as well as energy production. This is truly an economy-wide technoeconomic transition – which is why I call it the sixth wave disrupting the industrial system since the original Industrial Revolution.

Now other authors have addressed themselves to these questions but with differing emphases. Jeremy Rifkin is convinced that there is an industrial revolution involved here, but he sees it as the third such revolution – telescoping everything that has happened since the eighteenth century into two simple turning points, a first (industrial revolution) and a second (electrification). He insists that there is a third such transition underway, driven by technological changes with a principal focus on the Internet of Things (IoT) and Zero

Marginal Costs as the driving forces.[10] Now the IoT will surely have a profound impact in enabling people to take charge of many operations that have been the province of large corporations. But the IoT can also be viewed as enhancing the power of other large corporations – particularly of those that are investing large funds in the IoT like GE, Microsoft, Google and Intel. So while energy prosumers might be able to locate each other in a 'sharing economy' exchange of energy, I do not see this as the reason that will drive the diffusion of 6W processes so much as the fact that the technologies involved are manufactured to be cheap, clean, abundant – and safe.[11]

As for zero marginal costs (or more accurately, close-to-zero marginal costs), these too must certainly be viewed as a profound driver of the uptake of 6W technologies and products. There is no doubt that generating solar and wind power eliminates the cost of fuel from the energy equation and thereby makes such technologies much more attractive than their fossil fuelled competitors. The fact that sunshine and wind are free and can be harvested by devices that we build, and are operated with low marginal costs, is a profound advantage. But is it the principal driver of the uptake of 6W energy devices?

The feature that all 6W products and technologies have in common is that they address age-old issues of insecurity – food insecurity, water insecurity, energy insecurity and resource insecurity – and pose novel means of alleviating these insecurities. In their different ways they all substitute manufactured and artificial environments for traditional open air environments subject to adverse weather, physical conditions and dependence on water, soil and natural processes. Insofar as this is the message of the *Ecomodernist Manifesto* I agree with it and applaud the authors for putting their finger on the key issue.[12]

SIXTH WAVE TRENDS – DECOUPLING ECONOMIES FROM NATURAL CONSTRAINTS

There are many trends that drive the evolution of our global civilization – one being the processes of globalization themselves. There is elimination of ancient prejudices, and liberation of women from practices and ideologies that tie them

---

10. See Rifkin (2013; 2014).

11. I discuss these matters further below in the chapter on energy, where the case is made for a Global Energy Interconnection (GEI) that has greater salience than the IoT.

12. Here I am contrasting the *Ecomodernist Manifesto* with the arguments of other commentators like Jeremy Rifkin or Gaia-author James Lovelock.

to the home and to child bearing and child rearing (and prevent the onset of the demographic transition). What underpins many of these welcome shifts is a broad process widely known as modernization.

The features that all these 6W processes share is that they are products of manufacturing – in that they are clean and operated within a closed environment. They are *practicable* (in that the technologies already exist), *scalable* and *replicable* – and hence can be utilized in cities everywhere as the world population expands and urbanizes.[13] Above all, they present as favourable options for China, India and other emerging industrial giants, providing them with the means to resolve their issues of security of energy, water, food and resources supplies.

Another way of characterizing these processes is to describe them as shifting towards a design ethic of biomimicry or biomimesis – taking the biological world as fashioned through millions of years of evolution as guide to introducing and designing new technologies. Renewable energies are biomimetic, as are circular resource flows and water regeneration and desalination utilizing heat-driven processes that biomimic the evaporation-driven water cycle. Even synthetic meat culture and creation of artificial dairy products can be said to be biomimetic in that they are guided by nature in their ways of constructing muscle tissues and blends of proteins that can substitute for the animal-derived originals.[14]

In this book I am focused on the dominant technoeconomic trends of our time, which may be called ecomodernizing trends, and I ask to what extent the successful industrialization of large countries like China and India and Brazil depends on the strategic choices they make as they embark on their modernizing journey. Along with South Africa these may be called the BICS countries, with reference to what Goldman Sachs christened the BRICS – an acronym which included Russia. (Let us agree to exclude Russia because it remains tied to fossil fuels and shows little inclination presently to develop energy alternatives like renewable power or resource alternatives like the circular economy.) The BICS countries are becoming the centre of gravity of

---

13. These features of being practicable, scalable and replicable are those used explicitly by the administrative committee of the joint Sino-Singapore eco-city of Tianjin – as discussed in the penultimate chapter. I am taking these features as characterizing 6W processes generally.

14. I discussed biomimicry at length in *Greening of Capitalism* (Mathews 2015). My sister Freya Mathews has discussed the philosophical underpinnings of biomimicry (F. Mathews 2011).

world manufacturing (Great Convergence) and are now becoming the drivers of investment in new 6W technological processes, through their creation of new investment vehicles such as the New Development Bank on the one hand (a BRICS initiative) and the Asian Infrastructure Investment Bank (AIIB) on the other. These banks are expected to take over from the World Bank as sources of green infrastructure funding in the next couple of decades.[15]

The major trends worth focusing on are those that decouple economies and economic processes from natural constraints. It is China and India that appear to be driving the uptake of these new systems, with strategic choices that are distinctive and differ in many ways from those outlined by the authors of the *Ecomodernist Manifesto*. Their choices impact both on their own economies and on the rest of the world as their actions drive the expansion of markets and hence the downward trend of costs and therefore prices. It is little wonder then that these countries are greening their economies as fast as they can manage the process – with all the technological, economic and geopolitical constraints (such as trade conflicts) involved. There really is no secret as to why China, India and other industrializing countries are choosing the green growth option with distinctive strategic choices that reflect their historic positions. We start by seeking to analyse just why they are making these particular choices – and what the impact is likely to be.

---

15. See the argument of the paper 'The AIIB and investment in action on climate change', by Darius Nassiry and Smita Nakhooda, ODI, April 2016, at: http://www.odi.org/publications/10374-aiib-and-investment-action-climate-change.

CHAPTER 5

NO WONDER CHINA AND INDIA ARE PURSUING GREEN GROWTH STRATEGIES SO VIGOROUSLY

The argument so far is that ecomodernization will proceed because of its superior attributes, namely in decoupling economic activities from their natural moorings and thereby being able to benefit from technological advantages in terms of greater eco-efficiencies and lower costs. But what drives these changes is normally left unexplored. In the *Ecomodernist Manifesto* there is a great lacuna at the core, with a big question mark: is it solely a moral imperative that will drive the transformations described in food, water, energy and resource production?

This is where China and India enter the picture. In addition to adopting an ecomodernizing platform (= green growth) for their own benefit, their actions in doing so have powerful repercussions on the world as a whole. As China becomes the world's renewables superpower, it expands the market for renewables and low-carbon technologies, which in turn leads to greater specialization and further efficiencies being captured, leading to lower costs and lower prices that translate into further specialization and greater efficiencies – and lower costs. And so on, round and round, in a process best captured by non-mainstream economists as *circular and cumulative causation* (C and CC).[1]

The core of my argument is that China and India are adopting ecomodernizing strategies for their own benefit (enhancing energy, spillover food, resources and water security), but that as they do so they drive spill over effects around the world in terms of reducing costs, captured in the

---

1. See Toner (2001) for an illuminating discussion of Circular and Cumulative Causation and why it disappeared from mainstream economic analysis. The concept was used by Kaldor (1970) in his Address to the Scottish Economic Society on regional policies.

learning curve. And these reducing costs make it more likely for firms in other parts of the world to pursue similar strategies, bypassing the difficulties encountered in use of fossil fuels, thereby reinforcing the ecomodernizing tendencies that are already underway. The advantages in terms of lower carbon emissions are indeed a fortunate side-effect of this process. This is a most convenient truth.

We started the discussion with the process of 'shifting wealth' (OECD) or Great Convergence, which in turn creates enormous energy and resource demands that feed insecurity if the conventional 'business as usual' model is pursued.[2] Instead China is pursuing a 'green growth' strategy, as is India with a lag of a few years, through which decoupling is being achieved and energy and resource security is being enhanced. China and India are utilizing their newfound positions of prominence in the manufacturing world to pursue fresh strategies of green growth

CHINA AND ITS GREEN GROWTH STRATEGY

China has been setting ambitious targets for the development of its green economy, starting with the 11th Five Year Plan (FYP) (2006–2010) then in the 12th FYP (2011–2015), where the targets for 2015 can be checked against real accomplishments, and now in the 13th FYP covering the years 2016 to 2020. The headline report is that China intends to be far and away the world leader in water, wind and sun power generation by 2020, with installed power generation capacity of 750 GW – or three quarters of a trillion watts of clean and renewable power. If this trend continues (and there is every reason for believing that it will not just continue, but intensify) then China would be the world's first country to build 1 trillion watts of clean, renewable power before 2025, that is, within the next decade. That means saved carbon emissions from coal-fired plants that would be generating 1 trillion watts of dirty power; it means saved import payments for fossil fuels (coal, oil, gas) to the tune of 1 trillion watts of power capacity; and of course the intangible benefits of creating the world's most competitive export platform for clean, green energy systems. Above all it means that China will be able to drive the modernization of its economy with clean power as it becomes one of the most electrified industrial systems on the planet.

---

2. For a review of the Great Convergence that links it through demographic trends to the earlier Great Divergence, see Korotayev et al. (2016).

Target of 750 billion watts of clean, green power in China by 2020

No other country comes close to this Chinese target of installing 750 GW of clean energy from water, wind and sun by 2020. By contrast the EU was able to install 12.8 GW of new wind capacity in 2015 to bring the total installed wind capacity to 142 GW.[3]

China's 2020 targets

Solar 160 GW
Wind 250 GW
Hydro 340 GW
Total   750 GW[4]

Just in the past five years, China has added over 200 GW of clean energy capacity, or an average of over 40 GW per year. This supports the assertion that China is likely to reach a renewable power capacity exceeding 1 trillion watts (1 TW) before the year 2025 – or within a decade. This will be a milestone of enormous significance.

As China resorts increasingly to green power, so it will drive emulation around the world. So it is likely that by the late 2020s the world as a whole should have built several terawatts of clean power (largely solar and wind) and should be enjoying the newfound energy and resource security that would come from this. The impact on the fossil fuel industries will be profound, as the shift to renewables for power generation can be expected to kill off the coal industry; the shift to EVs in transport can be expected to drastically reduce oil consumption and thereby have profound effects on the oil majors; and the shift to intensive food production without fertilisers, pesticides or herbicides can be expected to have profound effects on the agricultural chemicals industry. These are just some of the disruptions that can be anticipated.

Examining the case of energy first, with my collaborator Dr Hao Tan I have been following the changes in China's production of electric power as proxy for its shift in energy generation more generally. We see a significant change in China's energy patterns headlined by a strong shift towards the use of renewables, namely electric power generation from renewable sources

---

3. See the data from the European Wind Energy Association, at: http://www.ewea.org/statistics/european/.

4. The 13th FYP for energy issued in late 2016 downgraded these targets slightly. The revised targets are: solar 110–150 GW, wind 210–250 GW, hydro unchanged at 340 GW,

FIGURE 5.1. China: Trends in power sources generated from water, wind and sun (WWS), 1990–2015.

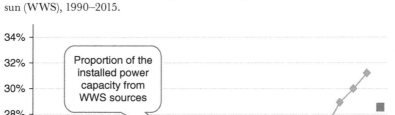

SOURCE: Mathews and Tan 2015.

such as wind, solar PV and water (hydro). This is captured most clearly in the changing proportions of power generated from WWS sources vs power generated from thermal sources – as shown in Figure 5.1.

This chart makes it very clear where China's energy system is headed. China is increasing its proportion of electric power generating capacity utilizing WWS sources from around 21 per cent in 2006–2007 to 32 per cent in 2015 and an anticipated 36 per cent by 2020.[5] Once China has passed the 40 per cent mark for proportion of power generated from WWS sources in the 2020s, it could be safely assumed that it will continue in this vein through logistic industrial dynamics and will pass the 50 per cent mark sometime in the 2030s, if not before. It would by then have a predominantly green electric power generation system – the first major industrial country in the world to achieve that distinction.

Like all industrial powers that preceded it, China initially built a power system needed to drive its manufacturing system utilizing fossil fuels, mainly coal. The coal-driven electric power system grew rapidly – particularly after 2001 when China joined the WTO, as seen clearly in Figure 5.2.

---

with total 660–740 GW. These revised targets which are introduced no doubt to ensure fulfilment by 2020, are still well in advance of those of any other country.

5. See the discussion by Hao Tan and myself in our book on *China's Renewable Energy Revolution* (Mathews and Tan 2015).

FIGURE 5.2. The black face of China: Coal-fired power generation, 1980–2015.

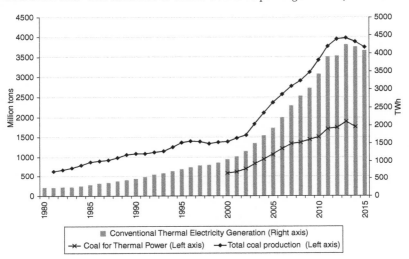

SOURCE: Mathews and Tan 2015.

There are two striking features of this chart worth noting. One is the rapid rise in coal consumption by the electric power generation system – particularly after 2001 when China joined the WTO and declared, in effect, that it was 'open for business'. This is the 'black face' of China that is responsible for so much particulate pollution, making the air in cities like Tianjin and Beijing frequently unbreathable.

The other striking feature is the levelling off in coal consumption around 2012/2013, with coal consumption actually falling in the years 2014 and again in 2015, showing that the trend is a strong one. This reveals the power exercised by government in China, where the authorities are not afraid to intervene in the economy to correct what is viewed as a major anomaly. There is indeed a 'new normal' operating here.[6]

The shift towards greater coal consumption as revealed in changes to estimates of coal consumption released in 2015 is shown in Figure 5.3 – which reveals that China's dependence on coal in the past was even worse than widely believed. But the revised data also reveal that the levelling off and reduction in coal consumption in the last two years is maintained.

6. See the paper by Green and Stern (2016) making this point with regard to China's dramatic turn to clean sources of energy.

FIGURE 5.3. China: Revised coal consumption data.

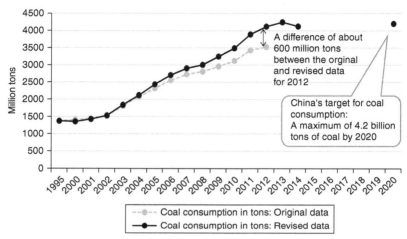

SOURCE: Mathews and Tan 2015.

Now if China were to continue with its early dependence on fossil fuels, particularly coal, then the country would become more and more dependent on imports and on extracting coal and fossil fuels from the world's geopolitical hotspots. This would have serious repercussions and be a major threat to world peace. Instead, as revealed in Figure 5.1, we see that from a low of 21 per cent in 2007, the proportion of electric power generating capacity utilizing renewable WWS sources increased to reach 32 per cent by 2015. [7]

So China has already emerged as the world's powerhouse for renewables. After building up its renewables capacity faster than any other country through unprecedented investments in wind power, then solar PV power, and in the smart grid, it now exceeds all countries in terms of its total renewables capacity based on water, wind and sun. It has an official target for renewables capacity of 550 GW by 2017, and should (if present trends continue) be exceeding 750 GW by 2020 (the official target of the ND&RC). Reaching 750 GW by 2020 would make China the undisputed superpower of renewables. At this rate it would be at or above 1000 GW – or *1 TW – by 2025 or earlier – that is, within a decade.* So within less than a decade China would have revolutionized the

---

7. In terms of electricity generated, in 2015 renewables WWS sources accounted for 25 per cent of total power generated.

world's energy system, as well as its own, by building a formidable renewable power system. China is meeting, and surpassing, the 'terawatt challenge'.[8]

And it is doing so through strength in manufacturing. Its rapid expansion of a renewables sector is based on reliance on the manufactured energy sources of wind, solar PV and hydro – water, wind and sun. Nuclear power is part of the mix as well, but on nothing like the scale of power from water, wind and sun. These are safe sources, they are reliable and above all they are scalable (and infinitely expandable) because they are products of manufacturing, not of mineral extraction. The more China builds its renewables powerhouse, the more it enhances its energy security and acts to curb the shocking levels of particulate pollution caused by its burning of fossil fuels.

The 2015 data reinforce this favourable trend. We can use the capacity additions made in the year 2015 as indicating where the leading edge in the system is moving. In 2015 China added generating capacity of 72 GW from non-thermal sources (34 GW from wind, 14 GW from solar, 17 GW from hydro plus 6 GW from nuclear) compared with 74.5 GW from thermal sources Thus China is close to the tipping point where non-thermal capacity added exceeds thermal capacity added.[9] *China is adding more than 1 billion watts (1 GW) of clean new power capacity every week.* This shows clearly the direction in which the system is headed, as well as the rate of change.

As for the total system of electric power generation, it has changed from being dependent in 2008 on thermal sources for 81 per cent of its generating capacity, falling to 73 per cent in 2015 – a reduction of 8 per cent in just seven years, or more than 10 per cent change in a decade. At this rate China will be down to sourcing less than 50 per cent of its total electric power from thermal sources by the 2030s – by which time it would be described accurately as more of a green electric power system than a black. It would be the first in the world amongst major industrial powers to be so described.

Let us ponder that for a moment – China's electric power system generating more power from renewable sources (WWS plus a bit of nuclear) than from coal and thermal sources (counting oil, gas and coal) – a transformation that is well under way, with the leading edge of the energy system already more green than black (where new capacity added from WWS sources is outranking thermal capacity added). As the capacity added becomes more green than black, the total system changes; it can be anticipated to be more

8. Smalley, Future global energy prosperity: The terawatt challenge, *MRS Bulletin* 2005.

9. All data are taken from my 2016 posting to *Asia Pacific Journal: Japan Focus*, at: http://apjjf.org/2016/17/Mathews.html.

green than black by the 2030s, that is, well before mid-century. This is in itself an unprecedented rate of industrial change. We have been told by energy scholars such as Smil that energy systems take decades to change.[10] The modern fossil fuel system, for example, took close to 100 years to oust the former system with its organic sources, and current shifts in fossil fuels themselves, for example, from oil to natural gas, are likewise projected to take decades. Yet here are renewables in China reaching a tipping point within just a couple of decades. This is the power of manufacturing and logistics dynamics demonstrated in all their grandeur.

Most observers immediately extrapolate from this shift away from fossil fuels to carbon emissions, arguing that China's carbon emissions could peak in less than a decade after that point – still within the 2030s. (In fact they are likely to peak much earlier – perhaps as early as 2020.) But it is not reduction in carbon emissions that I am suggesting drives this change, so much as the dramatic improvements offered in energy security and in terms of reducing particulate pollution.

WHAT ARE THE OPTIONS AVAILABLE FOR CHINA?

When the world's largest industrial revolution is considered from China's perspective, what exactly are the options available? So far, China has been placing most emphasis on the black energy strategy, that is to say focusing on building a huge fossil-fuelled power system that would become (and has become) the largest in the world. But the country has clearly run into the environmental limits of such a strategy. No other country on the planet suffers from such bad pollution – of air, of water, of soil – as China. And the Chinese leadership knows better than anyone else what might be the political limits of tolerance in China for the filthy air that people are required to breathe. So an alternative is needed. What are the options?

One option that might be considered attractive to some is that of carbon capture and storage and 'clean coal' technology for power generation. But this is an unlikely scenario. Firstly such technology addresses the carbon pollution (carbon emissions and their impact on climate) but not so much the particulate pollution, which is the real problem from the Chinese perspective. Secondly these solutions would involve China in importing advanced technology (e.g., for scrubbing emissions from thermal power plants) from countries like Germany and Japan. The third and most powerful reason that this pathway might not be supported is

---

10. See Smil 2005.

that this option would not capture for China the learning curve advantages that would flow from manufacturing its own energy devices. Neither would it square with China's goal of indigenizing its own technological innovation.

For similar reasons it is unlikely that China would wish to follow the pathway of nuclear power – even if this option is widely promoted by informed observers in Europe and the US such as James Hansen.[11] It is true that China is building more nuclear reactors today than any other country – but it is likely that this is more a business decision than a domestic environmental strategic decision. Hao Tan and I have provided data that demonstrate that China has been building more wind power capacity than nuclear capacity, and actually generating more electrical energy from wind than from nuclear sources – a trend that is very likely to continue.[12] In China's case the reason for this preference is no doubt inked to the fact that wind power and solar power technologies can be indigenized and expanded rapidly in China whereas nuclear technology is much more recalcitrant and harder to transfer. That China is devoting considerable resources to the nuclear option (and to newer generations of reactors) is evidence of an openness to keeping several energy options open – not of having made a choice for or against any specific technology.

Another option for China is to reduce its resource and energy dependence by opting for zero growth. Although this is a popular perspective amongst Western environment groups, who argue that on a finite planet there cannot be exponential growth forever, it is obviously not viable for China, which depends on economic growth to lift its population up to middle-income status. Of course all countries as they advance in terms of per capita income and industrial strength will eventually have to phase out extensive growth – but China has not reached that point yet.

It seems clear that the best option for China is green growth, or what the Chinese themselves call (somewhat awkwardly) 'ecological civilization'. This refers to an increasingly intensive model of economic growth, achieved by a switch to resource regeneration rather than endless resource throughput (i.e., a switch from a linear to a circular economy) and a switch to renewables rather than fossil fuels, making for a smaller footprint arising from China's industrial activities.[13] It is this model that I am referring to as ecomodernization or the global green shift.

---

11. See the statement by James Hansen and other nuclear physicists on nuclear power being the only path forward on climate change (and for China) in *The Guardian*, 3 December 2015, at: http://www.theguardian.com/environment/2015/dec/03/nuclear-power-paves-the-only-viable-path-forward-on-climate-change.

12. See Mathews and Tan 2015.

13. There is now substantial scholarly research on China's prospects for a clean energy transition. For an exposition utilizing the SWITCH model as applied to China, see He et al. (2016).

How China stumbled upon this particular option as its preferred way forward is an interesting question in itself. It is surely partly a result of an intense pragmatism – a willingness to judge strategies in terms of their results rather than their ideological underpinnings. And green growth certainly delivers – in terms of the immediate goal of clearing the skies, as well as in the medium-term goal of enhancing energy security and resource security. It also delivers in terms of building export platforms for the future, in anticipation of the likely emergence of renewables as the dominant energy industries of the twenty-first century. Apart from this pragmatic outlook, perhaps what also contributed to China's pursuit of a green option as alternative to the black fossil fuelled option previously followed was a desire to avoid the kind of terrorist entanglements that were clearly evident in the US as it suffered the Twin Towers catastrophe of 11 September 2001. It was only two or three years after these events in New York that decisions were made in China that launched a serious build-up of (manufactured) renewables as alternative sources of energy security, taking China away from dependence on oil imports from the Middle East. This is unlikely to have been coincidental.[14]

Are bankruptcies and overcapacity in China's renewables manufacturing industries a sign of weakness?

China has utilized industrial strategy to good effect in fashioning new industries based on renewable energies and resource recirculation. But critics point to bankruptcies and overcapacity. It is true that there have been bankruptcies in China's solar PV industry, as well as widespread overcapacity. This is sometimes interpreted as meaning that China has made a bad choice in promoting this industry. But these developments should be viewed as symptoms of healthy industrial dynamics. Consider the analogous situation in the US automobile industry in the 1920s, where hundreds of companies

---

14. Much more could be said on these points. It is true that China's involvement as oil importer from both Iraq and Iran has increased since 2001 – but that can be attributed to China as a latecomer to the global oil markets pursuing a strategy of taking on any sources of supply as they become available. In similar manner China has also raised its level of imports from countries such as Ecuador and South Sudan – with all their civil war and geopolitical complications. As the years go by and the energy security implications of China's choice of renewables as desirable option become clear, no doubt the Chinese leadership is confirmed in the wisdom of its choice.

came into existence supplying component parts or final vehicles in the Detroit area, which were then were weeded down to the Big Three and a few other independents (all of whom had stopped manufacturing by the 1950s). The US industry was consolidated through mergers, acquisitions, bankruptcies and exits from the industry – making for greater efficiencies, cost reductions and development of industry-wide standards. The same process is found in other manufacturing industries – and can be anticipated as unfolding in the renewable energy industry in China.

Bankruptcy laws operate like the capitalist equivalent of the biodiversity created by natural selection in the biological world. By having the legal option of bankruptcy, companies are able to rescue themselves from creditors and allow the established patterns of production to be changed and adapted to new conditions. China is following the rest of the industrial world in discovering the benefits of bankruptcy law in facilitating industrial adaptation, and so the appearance of cases of bankruptcy in an emerging industry like solar PV or wind power should be viewed not as a sign of weakness but on the contrary as an indication of strength, of healthy industrial dynamics. Bankruptcies and firm exits allow for the release of resources that would otherwise be tied up in unproductive arrangements, allowing new firms with new strategies to emerge. Just as biodiversity is the key to adaptive survival in the biological world, so bankruptcy allows for adaptation in the business world to allow firms to meet changing conditions. The biggest shift that is under way now is the green shift, with its accommodation between economics and ecology – and healthy industrial dynamics promise to enable firms in China to adapt to meet the challenges involved.[15]

The pollution constraint

China has telescoped development processes that took centuries to accomplish in other parts of the world into just three decades. So it is not surprising that China is now experiencing some of the worst pollution crises

---

15. By contrast the high level of curtailment in the Chinese renewables sector is a sign of weakness and one which needs to be addressed by policy as a matter of urgency. Curtailment refers to electric power that is generated but is not fed into the grid, either because of poor connections or because the grid cannot accommodate the fluctuating sources of power. Whatever the cause, this is an issue that needs to be addressed by grid modernization and upgrading – an issue that Chinese State Grid Corporation is focused on. Curtailment represents a waste of energy production that the country can ill afford.

on the planet. One Chinese journalist who is hitting back and promoting a popular movement to combat the worst effects of the pollution is Chai Jing, with her video sensation 'Under the Dome'. After a few brief days enjoying huge popularity in China the *YouTube* video was taken down – but it is still of course available outside China.[16] Chai Jing emphasizes the point that China's smog is the result of a concatenation of pollution problems coming on top of each other – pollution from coal burning in heavy industry, pollution from dirty road vehicles, pollution from gasoline vaporization which adds further polycyclic aromatic hydrocarbons (all carcinogenic) to the toxic mix, as well as other sources. The clear message of the talk she gives is that China has the means available to tackle the pollution problems, but in practice at local level officials lack the political will to enforce the legal sanctions. A key episode in the film is the story of the petrol station owner who blocks an impromptu inspection of fuel dispensing equipment (which is clearly operating without a fumes trap) by telling the Environment Ministry inspectors that they 'have the responsibility but not the authority'. Chai Jing is calling for citizens in China to uphold that authority. She is in effect calling for a social movement that could emulate the effect just over half a century ago of Rachel Carson's *Silent Spring* in the then heavily polluted USA.[17]

Pollution problems are of course a major factor in driving China's government towards renewables – everyone, including senior officials, has to live 'under the dome' that is modern China. And China is demonstrating that a major industrial country can build a 1-trillion watt renewable energy system based on WWS sources within no more than a decade, swinging its power generation system away from dependence on fossil fuels with all their polluting and geopolitical threats and hazards towards reliance instead on manufactured energy generating sources. And as it swings away from the linear economy (with dependence on virgin raw materials extracted from the earth as well as dumping of wastes in the earth) to a circular economy, so its dependence on raw materials to drive this huge manufacturing system needed to produce energy devices will diminish. More and more of the materials required will be 'mined' from the circulation of materials in circular flows within its own economy. All of these dramatic changes are occurring in China, as the world's largest industrial power, within the space of a couple of decades. This breeds

---

16. See Chai Jing's talk on YouTube, at: https://www.youtube.com/watch?v=T6X2uwl QGQM.

17. See Carson (1962).

confidence that the era of the Anthropocene will be able to witness an earth-friendly energy and resources flow system, initiated first in China and then spreading around the world through competitive emulation.

INDIA'S RENEWABLES STRATEGY

From a slow start, India is now determined to become a world leader in green energy and green development. It is doing so not just because of concerns over climate change, but for reasons to do with energy and resource security and the building of an energy platform that will supply both domestic markets and export business as well.[18] India is using a full panoply of industrial strategies to achieve these ambitious goals, from market promotion measures including tax breaks and feed-in tariffs to industrial promotion such as local content requirements being attached to foreign direct investments – albeit attracting some opposition at the WTO, particularly from the USA.[19]

The most ambitious programme is the National Solar Mission, which in July 2015 was upgraded with a new goal of seeing 100 GW of solar power installed in India by the earlier date of 2019 – where 40 GW would be rooftop solar and 60 GW would be medium- and large-scale grid-connected solar power projects. These are extremely ambitious targets, upgraded from the original target of 20 GW by 2021–22 that had been announced in 2008 and amended in 2010. Indeed it puts India at par with China in terms of specific solar PV targets, where China had a well-known target for solar PV of 100 GW by 2020 and actually raised this to 160 GW by 2020 as part of the 13th FYP.

With the election of the Narendra Modi government in 2014, the stage was set for further detailed promotion of renewables and greening of the Indian economy generally. Modi himself has reiterated the point that his government's central goal will be to ensure 24/7 power for all Indians – and since coal is subject to supply and price fluctuations, the best way of delivering on such a promise is through promotion of renewables. The fresh targets announced are backed by administrative and financial commitments. The July 2014 budget of the Modi government had a provision for a doubling of the tax on coal, which would raise an extra $1.1 billion to fund clean energy projects. Green energy

---

18. For discussion of India's greening strategies, see for example Mattoo and Subramanian (2012) or Johnson (2015).

19. See the Dispute at the WTO involving US objections to India's National Solar Mission with its local content requirements, at https://www.wto.org/english/tratop_e/dispu_e/cases_e/ds456_e.htm (WTO 2016).

companies were at the same time offered a ten-year tax holiday in order to get themselves firmly established.[20]

There has been an important follow-up to the NSM in the form of direct support to farmers who are installing solar powered irrigation pumps, as announced in January 2016 by the Energy Minister Piyush Goyal. The plan envisages funding of US$11 billion over 3–4 years to roll out 30 million solar pumps, which would lead to substantial savings in subsidies and thereby pay for itself.[21] Here we see the benefits of a decentralized energy system as opposed to the centralized, high-density power system favoured by the authors of the *Ecomodernist Manifesto*.

The next move is doubtless for the Indian government to announce a National Wind Mission (NWM) to replicate the success to date of the National Solar Mission (NSM), with an anticipated target of adding an extra 60 GW of wind power by 2022. This goal, too, can be expected to be backed by comprehensive promotion policies encompassing tax breaks, facilitation in securing land and local permits, as well as promotion of the wind power manufacturing value chain in India (at present largely dominated by Suzlon). The essence of these renewables Mission programs (NSM and NWM) is that they are designed to provide investment certainty and real incentives for developers based on a clear understanding of what manufacturers and wind/solar farm developers need. The projects represent a substantial initiative on the part of the Ministry of New and Renewable Energy, itself a major institutional innovation, designed to create fiscal and monetary space for RE development separated from the influence of fossil fuels.[22]

India has learned from China the power of local content requirements (LCRs) as a tool for domestic industry development. The provisions covering LCRs in the NSM were designed to avoid WTO entanglements, in particular having a state-owned entity being the purchaser of the solar energy generated and thereby being nominally in compliance with the WTO Government

---

20. See Johnson (2015) for further details.

21. See the report by Tim Buckley 'Wind and solar records tumble as China and India accelerate energy transition', 22 January 2016, at *RenewEconomy*: http://reneweconomy. com.au/2016/69425

22. Current levels of Renewable Energy (RE) capacity in India were (at March 2015): wind power capacity 23.4 GW; solar PV capacity 3.7 GW and total RE capacity 35.8 GW. The ambitious NSM and (probable) NWM targets would have to see an extra 10 GW of solar and 10 GW of wind capacity being added each year between now and 2020. This in itself can be viewed as a major industrialization effort.

Procurement Agreement. Even the name of the Indian programme, namely the NSM Procurement Program, emphasized this aspect and signalled India's strategy if required to defend the programme in Geneva. Nevertheless the United States objected to the LCR provisions on grounds that they create trade barriers to exports of US renewable energy products and technology (which is, after all, their goal). In fact the US lodged two successive objections in a case where the WTO declared in February 2016 that India's NSM violated WTO rules and would have to be disbanded.[23] India is of course appealing the decision, which on the face of it would prevent any country from utilizing tools like local content requirements to facilitate the building of a renewables devices industry in its own country – a measure that runs directly counter to the commitments made by countries to decarbonize their energy systems at the Paris climate conference of December 2015. However the Indian government is clearly determined to see the issue through and continue its strong support for building renewables industries, and is unlikely to allow this hiccup at the WTO to curb its aspirations.

---

23. For commentary see Clean Technica, at: http://cleantechnica.com/2016/03/15/indias-dcr-woes/. My own comments can be found at Mathews (2016b) and in Chapter 8.

CHAPTER 6

FINANCE NOW PLAYING A CENTRAL ROLE IN THE GREEN SHIFT

It has always struck me as anomalous that along with the UN-sponsored Conferences of the Parties under the Kyoto Protocol, with their ever-intensifying calls for something to be done about climate change, when it came to the question of finance the debate seemed strangely muted: the UN appeared unable to see further than tax-based, public finance as source of funds. Yet if climate change were a consequence of our fossil-fuelled industrial system, under the control of capitalists, then it is to capitalists that the world would have to look for a solution. Why were the biggest sources of capital on the planet – the bonds and equities markets – not involved front and centre in the UN climate debates?

Finally the situation is changing. Now the role of the capital markets is becoming clearer as financial instruments like green bonds are being issued and are attracting the attention of long-term institutional investors like pension funds and insurance companies. From early 'toe-in-the-water' initiatives with green bonds by the World Bank and European Investment Bank (EIB) in the 2000s, the pace has quickened. Green bonds totalling $36 billion were issued in 2014, then $42 billion in 2015 and now Moody's Investors' Services see the likely total in 2016 as approaching $50 billion, while the Climate Bonds Initiative sees the 2016 total as likely to be closer to $100 billion.[1] Finally, it seems that some serious levels of finance are flowing to clean and green investment projects.

Of course these issuances are not yet hitting the trillions that will be needed to drive a serious shift from one kind of energy and industrial system

---

1. See the website of the Climate Bonds Initiative: https://www.climatebonds.net/ [Disclosure: I am a member of the CBI].

to another. But they are moving in the right direction and are being issued at scale. Soon the question of whether funds should be investing their capital in risky, fossil-fuelled assets that are likely to become 'stranded' as their risks become clearer, or alternatively should be investing their funds in safe, reliable and productive green assets that promise regular returns, is likely to become the central question in the climate debate.[2]

Before that time comes, China and India are already laying their bets and are embarking on wholesale greening of their financial systems. As in all aspects of the greening of the global economy, China is emerging as a leader in the financial aspects of the process, understanding that ambitious investment strategies need to be financed if they are to be successful. Brought together by Dr Ma Jun of the People's Bank of China (PBoC), the Green Finance Task Force in China issued its long-awaited report 'Establishing China's Green Financial System' in April 2015 – making China the first country in the world to set specific guidelines for the issuing of green securities.[3] The report sets out an ambitious agenda for how China can green its rapidly developing financial and capital markets, making use of policy, regulatory and market-innovations. The report notes that China will need investment each year of at least 2 trillion yuan (US$320 billion) or more than 3 per cent of GDP, for at least the next five years. This is no doubt a commitment at the heart of the 13th Five Year Plan – and one that is driving China's adoption of a green growth strategy.

TAPPING THE CAPITAL MARKETS: THE KEXIM GREEN BONDS

The greening of financial markets took off slowly – retarded no doubt by the incapacity of the UN climate conferences to come to grips with the issue. Things changed dramatically in February 2013, when a commercial bank – the Korean Export Import Bank – issued a $500 million green bond. The funds raised were earmarked for financing of Korean low-carbon initiatives, including renewable energy, energy efficiency and clean water projects undertaken by Korean firms around the world. The bond was targeted at and taken up by institutional investors. Kexim was the first national commercial

---

2. The concept of 'stranded assets' as developed by the Carbon Tracker Initiative in London has proven to be influential. For details see the CTI webpage: http://www.carbontracker.org/report/unburnable-carbon-wasted-capital-and-stranded-assets/.

3. See the report at: https://www.cbd.int/financial/privatesector/china-Green%20Task%20Force%20Report.pdf.

bank to issue such a green bond – catapulting Seoul to a leadership role in green finance. The bond was offered globally, to US Securities and Exchange Commission standards, with book runners Bank of America Merrill Lynch as well as the Scandinavian bank SEB Enskilda. As a global security, it commanded a strong resale value, enhancing its credibility in the eyes of institutional investors. The bond was offered for sale on international markets, and was oversubscribed, revealing that medium-term green investments could henceforth be viewed as safer than fossil-fuel investments. There was third party assurance that the funds raised would be disbursed to genuinely green projects.

The Kexim Bank was so pleased with the 2013 green bond issue that they entered the market again two years later, in February 2015. This was a second bond offering, again targeted at institutional investors, this time to the value of $400 million, offering investors a 5-year term with semi-annual coupon payments of 2.125 per cent. This second issue was also oversubscribed, and largely taken up by institutional investors from Asia, revealing that they are becoming more comfortable with green debt securities.

This is significant because it shows Kexim as being satisfied with the first issue and willing to come back for a second tranche. All the $500 million in funds raised from the first issue had been disbursed on green projects being undertaken by Korean firms around the world, and the bank was ready to repeat the exercise with a further $400 million issue. This means that Kexim has been making use of a 'treasury' of close to $1 billion to finance green projects wherever Korean firms are involved.

These bond issues by Kexim demonstrate that institutional investors are prepared to purchase green financial securities from reputable banks if presented in the right way, with suitable global reach and certification and at investment grade. So – green bonds are moving from the realm of being curiosities to become mainstream financial products.

* * *

Bonds are the core of the capitalist system. It takes countries decades, if not centuries, to build effective bond markets. They enable governments and businesses to raise funds, on the strength of their credibility and reputation. Bonds are 'investment grade' securities, meaning that they are only offered for large amounts (the $900 million of the Kexim Bank green bonds is typical). Their value for green finance is that they can aggregate across a large number of small projects. The diseconomies of insufficient scale associated with small projects are decisively overcome by a green bond that aggregates such projects together.

Thus the financing of clean tech projects via green bonds promises cheap capital, since the interest charges will be lower for projects in aggregate than for conventional bank finance supporting individual projects. This means that renewable energy and energy efficiency projects that might otherwise be out of the running because of the high cost of capital can become viable. The diffusion of green energy and resource projects is therefore accelerated.

The contrast with carbon trading has to be underlined. The idea that pollution allowances could be traded and that the ''carbon markets' so created might drive investment in the desired direction, has now been shown to have little if not zero potential. The dismal performance of the Emissions Trading Scheme (ETS) in Europe and collapsing carbon prices elsewhere certainly attest to that. Green bonds by contrast address the financing issue directly and effectively without the need for intermediaries.

Bonds are serious financial instruments that are not to be played with. If a country's bonds lose their value, then the country faces ruin. (Technically, it would be unable to meet its payments and would have to default – a desperate step.) Hence, a green bond issued with a national government's imprimatur (as was the case with the new green bond issued by the Kexim Bank) means that the bond would hold its value only if the projects really were an investment in a green future and really would have the backing of the government. The bond markets would see through any shenanigans and punish the issuer severely.

The enormous investment potential of the bond markets is there to be tapped to finance green investments – but had been done so only in a minimal way until April 2013 and the issue of the Kexim bond. The ideological insistence of the UN and the parties to the Kyoto process that all green investments should emanate solely from tax-based public sources (which could manifestly not finance the transition in any realistic manner) was finally overcome.

So the big guns of capitalism are now being employed in financing clean technology projects via green bonds. And the big investors – institutional, pension and insurance funds, which have between them over $70 trillion in investable funds, according to the OECD – are now to be actively involved. To tap into global bond markets is a real form of green finance – and one where Seoul may just have seized the initiative away from New York, Frankfurt and London.

GREEN BONDS EXPANSION

For decades the world laboured under the Kyoto process with its insistence that all funding for the needed transformations was to come from public finance

– that is, from governments supplying tax-based funding. In meeting after meeting of the parties, all the way up to Paris in December 2015 there was a focus on some kind of green fund – but never on the role of the private sector in investing in green projects. This may be viewed as the other side of the mainstream economics focus on mitigation of climate change as a cost – as a cost, it carries no incentive to invest. But when viewed as a transformation of the industrial system driven by green investment, then the present focus on public, tax-based funding recedes into the background.

The first authoritative estimate of the appropriate balance between public and private funding for the changes needed can be found in the report from the Green Finance Task Force coordinated by the People's Bank of China (PBoC), on *Establishing China's Green Financial System* (April 2015). In this report it is stated that no more than 15 per cent of the needed funding could be expected to come from tax-based public finance – meaning that 85 per cent at least of the needed funding would have to come from the private sector. The Chinese report then goes on to estimate that up to 2 trillion yuan would be needed each year for the next five years 2016–2020 – or 10 trillion yuan altogether (US$ 1.5 trillion).That places the focus of interest immediately on the means through which such huge sums might be raised – on green bonds, on green banks, on green equities and all the other measures discussed in the comprehensive Chinese report.

The global financial capital markets are vast – amounting to around $212 trillion at last count by the World Bank. The stock markets of the world (equities markets) account for $54 trillion, while bank loans account for another $64 trillion – leaving bonds (debt securities) accounting for the biggest slice, at $93 trillion.[4] These huge aggregates of capital reveal that capital shortage is not the problem in greening the world's economy; the issue is to develop the debt securities that will attract institutional investors who are always looking for a safe haven for their sums held under trust.

Compared with these huge sums potentially available in the capital markets, the sums raised so far by instruments like green bonds seem small indeed. The first corporate green bonds were issued in November 2013, creating a total market size for 2013 of $11 billion. The market trebled in size in 2014 to $36.6 billion issued and thence to $41.8 billion in 2015, while the Climate Bonds Initiative organization in London has announced its expectation that issuances for 2016 will exceed $100 billion (Figure 6.1).

---

4. These data are drawn from the World Bank 2015 publication *What Are Green Bonds?* (available at: http://treasury.worldbank.org/cmd/htm/What-are-Green-Bonds-Home.html).

FIGURE 6.1. Growth in green bonds issued, 2012–2015.

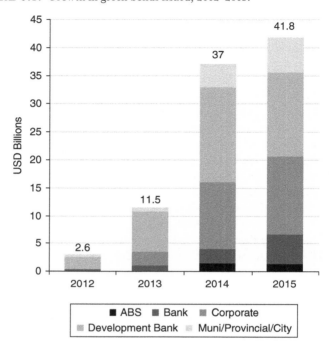

NOTE: ABS, asset-backed securities.
SOURCE: Climate Bonds Initiative. Data as of 31 December 2015.

The first quarter of 2016 has witnessed a real take-off in the market for green bonds, with total issuances exceeding $16.5 billion. This growth was driven partly by issuances in China, which accounted for half the bonds (including clean transport bonds needed to finance high speed rail). Moody's Investment Services expects to see $50 billion in green bonds issued in 2016, indicating how observers see the market as moving.

CHINA AND THE BUILDING OF A GREEN FINANCIAL SYSTEM

As in all aspects of the greening of the economy, China is emerging as a leader in the financial aspects of the process, understanding that ambitious investment strategies need to be financed if they are to be successful. Brought together by Dr Ma Jun of the PBoC, the Green Finance Task Force in China issued its long-awaited report 'Establishing China's Green Financial System' in April 2015 – making China the first country in the world to issue specific guidelines on the issuing of green securities.[5]

China is adopting a realist perspective on sources of green finance, where the 2015 report states that no more than 15 per cent of all green investment can be expected to come from fiscal sources (i.e., tax-based investment). This means that the bulk of the financing – or 85 per cent – is expected to come from the private sector, through various green finance channels. These are listed as involving green bank loans, green funds and green bonds.

Ma Jun, head of the research bureau of the PBoC and moving spirit behind this important initiative, lists six core principles of greening of finance in his Foreword to the report. Ma Jun's six principles are that China's green financial system should move towards:

1) Building new channels for green investment, and not just restricting polluting investment;

2) Opening up new channels through new specialized green lending and investment institutions (such as a green bank), and not just relying on existing banking channels;

3) Steering private capital to the greening of industry, reducing reliance on administrative orders;

4) Ushering in a range of new green instruments such as green bonds, green stocks, green funds and green insurance, and not just providing green loans;

5) Changing the behaviour of financial institutions through financial and legal measures, with public funds aiming to leverage private funds up to tenfold; and

6) Providing necessary financial infrastructure that will enable green investments to thrive (such as green credit ratings, environmental impact data) rather than just offering administrative support for green investment.

This national strategy – the first of its kind in the world – underlines how seriously China is taking its role in greening its economy. The report proposes three major institutional innovations including creation of green banks (e.g.,

---

5. See the report at: https://www.cbd.int/financial/privatesector/china-Green%20Task%20Force%20Report.pdf.

the proposed China Ecological Development Bank and regional-level green banks); creation of green funds (i.e., green industry funds and public-private partnership arrangements); and a process of greening the existing development banks (such as the China Development Bank allocating part of its lending portfolio to targeted green investments).

The report goes on to specify how China needs to develop specific green financial instruments, including 'discounted green loans' (i.e., offering bank loans at differential interest rates depending on whether projects meet green targets); permitting Chinese banks to issue green bonds, thus tapping into the debt securities market (and helping to grow it in China); and green IPOs, that is, improving the mechanism through which firms' environmental performance is communicated and recognized in equity markets.

The report lays out a theoretical framework that helps make sense of its specific proposals and policy guidelines. Three principles inform the whole report, namely that:

1) The return on investment in green projects needs to be enhanced – by increasing revenues from cleaner products and projects, lowering taxes on such entities and reducing their costs and risks;

2) By contrast, the return on investment in polluting projects needs to be lowered, by reducing perverse subsidies, raising taxes on pollution and raising costs of non-compliance with environmental standards; and

3) Raising awareness of and responsiveness to these market signals by investors, companies and consumers, through such measures as environmental impact data, mandatory risk assessment disclosure and creation of green stock indexes.

One has to admit that this is a comprehensive survey of the issues raised in driving finance to the new tasks involved in greening the economy. And its publication has been followed by financial action. The *Agricultural Bank of China* was the first Chinese financial institution to venture into the new space, raising $1 billion from a three-part green bond in October 2015.[6] The green bonds market in China is set to grow significantly as the government has given the go-ahead to banks to launch large issues. The *Shanghai Pudong Development Bank* came out with a green bond worth 20 billion Yuan (US$4.3 billion) in January 2016.

---

6. See the Reuters report, at: http://www.reuters.com/article/china-bonds-offshore-idUSL3N12E1N620151014.

In its cautious but determined way, China is moving towards a quota for banks totalling 300 billion Yuan (more than US$45 billion) in green bond issues.[7]

China's actions and proposals may already have sparked action in Japan – which has otherwise remained on the sidelines in the greening of finance. In October 2015 Japan's *Sumitomo Mitsui Banking Corporation* raised $500 million through the sale of green bonds, becoming the first Japanese bank to issue such green debt instruments in dollar form. So now there is a healthy competition opening up between Japan and China over who can green its finance system first. So far the Chinese are winning.

---

7. See the report at: http://cleantechnica.com/2016/01/25/two-chinese-banks-set-issue-green-bonds-worth-15-billion/.

CHAPTER 7

CAN THE CHINA MODEL
BE UTILIZED BY OTHER
INDUSTRIALIZING COUNTRIES?

There was a time when industrial development and energy were discussed in separate categories. The prevailing orthodoxy, which governed the 'East Asian Miracle' of Japan's industrialization, followed by that of Korea, Taiwan and Singapore, was that integration with the world's fossil-fuel economy represented the optimal path forward. Grow rich with coal and oil, and then diversify – this was the formula. It worked because as a group, the East Asian 'tigers' could not put too much strain on global fossil fuel supplies. But in the twenty-first century, as giants like China and then India and Brazil and South Africa are moving along the industrialization pathway, their energy choices are becoming critical – for themselves and for the planet.

Let us call these the BICS countries, as opposed to the BRICS – leaving out Russia which is a special case through continued dependence on fossil fuels. The BICS countries have a population numbering 2.7 billion (around a third of the total world population of 7.3 billion), and at this scale the pathway to industrialization cannot ignore the means through which the process unfolds. If the BICS countries were to follow the 'Business as Usual' pathway, with its strategy of exploiting access to fossil fuels wherever they can be found and are politically/economically available, they would run into serious geopolitical tensions well before the fuels ran out.

The Western countries as they industrialized were able to tap resources from around the world, via colonialism and imperialism, while they exploited their own coal and oil reserves without any sense that they might be finite. And carbon emissions with their deleterious planetary climatic impact were not considered a problem. Obviously enough, these conditions do not apply today.

The emerging industrial powers, led by the BICS countries, have to invent a new development model that will enable them to bring ten times as many people to the rising income levels enjoyed by industrialized countries, while having to respect much tighter constraints on resources and fossil fuel usage. Without a 'circuit breaker' this challenge does not add up – the BICS countries would be trying the square the circle. The result would be heightened geopolitical tensions leading to war, revolution and terror, quite apart from ecological damage of unimaginable proportions.

But there is a circuit breaker – and it is green development. Its core is green growth. In their various ways, the BICS countries are all pursuing some variant of green growth alongside the fossil-fuelled and resource profligate model of development. This is their feasible pathway to industrial development. When one reflects on the issues involved, what other pathway is there?

The positive future-oriented scenario is one in which these countries maintain their focus on and commitment to green development, because of their overwhelming national interests in doing so. It is an argument that starts with the interests of the emerging industrial giants in finding a feasible pathway for completing their industrialization, rather than with international conferences on climate change. The sceptical view is that these countries are doing too little, too late to reverse their previous fossil-fuelled trajectory. Our scepticism is reinforced by the carbon lock-in that still prevails in the West. The US for example (pace the eleventh hour efforts of the Obama administration) is fixated on its 'energy revolution' involving coal seam gas and shale oil – fossil fuels that have only become accessible in the past decade because of technological developments, and which as high cost businesses were severely curtailed because of falling oil prices. Japan has continued to focus on nuclear, despite Fukushima, – with all the cost overruns and delays entailed. And the EU remains divided between the renewable energy optimism of Germany, with its optimistic *Energiewende*, and the fossil fuel/nuclear hard line of the UK, Poland et al.[1]

Moreover the efforts of the BICS countries to promote renewables and low-carbon development are not supported internationally – even with all the rhetoric on carbon reductions emitted under the Kyoto process and culminating in the Paris Climate Declaration of December 2015. In place of

---

1. The Conservative German government swung against nuclear power in 2011 and introduced the *Energiewende* ('Energy Transformation') with a strong emphasis on renewables but also a lingering attachment to coal. For objective evaluations see Morris and Pehnt (2012) and more recently Renn and Marshall (2016).

promoting diffusion of clean and low-carbon technology, the industrialized countries are actively seeking to impede it through trade sanctions. China for example has been 'punished' for promoting its solar PV industry by other countries, led by the US, the EU and Japan, with their imposition of counter-tariffs on solar PV imports that have caused great disruption to China's PV industry. In India attempts to grow a solar PV industry in emulation of China, utilizing local content requirements, feed-in tariffs, tax breaks and other tools from the industrial strategy toolkit, are also being hindered by trade actions brought to the WTO.

Whether these international trade complications could derail current efforts by the BICS countries to green their industrial development is an important topic addressed in this book. But the case for the success of these emerging countries' greening strategies is overwhelmingly based on the fact that renewables today offer the most cost-effective means of building energy systems. Whereas in previous decades the case that coal could provide the cheapest form of energy (and electric power in particular) was decisive in determining energy strategies, today the situation is reversed, with renewables providing the cheapest option – or are about to do so as the learning curve continues to drive down their costs. A similar argument applies to the reducing costs of resource regeneration via the Circular Economy as opposed to virgin extraction. These developments constitute a truly world-historic change that can transform development possibilities, in the BICS countries and beyond.

ADVANTAGES OF GREEN GROWTH DEVELOPMENT STRATEGIES

In addition to avoiding the problems or impossible options created by the 'business as usual' development pathway, an alternative based on green development offers many advantages to developing countries that look to raise their living standards through industrialization and industrial catch-up with the West. Assuming that the strategy is directed towards building cleantech industries, and not just cleantech markets, we can identify at least nine inter-related advantages of moving towards green growth (GG) pathways.[2]

---

2. The following section is based on my paper published in *Seoul Journal of Economics* (Mathews 2013b).

Renewable resources are available to all

A GG pathway will be based on technologies that capture renewable flows of energy or reduced resource input requirements, and thus will be based sustainably on endlessly renewing resources. These resources are abundant – particularly in tropical developing countries – and widely dispersed, meaning that countries can frame their strategies without regard to accidents of geography. A GG pathway provides a secure and sustainable foundation for a development strategy – as opposed to the insecurities, costs and foreign dependence associated with the 'Business as Usual' (BAU) pathway. Since the renewable resources are widely dispersed and hence open to all, they do not privilege some countries or regions by geographic accident. And since the capture of renewable energies and the recycling of resources calls for sophisticated technologies, the latecomer pursuing them is required to think in terms of development as the building of technological capabilities complementing the diffusion of technologies – rather than just on extracting wealth from quarries, mines or plantations.

Green development is biased towards rural employment generation

Green development (GG) pathways will bias countries to sustainable income generation, employment generation, and particularly rural employment generation and protection, thus easing the transition from rural- to urban-based manufacturing. Social and economic polarization can therefore be mitigated by GG strategies – while enjoying all the advantages of urban, manufacturing-based development.

Cost disadvantages can be overcome

GG pathways incur initial costs which can exceed those associated with cheap fossil fuels – but offer medium- and long-term sustainable advantages. The short-term costs can be met by smart finance and tax relief policies. The medium- to long-term advantages are securely based on learning curves that relentlessly reduce costs, as opposed to rising costs of fossil fuel and resource inputs. This is a far more favourable development strategy than one based on imports of fossil fuels, no matter how cheap they may be in the short term.

Green growth pathways offer unlimited catch-up and technological leapfrogging possibilities

Capture of catch up and leapfrogging opportunities lie at the core of all successful development strategies. Whereas the East Asian countries like Taiwan or Korea were able to catch up in prevailing sectors such as electronics, semiconductors and telecommunications, today's developing giants like China, India, and Brazil need to focus on new technological sectors, of which renewable energies and industrial ecology (transforming one firm's waste into another's inputs) promise to be most capable of generating industrial advantages.

Green and black development complement each other

A GG pathway offers resource-abundant countries (e.g., most tropical developing countries) a sensible and logical path forward by tapping initially into their own resources and seeking investment to add value to these resources as a first step in successful industrialization. Thus countries such as Mozambique, where a long history of terrible civil wars delayed development, has over the past decade recovered its economic momentum and is actually building on extensive fossil fuel resources to create a modern economy peopled by modern firms, generating employment and exports. This is done in 'black economy' terms. But at the same time it is providing a means to finance green development initiatives, including hydroelectric, solar and wind power initiatives, and the beginnings of a new front in agriculture devoted to bioenergy and biofuels.[3] These considerations are the very opposite of those underpinning the notion of the 'resource curse' – where development of a mono-resource (usually by foreign capital) is allowed to outweigh all other development options.

Green growth generates export earnings and reduces import charges

A GG pathway offers the prospect of generating a double dividend in the form of reducing import costs and generating export earnings while building business

---

3. On Mozambique's energy choices, see Cuvilas et al. (2010).

experience. The generation of export earnings creates the funds needed to buy equipment and enter into modern manufacturing activities, thus building a wave of development across the economy. The reduction and avoidance of costs incurred through fossil fuel imports again releases further funds for investment in domestic development, and reduces costs for domestic industry which is otherwise made uncompetitive abroad through high fuel and power charges (not to mention power blackouts and brownouts). Green development through circular economy initiatives (e.g., recycling and industrial ecology linkages) offers the prospect of reduced dependence on resource imports and strains on the balance of payments, which can drag down countries aspiring to middle-income status.

A green growth pathway generates increasing returns through cross-linkages

A GG strategy offers numerous and growing possibilities for building cross-linkages that generate increasing returns and underpin an economy's growth. As opposed to resource extraction activities, which stand alone with few (if any) connections to the domestic economy, the pursuit of renewable energy and cleantech industries brings to the fore the construction of value chains and their cross-linkages. Policies designed to create domestic supply chains and supply clusters come to the fore. This generates a renewed emphasis on what (in development circles) used to be called the *Big push* – meaning that development could be expected to succeed only when several industries providing markets for each others' products were developed simultaneously.[4] Now the same idea can be translated into green development terms. Criss-crossing value chains constitute the skeleton of a successful industrial economy, and a bias towards clean technology industries can create the momentum for such wealth-generating linkages.[5]

---

4. See Rosenstein-Rodan (1943) for the classic statement of this position.

5. I say 'can create' rather than 'does create' because obviously the cross-linkage advantages are secured only by smart policies that seek to create such linkages; in the absence of such policies, critiques of green growth such as those by Resnick et al. (2012) carry weight.

Insertion in global value chains

A GG pathway offers opportunities for local firms to embed themselves in global value chains and to create their own local supply chains – as witnessed in the domestic value chains being created in China and India for solar cell and wind generator construction, and in Brazil for bioethanol and now biodiesel processing. A GG pathway likewise reduces the prospect that developing countries will be locked into a single monoculture (e.g., resource extraction) given that it is technologically based rather than extraction based, and offers business opportunities for local firms.

Green growth provides a bias towards innovation

Finally, a GG pathway creates a bias towards innovation – rather than simply passively accepting and riding on innovations generated elsewhere in resource extraction industries. The focus on technology and technological capabilities acquisition is just what a developing country needs. The bias towards keeping up with renewable technologies as they are developed around the world puts the developing country in good company – and sets it up for waves of technology diffusion (encouraged through public research institutes such as ITRI in Taiwan or EMBRAPA in Brazil) that drive the development trajectory, and prevent it from being 'stuck' at any point or level.

These are all potential advantages that are available to latecomers – provided they develop smart strategies for taking advantage of these opportunities, and for getting around the barriers raised by fossil fuel dependence and 'carbon lock-in', and are prepared to invest resources in their own development of technical capabilities and innovation. And they are available to countries at all levels of development – from the poorest and least-developed (provided they have state institutions that can act to shunt the economy onto a green trajectory) to those at mid-level where aspirations to become integrated in global value chains are strongest.

It is not just China and India that are exhibiting the hallmarks of green growth. As opposed to those who argue that poor countries today need to go through their own phase of using fossil fuels, it is indeed the developing countries that switch to green growth that are likely to benefit the most. Let us take an example to see how the process is likely to unfold.

PROSPECTS FOR GREEN GROWTH IN DEVELOPING
COUNTRIES: MOROCCO AS EXEMPLAR

Morocco is an excellent example of a developing country that has made a smart move to exploit its abundant natural resources – wind and sun – to build an energy system that is no longer dependent on imported fossil fuels, and which gives the country energy security and builds an export platform for the future. Morocco is the only North African country not to have extensive oil deposits – and this is now turning out to be a blessing because it has sharpened focus on building renewably powered systems. Its dependence on imported fossil fuels was extreme: 97 per cent of all its energy needs were imported in 2009, the year its alternative strategy was initiated. This was also costly: the import burden came to Dh 62 billion (US$6.2 billion) per year. Subsidies paid to fossil fuels varied between $1 billion and $4 billion per year.

In 2009 there was an abrupt change of course, signalled by a statement from King Mohammad VI, demanding that government officials prioritize renewables and energy efficiency and move away from dependence on fossil fuels. An ambitious target of 6 GW renewables capacity by 2020 was set – 2 GW from solar, 2 GW hydro and 2 GW from wind power. This represented a completely new WWS strategy, to be pursued at scale. The target represented no less than 42 per cent of Morocco's electrical capacity. Energy security and job creation were top of the priorities for the new direction. The first steps to reach these targets were institutional. The monopoly power of the existing state utility electricity producer was broken in a new law that opened the power generation market to private players. Two new institutions were created. The first, an agency for the development of renewable energies and energy efficiency, was charged with overseeing RE development in Morocco. The second, the *Moroccan Solar Energy Agency* (MASEN) was created also in 2009 to guide development of the solar power sector. The senior officials at Masen launched a competitive financing model for solar power that has proven to be extremely effective.

MASEN is a public company 25 per cent owned by the Moroccan government. It has been tasked with the launch of a sophisticated solar development plan where the focus has been on large-scale Concentrated Solar Power (CSP) projects. The first project launched by MASEN has been the Noor project, a 500 MW CSP project being built near the town of Ouarzazate, in three stages. Noor 1 was actually completed and launched in December 2015. It is to be followed by Stages 2 and 3 where different CSP technologies are to be utilized – Noor I commissioned by 2015 with parabolic trough mirror technology, with Noor II utilizing power tower CSP technology and Noor III to try a further variant. This is a smart strategy designed to set up experiments in Moroccan conditions at scale, to establish which options are superior. The Noor I plant employs molten salt technology providing three hours of energy storage, or power generation after sunset. The final Noor project is expected to have near 24/7 operation as a result of molten salt energy storage technology. This is an excellent example of developing country leapfrogging to the most advanced technology available.[6]

The Noor project is underpinned by a sophisticated Build-Own-Operate-Transfer (BOOT) approach and risk sharing arrangements, indicating the financial sophistication of the project. It involves MASEN itself and a favoured tenderer (the solar power company) supported by a 25-year fixed term Power Purchase Agreement (PPA). The Moroccan government undertakes to pay MASEN the difference between the two contracts – ensuring that international players would be prepared to enter the bidding process once it was declared open. The whole process was underwritten by a $200 million contingency loan facility (CLF) from the World Bank, awarded to the Moroccan government.[7]

In another smart move, MASEN is empowered to be the consolidator of concessional loans provided by various multilateral lending agencies, including the World Bank, the European Investment Bank (EIB) and the African Development Bank (ADB). Morocco amassed a $9 billion 'national solar fund' to act as guarantor of the risk-sharing financing arrangements of the entire solar plan involving the Noor I project and subsequent developments. With this scheme in place, competitive bids were sought at a public auction, with the winners being a consortium headed by ACWA from Saudi Arabia and

---

6. Contracts for Noor II and Noor III were awarded in January 2015 to the ACWA/Sener consortium, covering the Noor II phase – a 200 MW parabolic trough technology CSP plant with 7 hours energy storage from molten salts – and the Noor III phase – 150 MW CSP tower technology with again 7 hours molten salt energy storage. For Sener (the Spanish engineering giant) the Noor I and Noor II parabolic trough mirror technology is a further evolution of the technology deployed in the Spanish Valle plant; while the Noor III CSP tower technology will be an evolution of the system pioneered by Sener in the Gemasolar plant in Seville, Spain.

7. See the description provided in the Green Growth Best Practice paper from Frisari and Falconer (2012 and 2013).

Sener from Spain. A world best winning tariff of just 18 cents per kilowatt-hour
(kWh) was offered.[8]

The Moroccan Noor project has been assisted by the falling costs of CSP
projects since the project's announcement in 2009. There is full support for
the project in Morocco, led by the Ministry of Energy, Mining, Water and
Environment, in the expectation that costs will continue to fall.[9] Now, as
a demonstration of its commitment to green growth and development of
renewables, Morocco was in fact host to the UNFCCC 22nd Conference of
the Parties meeting (the first after Paris) that took place in November 2016.

Noor I is now the world's largest CSP plant. Its first phase generates power
at 160 MW and covers an area of 2.5 km^2 – so this sets a new benchmark for
the land 'cost' of concentrated solar power, at 1.6 ha/MW [or 16 km^2 per
GW].[10] The 'land cost' is precisely 15.6 km^2 needed for 1 GW power, or around
16 km^2 as utilized in the calculations of land area required by 'Renewistan' in
Chapter 13.[11] Expanding at the same ratio, a powerful generating capacity of
10 GW in Morocco would call for land of 156 km^2 – a tiny speck in the desert
when compared with Morocco's vast land area of 446,000 km^2. An alternative
sense of land 'cost' is provided by the Shams 1 CSP plant in the UAE, where the
100 MW facility calls for land of 2.5 km^2. Scaling this up to 1 GW would call
for 25 km^2, and to 10 GW for land area of 250 km^2 – or marginally more than

---

8. The results were announced in 2013 – a very short time for implementation of the
agreement by international standards. The winning tariff was 18.4 cents per kWh [US$0.184
per kWh (or US$18.40 per MWh)], which is what the winning consortium would expect
to be paid for power generated. The ACWA–Sener consortium is expected to generate
power and sell it at a guaranteed price of US$0.18 per kWh (US$184 per MWh) according
to a Purchase Price Agreement (PPA) valid for 25 years. The levelized cost of electricity
produced by Noor I with an internal rate of return (IRR) of 13.1 per cent is estimated to
be US$ 185 per MWh. This is a world record low contract price for power generation.

9. See the explanation from the Moroccan Environment Minister, Dr Hakima el Haite,
at: https://www.youtube.com/watch?v=WNbQD0klXRU.

10. According to observers from the San Giorgio Group, the energy generated by the
Noor I complex is in excess of the amount predicted, because of streamlining of mirror
placement, and as of 2013 amounted to 425 GWh in a year. This represents a world
class capacity factor of 32 per cent [160 MW generating 425 GWh in a year, or 1 GW
generating 2850 GWh in a year, as compared with a generation level of 8760 GWh at 100
per cent conversion]. See Frisari and Falconer 2013.

11. The calculation proceeds as follows. At 160 MW power rating needing 2.5 km^2, or 64
MW needing 1 km2, and inversely, 1 GW calling for land area of 15.6 km^2.

the comparable land 'cost' for the Noor I plant. This reveals how the Noor 1 plant has leapfrogged to be world leader – making it entirely appropriate to use this plant with its 'land cost' and capacity factor as benchmarks for calculations on the size needed by 'Renewistan' (as computed in Chapter 13).

Noor I has called for the manufacture of 500,000 mirrors. Much of this work is already being done in Morocco, with local content reaching a level of 30 per cent. Thus the project is playing a profound industrial development role, in creating both jobs and local value chain for the manufacture of the mirrors and lenses needed to generate power utilizing CSP technology with molten salt energy storage. Morocco is building not just an important source of industrial power but an export platform for the future.

CHAPTER 8

GREEN GROWTH DEVELOPMENT STRATEGIES, LOCAL CONTENT REQUIREMENTS AND WORLD TRADE

World trade should be one of the principal drivers of the global green shift. There is global free trade for all the fossil fuels – coal, oil and gas – with vast supporting infrastructures and well-functioning commodities and futures markets. But there is as yet no comparable free trade in renewables devices and renewable power. Indeed the opposite is the case. A rash of disputes over green energy promotion, both brought before the World Trade Organization (WTO) and by countries imposing unilateral 'trade remedies' on each other, threaten to subdue countries' enthusiasm for building green industries. These disputes have come to a head in the past few years, leading scholars to label them as the 'next generation' of trade and environment conflicts and viewing them as imposing a serious risk of reversing whatever gains might be made in the forums established within the terms of the UNFCCC.[1] Indeed there is a very real danger that actions brought against countries in the name of upholding the principles of free trade might jeopardize the gains won at the Paris climate conference staged in December 2015. What was won within the arena of the UNFCCC might be lost again within the arena of the WTO.

The new trade disputes trace their origin to the rapid rise of green industrial policies being pursued by new industrial powers such as China, India, Brazil and South Africa, but also by state- and provincial-level governments in the EU, Canada and the US. While legal scholars have advanced various ways of dealing with these disputes and their serious ramifications for efforts to advance decarbonization, these suggestions have

---

1. See for example Wu and Salzman 2014; Bigdeli 2014.

mostly involved reforms to WTO law and its various recognized exceptions, as well as to national-level trade remedies processes such as imposition of Countervailing Duties (CVDs).

What is missing in the various proposals advanced so far is a recognition of the importance of supranational endorsement of any particular country's imposition of promotional measures such as local content requirements. Such a policy goal might be pursued through promotion of green energy and cleantech industries viewed in the form of a global public good resulting in the mitigation of climate change. Such public goods have long been recognized by the WTO as justifying temporary relaxation of world trade disciplines. The time has surely come to add the global 'public good' of mitigation of climate change to this list. The goal would be given much added credibility if it could appeal to the newly adopted Paris Climate Agreement as a clearly stated collective aspiration of humanity.[2]

LOCAL CONTENT REQUIREMENTS AND 'NEXT GENERATION' TRADE DISPUTES

The imposition of *Local Content Requirements* (LCRs) as a means of promoting green industries by China, India and other countries traces its origins to China's active development of its wind power industry in the 1990s. In the late 1990s there were targets for wind power development and local content targets that came to be formally implemented in the Wind Power Concession Programme launched in 2003 by the National Development and Reform Commission. This programme saw local content requirements specified for projects of between 100 and 200 MW being set initially at 40 per cent and rising to 70 per cent, with the clear goal of building a local green wind power supply chain. The programme was indeed successful. Under international protest the programme was discontinued in 2009 (revoked by ND&RC Notice 2991 in November 2009) – but already the programme had had its effect, and was being superseded by financing arrangements that likewise required local wind power projects having to meet specified grid-connection targets in order for funding to be approved. China's wind power generation and wind turbine manufacturing sector emerged as world #1 in the 2000s – widely attributed to the success of the wind power promotion programme with its strong reliance on local content

---

2. The section that follows draws on my recent paper 'Global trade and promotion of cleantech industry: A post-Paris agenda' published in *Climate Policy* (2016b).

requirements. The programme did not result in a formal WTO dispute because China discontinued the programme after judging it to be a success.

The next decade saw many more LCR provisions being implemented, by EU countries such as Spain and by US states including California, as well as by Canadian provinces such as Ontario and Quebec. These programs have provoked numerous counteractions taken within the trade arena. Japan took action against Ontario's Feed-in-Tariff (FiT) provisions coupled to Local Content Requirements (LCRs), despite their success in helping to build an effective renewable energy system in the province and reducing carbon emissions. The dispute went to Geneva and the Ontario programme was deemed WTO-incompatible by an Appeal Board hearing in 2013.[3] Since then there have been further actions taken against China's promotion of both its wind turbine industry through LCRs, and its solar PV industry through local subsidies and tax breaks (in separate actions brought by the US and the EU); and against India's National Solar Mission (NSM), which had been framed as a means of bringing India into the mainstream in transitioning to a clean energy future (an action brought by the US).

The case of India may be taken as exemplary, both because it stands as a clear model for other countries and because its details have been reviewed by a panel of the WTO and a (negative) finding reported in 2016.[4] The LCR provisions of the National Solar Mission are quite explicit – and have provided a template also for the anticipated National Wind Program. The National Solar Mission was launched originally by the Singh administration with its comprehensive national development goals being made very clear.[5] An initial total of 10 GW was to be installed over five years, subsequently upgraded to reach a new 100 GW target by 2019. India has learned from China the power of local content requirements (LCRs) as a tool for domestic renewable energy industry development.[6] India has appealed the WTO decision. In April 2016 it

3. For the text of the WTO Appeal decision, see WTO (2014), and for commentary see Charnovitz and Fischer (2015).

4. See the WTO report on the India case, 'Dispute settlement: Dispute DS456 India – certain measures relating to solar cells and solar modules', available at: https://www.wto.org/english/tratop_e/dispu_e/cases_e/ds456_e.htm.

5. For background on the issues see Johnson 2015; as well as Kent and Jha 2014.

6. On India's strategies including use of Local Content Requirements, see Johnson (2015); and Chaudhary et al. (2015). India actually has long experience of local content requirements, having used them to promote the automobile industry – again attracting WTO disapproval.

was supported by China – so now there is a strong China–India axis opposing the WTO's use of trade remedies against attempts to build renewable power industries through use of LCRs.[7]

Brazil utilized a smart combination of strategies to enable it to catch up in renewables and build its own renewable power industries. These strategies include guaranteed power purchase agreements (PPAs) and power-contract auctions to boost the market for renewables, as well as the use of indirect local sourcing requirements imposed outside the trading system (where they would attract attention from trading partners) but instead indirectly through the financing mechanism, operated by the Brazilian National Development Bank (BNDES).

While South Africa is not in the same league as Brazil, India and China in terms of its energy transition and its economic potential, there are good reasons for including it in this overview because it is grouped with the BICs in Goldman Sachs-inspired analyses of emerging markets, and because it is party to the launch of the BRICS-countries' newly created infrastructure investment bank (the New Development Bank, launched formally in Shanghai in July 2015).[8] Wind farms are now proliferating in South Africa, providing enhanced energy security and a growing market for wind turbine products as well as local employment for workers who would otherwise remain unskilled and unemployed.[9] It is LCRs that have demonstrated their capacity to facilitate the building of green energy industries in South Africa, a country that has traditionally been dominated by fossil fuels.

It is clear that the major industrializing powers are now embarking on serious programs to build up their renewables sectors, and that they are doing so through smart use of green industrial strategies. The issue is: how are these developments to be made compatible with the world trading system?

---

7. On China–India cooperation see: http://www.dnaindia.com/money/report-china-supports-india-s-stand-on-wto-solar-case-2199408

8. See Reuters story: http://in.reuters.com/article/2015/07/21/emerging-brics-bank-idINKCN0PV07Z20150721

9. The Cookhouse wind farm for example is the largest built so far in Africa, with 66 2-MW turbines spinning to generate power at 138 MW; it started feeding power into the grid at the end of 2014. Wind energy costed at less than 5 US cents per kWh means that the farm generates power at around half the cost of coal.

GREEN REFORMS TO THE WORLD'S TRADE SYSTEM

Let us agree that countries that seriously tackle the challenge of cleaning their energy systems have to employ some form of green industrial policy. These industries cannot be established by the simple expedients advocated by mainstream economics, such as product and technology substitutions being induced by (say) carbon taxes. Instead industrializing countries have learned to utilize one or more of the various industrial strategies involving subsidies, low-interest loans, tax breaks, feed-in tariffs and above all local content requirements which have proven themselves to be powerful means, when employed judiciously, to build new cleantech value chains and firms that produce cleantech products. I am not advocating that newly industrializing countries like China and India be allowed to build renewable energy industries that will then destroy such industries in already developed countries.[10] Rather, it is a question of promoting the diffusion of cleantech industries and encouraging the planting of such industries in countries around the world – subject to WTO oversight to ensure that competition remains reasonable and does not become predatory. How the advanced countries should respond is a separate matter. Clearly if they are exposed to stringent competition from emerging countries utilizing various forms of industrial policy then they need to employ counter industrial policies to promote their own innovative products and industries. New generations of solar PV power, for example, such as perovskite cells, could be promoted by advanced countries through innovation strategies, with a view to securing positions of leadership in these emerging sectors and requiring Chinese and Indian firms to pay royalties as they race to catch up with such innovations. But there are few voices in the West advocating such industrial strategies.

One of the few attempts to reconcile WTO agreements with global climate concerns is the 'Greenprint' offered in realistic fashion by Indian–US scholars Mattoo and Subramanian (2012; 2013). They frame the problem (as I do here) as requiring a fresh start for climate negotiations based on recognition of the newly important role played by the industrial giants China, India, and Brazil, and recognizing that a change in WTO rules is needed and justified to allow countries to take the steps required to build green industries. Mattoo and Subramanian argue that production subsidies for specific green products and

---

10. See Frey 2016; Chufart-Finsterwald 2014.

technologies – paid under such provisions as Feed-in-Tariffs and direct support
for renewable energy industries – should be deemed permissible for a specified
period. Export subsidies should not be prohibited, they argue, but (depending
on the circumstances) should be designated as 'actionable' (which means that
they can be challenged if a case can be made). Without specifically mentioning
LCRs Mattoo and Subramanian paradoxically recommend no change for
existing trade rules covering 'subsidies contingent upon the use of domestic over
imported goods'. On the face of it this would allow the current spate of trade
disputes over LCRs to continue unabated, and possibly exacerbate them.[11] What
is needed, I suggest, is a process that allows the principal issues before the two
global bodies concerned, the UNFCCC and the WTO, to be directly addressed.

INTEGRATING THE WORLD'S TRADE AND
CLIMATE REGIMES: A PROPOSAL

Various scholarly suggestions for integrating the role of the WTO with the
climate change regime have been advanced, with a focus on expanding the role
of exceptions to cover the public interest 'good' of climate change mitigation.
Howse (2010) provides one approach when he argues that the existing Article
XX of the GATT could be expanded to cover 'climate change mitigation' so
that countries introducing measures to support green industries would seek
exemption on these grounds. Art XX of the GATT lists measures 'necessary to
protect human, animal or plant life or health' as allowable exceptions to general
WTO discipline. A WTO decision to expand the coverage of Art XX in this
way would make it harder for countries to bring actions against proponents
of green industries. But it is still a weak defence: the country introducing the
measure is taking unilateral action and offers only its own assurance that the

---

11. By contrast, Wu and Salzman (2014) reject these kinds of reforms as being unrealistic,
and argue instead for reforms to the processes through which countries can impose Anti-
Dumping and Countervailing Duties (ADs and CVDs) on their own initiative, without
securing WTO endorsement. They target the US unilaterally imposed ADs and CVDs
against Chinese exports of solar PVs in particular, and argue that these were imposed
without adequate demonstration of trade damage and without adequate reference to
balancing considerations. They therefore call for reform of national-level processes such
as those operating in the US by the USTR and Commerce Department. But it has to be
said that if reforms at the level of the WTO would be difficult, these proposed reforms
to well-established US procedures would be even less politically palatable, driven as the
processes are by domestic economic interests.

measure is protected by Article XX. Something broader is clearly called for to stem the potential flood of green-related disputes.

One obvious candidate for supporting an extension of Art XX coverage is the UNFCCC itself. It is open to the UNFCCC to stipulate that certain measures taken in order to green industry are in the global public interest and deserve to be protected temporarily from action under WTO rules. A resolution adopted by a future Conference of the Parties could list such measures in an open and transparent fashion. It would then be open to the WTO as a global body to respond, by stating that it is prepared to recognize such a UNFCCC-based schedule as specifying measures that are taken in the public interest and are to be exempted from the usual rules of competition for a specified period (time, place, coverage). This would constitute a WTO–UNFCCC Global Climate Compact of far-reaching significance.

One practicable way forward would be for a future Conference of the Parties to adopt a resolution recognizing a group of green products and processes as being eligible for exemption from trade law for a set period (say five years). Based on the experience of China and India this would be time enough to enable countries that wish to take advantage of such an arrangement to build their green industries. Rather than leave individual countries on their own to argue their case before the WTO, such a resolution would lend the authority of the UNFCCC to the process, cutting through the complications raised by WTO procedures. The proposed Compact would establish once and for all that climate change mitigation is the ultimate 'public good' that needs to balance stringent application of trade provisions with exemption for certain designated products from the rules of full competition, for a designated period. [12]

The power of this proposal lies in the point that it promotes diffusion of green industries through allowed imposition of green industrial policy. It would not undermine WTO principles of free and fair trade, but would instead allow the WTO to (implicitly) recognize the UNFCCC as providing the authority needed to specify products or processes as being green, and give countries that wish to do so a window of protection to allow them to build the needed green industries. It would take the provisions of the newly adopted Paris Climate Agreement of 2015 beyond merely specifying reductions in carbon emissions towards engaging with the means that countries need to employ to embark on serious decarbonization of their energy systems.

---

12. I advance this proposal in the journal *Climate Policy* (Mathews 2016b).

The proposed Compact between the WTO and UNFCCC would be expected to drive investment, trade and industry towards low-carbon and zero-carbon activities – in serious and irreversible fashion. It would finally unleash the forces of capitalist competition to drive technological and production innovation in favour of reducing carbon emissions, as called for by the WTO itself, the World Bank and UNCTAD.[13] It would provide a fitting final piece of the needed global set of rules that would see the world make a successful transition to a greening of industry. And it would provide a fitting way forward beyond the 2015 Paris Climate Agreement.[14]

---

13. See WTO 2011; Charnovitz 2014; Cimino and Hufbauer 2014, representing perspectives from the WTO, the World Bank and UNCTAD.

14. In the context of this book, where climate change is not my central focus, it is also worth noting that a WTO-UNFCCC compact would not impinge negatively on efforts by industrializing giants to green their economies. On the contrary such a compact would support their efforts to enhance their energy and resource security by reducing the possibilities of their being charged at the WTO with breaching trade rules.

CHAPTER 9

FAREWELL FOSSIL FUELS

The supersession of one industrial mode by another involves a rise and at the same time a fall. Most of my efforts in this book are focused on explaining the rise of a new industrial system – one based on enhancing resource security via a Circular economy in place of linear resource throughput, and enhancing energy security via renewables that are generated from manufactured devices becoming the energy system of choice, over one based on extraction of natural materials. The complementary process involves the fall from dominance of the fossil fuels sectors, with all their vast hardware infrastructure of coal mines, oil and gas wells; tankers, pipelines, ports and terminals, processing and refining operations, and ultimate distribution – no less than their software infrastructure of commodities markets and futures markets, huge R&D and exploration budgets, global branding and marketing, use of new technologies like Global Positioning Satellite procedures and horizontal drilling, and all the rest of it. This is indeed a vast industrial system of daunting scale and complexity that is in place – but which is now in the process of decline. I examine the evidence and defend the proposition that fossil fuels are in terminal decline in this chapter.

DECLINING INDUSTRIES

For all the seeming dominance of the vast industrial infrastructure and superstructure created for fossil fuels, it really is in decline – indeed, in terminal decline. This is certainly the case for the *coal industry*, with once-dominant firms now seeking refuge in bankruptcy as their share prices collapse amidst plunging prices for coal, reduced levels of consumption (drastically reduced levels of consumption), reduced production, employment and investment and falling levels of trade, affecting all countries involved in the world of coal. Once 'King Coal' is king no longer. In the US, to take a prominent example, the world's one-time largest coal producer, Peabody Energy, watched as its share price collapsed, from a market cap value of $20 billion in 2008 to a penny stock, and it was eventually forced to file for bankruptcy protection in March 2016. Other US coal companies like Arch Coal, Patriot and Alpha Natural Resources have followed the same trajectory.

In the EU the long-term decline of coal (over decades) is now being accelerated by the rise of alternative sources of power generation. In the UK, where coal has been in decline for decades, there have been days in the year 2016 where power was generated with zero contribution from coal – a glimpse surely of the future. And in China, where enormous efforts were devoted in the 1980s and 1990s to building a viable national coal industry, focused on the operations of Shenhua as lead coal producer and importer, equally large efforts are now being devoted to phasing out the industry in favour of energy alternatives. China has not just arrested the growth in its coal consumption in the power generation industry but has actually reduced its absolute levels of consumption for the first time ever. China has drastically curtailed its coal imports, and is closing many of its port operations – as it raises employment and investment in alternative energy activities. In China the drive to discontinue the coal operations is coming from central political choices involved in the swing away from coal because of the filth of its pollution. Coal is viewed as the means through which the country escaped from poverty – but it has now served its purpose and it is time to move on to cleaner sources of energy. China is concerned to ensure that the shift from one primary energy source to another is accomplished with minimal social dislocation.

Of course China could choose as energy option for the future clean coal technology (as developed for example in Germany) as well as carbon capture and storage – with a view to cleaning up its emissions without changing the fuel base. This would have the effect of tackling immediate particulate pollution problems as well as carbon emissions – but it would not have any impact on China's strategic goal of enhancing energy security through switching from minerals extraction and processing(with its increasing costs and diminishing returns) to generating energy from manufactured devices that feature diminishing costs and increasing returns. Nor would it allow China to benefit from reducing costs associated with manufacturing learning curves. Indeed it would condemn China to be a technological follower indefinitely and negate the goal of indigenizing energy technology through innovation. So it is hardly surprising that China is not setting such a course as its preferred means of adapting to the decline of fossil fuels.

OIL AND GAS INDUSTRY PROBLEMS

Things are little better in the oil industry, which by mid-2016 globally had been going through seven successive quarters of recession. Again levels of production were down, as were consumption levels, and the share prices and capital values of some of the world's largest oil companies were plunging. Alberta's dream of becoming the 'Saudi Arabia of tar sands' and the new major oil producer of the Western world was going up in smoke – literally. Wild fires in Alberta have been burning out of control and consuming the tar sands operations promoted so carefully over the past decades in Canada. In mid-May the work camps of major tar sands companies Suncor Energy Inc. and Syncrude Canada had to be evacuated – and were to be closed down until it was deemed safe to reopen them.[1] The worst case scenario is that the fires would have completely destroyed the tar sands operations. Nothing could underline more dramatically the risks associated with building energy futures on extraction activities such as fracking – as opposed to the relatively safe methods of power generation from renewables based on manufacture of renewables devices. By mid-May no fewer than four companies – BP, Phillips, Suncor and the Chinese-owned CNOOC Nexen – had issued *force majeure* statements to customers that conditions created by the fires would force them to cancel supply contracts. In the end the tar sands work camps of Suncor Energy and Syncrude Canada were defended by firefighters and the operations were saved – but the communities that lay at the heart of the industry had been destroyed.

These setbacks in Canada come on top of a year of declining oil and gas output and prolonged recession in the industry caused by a drastic lowering of the price of oil and cutbacks in consumption. The oil and gas services contractor Schlumberger reflects the general malaise; the company reported in May 2016 that its earnings had dropped 49 per cent in the first quarter and that since the peaking of demand in November 2014 it had cut 36,000 jobs, or 28 per cent of its workforce.[2] Oil prices have fluctuated wildly in recent years, falling from a high in November 2014 when prices exceeded $100 per barrel, to a level of between $30 and $40 in mid-2016 – thereby putting enormous pressure on the oil majors and the host of oil service companies that feed off the oil supply

---

1. See the report 'Major oil sands facilities, camps under mandatory evacuation order as fire rages', 17 May 2016, in *Toronto Globe & Mail*, at: http://www.theglobeandmail.com/report-on-business/industry-news/energy-and-resources/major-oil-sands-facilities-camps-under-mandatory-evacuation-order-as-fire-rages/article30057435/.
2. See the story in the *Wall Street Journal*, at: http://www.wsj.com/articles/schlumberger-profit-falls-49-as-revenue-slumps-1461272520.

chain. These price pressures have been exacerbated by the global oil cartel, OPEC, which has seen a prolonged struggle for power between Saudi Arabia on the one hand, and relative newcomers like Iran (within OPEC) and Russia (outside OPEC) on the other. Saudi Arabia in mid-2016 refused to reduce production as the price of oil fell (as would have been anticipated) and instead maintained high production levels to keep downward pressure on the oil price – thereby damaging the Iranian and Russian producers. Since the US would presumably have had to be in agreement on this strategy, it would have meant the US allowing the Saudis to come close to destroying the newly emerged US and Canadian shale oil and coal seam gas industries – another amazing facet of the global politics of oil. By the end of 2016 the price of oil was stabilizing – only emphasizing how unreliable an energy strategy based on oil must be.

Divestment

Adding to the troubles in the industry, there is now a firm movement worldwide for institutional investors to exit their fossil fuel shareholdings in favour of alternative energy holdings. Oil made vast fortunes for the pioneers in the US, such as John D. Rockefeller, who created the vast Rockefeller Foundation that is still active today – and associated family funds such as the Rockefeller Brothers Fund that have made waves by their divestment activities, moving out of investments in fossil fuels (to considerable fanfare). NGO funds with clout like the Bill and Melinda Gates Foundation, which only recently was stating its aversion to divestment from fossil fuels, was by 2016 divesting in a very big way – a good indication that the Gates and their fund managers had concluded that fossil fuels had no future.

IMPERFECT TRANSITION

Of course the fossil fuel era will not vanish overnight; there will be periodic revivals of fossil fuel interests and successes. This means that there will continue to be terrible accidents, fires, and explosions periodically erupting in coal mining, oil drilling and transport. Think of the US Upper Big Branch coal mine explosion that killed 29 men in 2010 (and for which the CEO of the company involved, Massey Energy, was sentenced to prison for wilful violation of mine safety standards).[3] Think of the BP *Deepwater Horizon* oil drilling disaster in the

---

3. The CEO, Don Blankenship, was sent to prison in 2016. Six years earlier he famously debated Robert Kennedy Jr over the environmental horrors perpetrated by the US

Gulf of Mexico in 2010 which turned out to be the biggest oil disaster in US history, killing eleven oil platform workers and releasing 4.9 million barrels of oil over an 87-day period when oil gushed unchecked from the wrecked drills on the seafloor.[4] The Hollywood movie *Deepwater Horizon*, released in late 2016, gives the full flavour of the enormous technical sophistication of deepwater drilling and the destructive effects when it all goes wrong. Ditto for the Prudhoe Bay oil spill in the Arctic (also involving BP) in 2006 that involved the leakage of 5 *trillion* barrels of oil (a million times worse than the Deepwater Horizon) and resulted in huge destruction of natural wildlife in the pristine Arctic area.[5] These disasters that have become almost commonplace will no doubt be regarded with mounting intolerance as energy alternatives to fossil fuels press their case.

There will continue to be terrible long-term health consequences for the workers in these fossil fuel industries (black lung from siliceous dust amongst coal miners; and bladder cancer from petrochemical workers exposed to aromatic hydrocarbons) and for the public more generally. There will continue to be the disastrous environmental impacts like destruction of coral reefs, deforestation and leaks of toxic mining materials into local rivers, causing widespread devastation – such as Texaco's record of failing to clean up its operations in Latin American countries like Ecuador. Now acquired by/ merged with Chevron, the company presents itself as a paragon of environmental virtue. The wider effects of fossil fuel leakages, and the impact of higher global temperatures induced by oil burning, such as the acid rain which has acidified lakes and devastated forests, will no doubt continue to exercise their influence.

There will continue to burn terrible oil refinery fires, like those that torched refineries in Puerto Rico, and in US states like Texas, California

---

coal industry – such as shearing off the tops of mountains – all of which he defended as standard business practice; he also referred to global warming as 'Obama's hoax'. For a report, see 'The death of US coal: industry on a steep decline as cheap natural gas rises', by Suzanne Goldenberg, *The Guardian*, 8 Apr 2016, at: http://www.theguardian.com/environment/2016/apr/08/us-coal-industry-decline-natural-gas.

4. A US government National Commission was established to investigate and report on the disaster. See the final report of the National Commission on the *BP Deepwater Horizon oil spill and offshore drilling*, at: https://cybercemetery.unt.edu/archive/oilspill/20121210200431/http://www.oilspillcommission.gov/final-report.

5. See the situation report by the Alaska Department of Environmental Conservation, 25 March 2008, at: http://dec.alaska.gov/spar/ppr/response/sum_fy06/060302301/sitreps/060302301_sr_23.pdf.

and Pennsylvania. Think of the fires at the former Texaco oil refinery on San Francisco Bay, where company officials have been charged with repeated wilful violations of safety procedures. There will continue to occur terrible explosions (unconfined vapour cloud explosion) like that which flattened Texas City, TX in 2005, killing 15 workers and injuring more than 179 others. The Texas City oil refinery had been acquired by BP from Amoco, as part of its absorption of Amoco in 1999. Or think of the fire that ravaged the Girard Point refinery of Gulf Oil on the Schuylkill River in Philadelphia, in 1975, causing the deaths of eight firefighters and which at one point threatened to engulf the entire city of Philadelphia. There will doubtless be more disasters like the oil spill from the Exxon-Valdez, caused by the rupture of the ship after it struck the Bligh reef in Prince William Sound in Alaska, in 1989.

No doubt there will continue to be geopolitical pressures arising from oil and gas extraction activities around the world, particularly as Chinese and Indian companies venture out into the world in search of hydrocarbon goodies and become vulnerable to the financial and environmental temptations of the industry. China for example thought it had a good source of oil in South Sudan – until an unanticipated civil war flared up and plunged the country into chaos. It is worth asking the question: How was this civil war started, and who stood to benefit?

Ecuador is another country where geopolitical pressures have exploded – once China became a customer for the country's oil exports. After assuming the presidency in 2007, Rafael Correa sought relief from the country's 'odious' foreign debts, and when this was refused the country defaulted, becoming a pariah in international credit markets. China took advantage of this situation to offer Ecuador credit – in return for oil. Chinese banks provided lines of credit and Chinese oil companies like China National Petroleum Corporation (CNPC) and PetroChina likewise provided loans as well as participating in construction of refineries and infrastructure. The terms of the agreement in-cluded sale of Amazonian crude to PetroChina. Thus China's international soft power has broadened as countries like Ecuador are drawn into its sphere of influence, with oil playing a major role in this process.

OIL IN THE TWENTIETH CENTURY: WARS, REVOLUTIONS AND TERROR

The oil wars of the twenty-first century – if China and India were to continue on a fossil fuel 'business as usual' pathway – would be expected to replicate the disasters of the twentieth century at an even greater scale of intensity and savagery. Oil was indeed at the source of many of the wars and revolutions of the twentieth century. In Mexico for example oil became a central player in the contending forces that broke out into the Mexican revolution of 1911, with Standard Oil and its affiliates being a major player.[6] Ever since Winston Churchill as the Secretary for the Navy in Britain (First Lord of the Admiralty) switched the Royal Navy from coal to oil in 1913, the transport of oil became a prime military target during the First World War and particularly in the Second World War when both Allies and Axis powers were vitally dependent on oil transport to sustain their military machines. In the African desert campaign, the brilliant German commander Rommel was not just outgunned by his British adversary General Montgomery, but was forced to concede battles for want of oil.

In the post war period the Middle East and the countries of the Persian Gulf came to occupy a disproportionate global influence based on their oil holdings. In Iran the democratically elected government of Mohammad Mosaddegh was toppled by a coup in 1953, instigated by the British with tacit CIA support, on account of Mosaddegh's threatened nationalization of the Anglo-Iranian Oil Company (forerunner of British Petroleum). This paved the way for installation of the Shah and his brutal pro-Western regime – until this in turn was toppled by the Islamic fundamentalist Khomeini regime in 1979. US–Iranian relations have been poisoned ever since – right up to 2016.

In Africa, oil has been at the core of the civil wars that have raged in Nigeria – first in the province of Biafra in the 1970s, and more recently in the Niger Delta. In the Delta area the oil majors have sought to maintain production while enriching a few in the Nigerian federal government, in the face of fierce resistance from Niger Delta provincial leaders. This pattern has been repeated around the world wherever oil wealth is monopolized by one group at the expense of others who feel they have rights to share in the wealth (or monopolize it). Then there were the oil wars in the Persian Gulf over the past half-century. These include the Iran–Iraq war of the 1970s, fought largely over who would have dominance in oil supplies, and then came the invasion of Kuwait by Saddam Hussain's Iraqi forces, leading to the US and Allied response known as the Kuwait War. The 1991 Kuwaiti oil fires, which turned the Persian Gulf into a blazing inferno, stand as a pre-eminent example of oil-related collateral war damage on a scale never hitherto experienced. Then there was the disastrous US invasion of Iraq in 2003, instigated (if never

---

6. For an insightful account see Rippy (1972).

officially admitted) by considerations of access to oil; it has been a final, bloody demonstration of how to confuse an energy strategy with a military strategy.

The most deadly terrorist organization of the late twentieth century was certainly Al-Qaeda, which arose in Saudi Arabia as an Islamic extremist organization opposed to Western oil interests in the country and the Saudi regime that was viewed as sympathetic to these interests. The most striking action undertaken by this group, under the leadership of Osama bin Laden, was doubtless the attack on the twin towers of the World Trade Centre in New York on 11 September 2001. It is worth recalling that this attack was instigated directly by a group intent on sowing terror in the US to highlight the character of the Western-supported oil regimes in the Middle East. Oil has thus been at the root of many of the wars, revolutions and terrorist actions of the twentieth century – and it will continue to be so in the twenty first century unless the grip of the oil and fossil fuels sector over industrial economies is loosened. China and India take note.

JAPANESE EXPERIENCE WITH THE ALLIED OIL EMBARGO

A story that China would be well aware of is that of the process through which Japan was led step-by-step into war in the Pacific and ultimately to declaration of war against the US in 1941. Japan acquired the extensive territory of Manchuria following its military victories over China in 1895 and Russia in 1905. At first Japan treated this new territory as a valuable source of raw materials but gradually it acquired greater significance in the eyes of the Japanese leadership. During the 1930s Japan took a militaristic turn and invaded China, taking advantage of this situation to set up a puppet state called Manchukuo in the region of Manchuria (in Northeast China) in 1931 (Figure 9.1).

Japan treated Manchukuo as a source of raw materials and accelerated its industrialization (providing a precedent for subsequent post-war Japanese industrial development and Korean industrialization as well after 1961). But Japan stumbled into an aggressive stance against the US, on which it was dependent for 80 per cent of its oil supplies.[7] This aggressive posture on the part of Japan led to the US and its allies denying Japan oil imports; these Allied embargoes threatened the country with economic and industrial collapse.

---

7. The companies involved were Stanvac, an affiliate of Standard Oil, and Rising Sun, an affiliate of Royal Dutch-Shell. For an outline of the story, see Sohn (2004), p. 71.

FIGURE 9.1. Manchukuo.

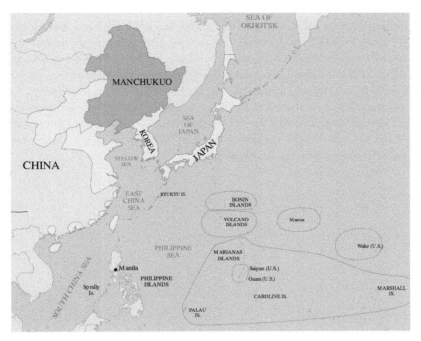

SOURCE: Available under Creative Commons from Pacific_Area_-_The_Imperial_
Powers_1939_-_Map.svg.

Japan took steps to expand its occupation of parts of Southeast Asia, rich in
oil, and sought to knock the US out of its sphere of influence in the Pacific
(what it called the East Asian Co-Prosperity Sphere) which, as we all know, led
to the bombing of Pearl Harbour and the entry of the US into the war – with
disastrous results for Japan. This little known East Asian story of oil, war, and
politics is no doubt a prime source of instruction for China today, and one of
the reasons behind China's aggressive build-up of renewable energy systems as
alternatives to oil and fossil fuels.

* * *

This first part of the book covers the major issues in the greening of the
world's industrial system and what is driving the process – involving the
greening of energy and materials systems as well as the mobilization of serious
finance. My argument is that while the West takes hesitant steps, China and
India are forging ahead, leading the way in the global green transition, and

demonstrating to other developing/industrializing countries what they can expect and hope for. We have also examined briefly the complementary difficulties of the fossil fuels industries and their terrible legacies – leading to a clear motive for China, India et al. to look for alternative energy sources and resource recirculation systems in the twenty-first century. We now turn to the details of the transition, examining the character of the ecomodernist/green shift that is underway, with a focus on the energy transition, resources, food and water issues involved. Our emphasis will be on understanding the drivers of the transition, and why they can be expected to effect a total green shift within just two or three decades at the most, to the point where ecology can meet the economy on favourable terms.

PART II

SIXTH WAVE ECO-INNOVATIONS

CHAPTER 10

GLOBAL POPULATION PEAKING ... AND URBANIZING

Trends in population are important – and provide a sound basis for discussion of all other resource and energy trends. Population dynamics set limits on other processes. Population trends befuddled earlier commentators and scholars who erroneously saw it as the fundamental driver to be limited before everything else. Now however there is a better appreciation of the peaking of population that UN demographers see as occurring by mid-century; global population is expected to stabilize at around 9 billion, and decrease thereafter.

The 'population bomb' scaremongering of the 1960s was based on initial exposure to rapid increases in global population, as growth rates were peaking. In fact world population increased from 3 billion to 6 billion from 1960 to 1999 – a doubling time of only 39 years. The rate of acceleration can be comprehended when we consider that the previous doubling time – when the world grew from 1.5 billion to 3 billion – took about 70 years (from 1890 to 1960). And the doubling time before that took about 150 years. Now if we trace the number sequence 150, 70, 39, the next number in the sequence would seem to be, say, 20 (as might be mathematically expected) but in reality it is more likely to be 100 or 1000 years, or infinity – in other words, it will never happen. Instead, world population will be expected to stabilize – according to the insights of the very important theory of the *demographic transition*. Based on UN population estimates, the growth rate of global population peaked in 1968 – the year of publication of the Ehrlichs' *Population Bomb*.[1]

---

1. See Goldstone (2010) for further twists to this story.

THE DEMOGRAPHIC TRANSITION

The theory of the demographic transition posits a very different process. It starts with a regime of high birth rates and high death rates – which characterized all countries prior to the industrial revolution and still characterizes some industrializing countries today. In this regime there are low growth rates, because deaths cancel out births. The transition begins with a decline in death rates (through modern medicine and improved public health measures) which leads to a rapid increase in population as birth rates exceed death rates. This is followed by a reduction in birth rates, not because of declining fertility but because as populations are urbanized and industrialized women express their preferences for fewer births – notwithstanding the teachings of major religions like Catholicism, Islam, and Judaism. So the low birth rates then balance the low mortality rates, and the population growth rate stabilizes once again at a low level.

There is overwhelming evidence to support the theory of the demographic transition, in both its dual phases. We can be confident that its prediction that there will be a peaking of global population at around 9 billion by mid-century or earlier will prove to be accurate.[2]

Other aspects of the Ecomodernization view follow from this. If population were to expand indefinitely, then there would no hope for curtailing the burning of fossil fuels with all their dirty emissions, as well as endless growth in water and resources use indefinitely, leading to impossibility of feeding such a burgeoning world population, But the fact that population can be confidently expected to peak at 9 billion changes everything. It means that technoeconomic measures of decoupling can be devised and put to work – as is really happening.

The first impact is in the growth of cities themselves – or what is called urbanization. Cities are the ultimate in creating an artificial environment where technologies allow urban life to be relatively decoupled from their natural moorings. Now the negative impact of expansion of cities on the environment is all too evident – witness the destruction of agricultural land, the paving of so much woodland, the pollution of watercourses, the expansion of non-sustainable landfill sites for waste disposal. Third world shanty towns are the symbol of these negative impacts.

At the same time some the positive effects that urbanization can be expected to have are clear. The ecomodernist Stewart Brand was one of the first to point to

---

2. See Lam (2011).

the potential that city life has to be less harsh on the environment than rural living. In his *Whole Earth Discipline* (Brand 2010) he argues that urbanization can have net favourable impact on the environment partly because population stabilizes and goes through the demographic transition first in cities, and because the exodus of populations from rural areas to cities reduces their negative impacts through strains on water supplies, fresh water and irrigation systems. Let us just take one horrifying story to back up Brand's thesis. In India one of the great (but barely mentioned) issues is defecation in the open air in rural villages, leading to pollution of water supplies by human fecal matter and consequent high levels of infection by organisms such as *Escherichia coli* particularly in young children. Indeed some health scholars have posited that India has a lower IQ nationally than would otherwise be the case because rural children have to spend much of their time fighting off *E. coli* infections that strain their resistance and retard their intellectual development. So urbanization in this case with its emphasis on provision of sewerage and fresh water supplies (even if delivered imperfectly) would constitute a huge boon for the country's children whose bodies would be able to concentrate on brain development rather than fighting off fecally delivered infections.[3]

Stewart Brand is something of an extremist when it comes to Ecomodernization. His title for the 2010 book, endorsing nuclear power, GMOs, and geoengineering is in my view somewhat exaggerated. It would seem to be enough to advocate and endorse what I am calling Sixth Wave (6W) technoeconomic transitions, with an emphasis on renewable energy, on production of fresh water through desalination, production of resources through circular economy measures and production of food through urban farming. This is all quite radical enough without going full bore for GMOs (to the benefit of Monsanto but few others) and geoengineering (a piece of scientific hubris that has no place in 6W thinking).

Leaving Brand's arguments to one side, there are so many ways in which cities can tame our species' adverse impact on the earth, particularly when we are discussing self-styled eco-cities. The rare attempts to create real eco-cities on the ground have few clear successes as yet, and some outright failures like the ill-fated Dongtan near Shanghai in China. There is also the top-down creation of Masdar in the UAE which is said to be struggling.[4] Meanwhile in

---

3. See the story in the *New York Times* by Gardiner Harris (13 July 2014), 'Poor sanitation in India may afflict well-fed children with malnutrition', available at: http://www.nytimes.com/2014/07/15/world/asia/poor-sanitation-in-india-may-afflict-well-fed-children-with-malnutrition.html?_r=0.

4. See the story in *The Guardian* at: http://www.theguardian.com/environment/2016/feb/16/masdars-zero-carbon-dream-could-become-worlds-first-green-ghost-town.

China eco-cities like the Tianjin eco-city have yet to prove themselves. But if eco-cities are given a broad definition and allowed to encompass greening of established cities, through creation of self-supporting neighbourhoods, sustainable transport, urban gardens and vertical production of food, all of which emphasize how the city can be the focus for the world's greening efforts, then progress is indeed substantial. I explore these issues further in chapter 17.

One prominent interpretation of eco-city design is associated with the notion of 'urban ecology' as developed for example by the American ecologist Richard Register.[5] His main line of argument is to see cities as the primary sites where living conditions can be reconstructed to be in better balance with nature. It raises the important point that a reengineered eco-city equipped with decoupled energy, water, resources and food production systems should have the space to allow for some re-greening. If the urban population is concentrated in parts of the city and services are concentrated in other parts, then that leaves considerable scope for reintroduction of green parkland, urban forests, tree-lined boulevards and other features that are a matter of green design. The goal should be to liberate the city from its tight coupling with nature – and thereby create space for greening that lends the city a pleasing aspect and provides the open space, fresh air and open country and woodland experience that people need for their well-being.

URBANIZATION AS ECOMODERNIZATION

Cities provide the ultimate in 'artificial living'. Just think of people working from an office as compared with earlier modes of labour – with the office's internal environment, usually heated in the winter and air-conditioned in the summer, as well as office equipment (printing, copying, IT) and telecommunications connections linking the office to the entire business world. Air conditioning on its own has been a huge boost for productivity in tropical countries. The founder of the first post-colonial government in Singapore, Lee Kuan Yew, is on the record as stating that it was air conditioning that had made all the difference in Singapore.[6]

---

5. See Register (1987) and Register (2006) for examples of his proposals.

6. As Lee Kuan Yew put it: 'Air conditioning was a most important invention for us, perhaps one of the signal inventions of history. It changed the nature of civilization by making development possible in the tropics. Without air conditioning you can work only in the cool early morning hours or at dusk. The first thing I did upon becoming prime minister was to install air conditioners in buildings where the civil service worked. This was key to public efficiency.' See http://www.huffingtonpost.com/nathan-gardels/lee-kuan-yew-remembered_b_6920292.html.

FIGURE 10.1. World urbanization, 1950–2015 (and 2050 projection).

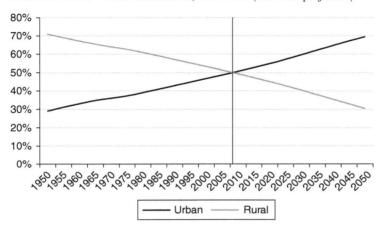

SOURCE: http://esa.un.org//unup/p2k0data.asp

Cities create the most 'decoupled' living environment that we can imagine. While the world has been living with cities now for several thousand years, the trend has picked up rapidly since the industrial revolution. The world was more urban than rural by 2010 – an extremely important milestone in the history of our species (Figure 10.1).

China as the latecomer to industrialization has experienced the most intense urbanization trends of any country preceding its modernization – and thereby showing the rest of the world what to expect. China is urbanizing and industrializing at the same time – at a pace unprecedented in history. In the space of just a few decades China has changed, and is changing, from a largely rural to a largely urban population. The figures speak for themselves. China was a largely rural country at the time of the revolution. It reached an urbanization level of 20 per cent by 1980; then 30 per cent by 1996; 40 per cent by 2002 and 50 per cent by 2011 – so by 2012 there were more people living in cities in China than in the countryside (Figure 10.2). The urbanization trend is expected to continue. According to the 12th Five Year Plan, China's urbanization level should have reached 54 per cent by 2015. The latest data released by the National Bureau of Statistics indicate that this target has already been exceeded, with China reaching 56 per cent urbanization level by the end of 2015.[7] By 2020 China's planners anticipate that 60 per cent of the population will live in cities.

---

7. See the press release from the National Bureau of Statistics, at: http://www.stats.gov. cn/english/PressRelease/201602/t20160229_1324019.html.

FIGURE 10.2. China: Urban residents and their proportion in the total population, 1949–2015.

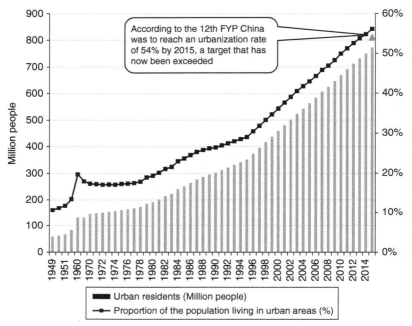

NOTE: The spike around 1957/58 is not an artefact of statistics, but the result of the decline of the rural population resulting from the three-year 'Great Chinese Famine' of 1958–1960, which was jointly caused by drought and by the policies of the Communist Party of China aimed at making a 'Great Leap Forward'.
SOURCE: Mathews, Hu and Tan (2016), based on data from the NBS (2015).

To gain a feel for this frantic pace of urbanization, which drives the greening of China's urban economy, consider the following. Over the decade 2005 to 2015 China raised its number of urbanized residents from 560 million to 770 million today. This means an increase of 210 million over the decade – or on average, 21 million newly urbanized people every year. This amounts to building seven new cities each of 3 million inhabitants, every year – a phenomenal rate of change. No wonder China is viewed as the urbanizing powerhouse of the planet, with a construction and housing industry to match.[8]

---

8. Behind China's rapid urbanization there lie some clever financial initiatives, including local authorities (municipal and provincial governments) reaping the returns to urbanization in enhanced land values which can then be channeled into investment in

Now the artificial character of cities is experienced in every aspect, from provision of power and water services, waste elimination and sewerage, public transport, public housing, extensive shared facilities for sport, recreation and entertainment. City life promises everything in comfort that is denied the rural dweller – which is why people gravitate towards cities as fast as they can when given the opportunity. This makes cities the ideal candidates for greening processes. Rather than being the foot draggers in terms of such issues as energy efficiency, over-use of transport, or exhaust pollution from automobiles, the city becomes instead the locus of reductions in energy intensity, water intensity, material intensity and buildings become the prime vehicles for greening. This is such a contrary view to the one that sees cities as concentrations of waste and pollution that it deserves highlighting as a principle, namely that as cities get bigger so they tend to get greener.[9] The greening of cities promises to make their role in countries' economic life already more significant as is becoming clear in countries like China as they rapidly urbanize – and become greener through urbanization.

CITIES AS WEALTH CREATORS

A rich literature has been documenting the central importance of cities in economic life. They have been magnets for the best and the brightest. Scholars from Alfred Marshall in the nineteenth century to Lewis Mumford and Jane Jacobs in the twentieth century and Richard Florida in the twenty-first century have sought to capture the 'extra' that industrial agglomerations of firms (in the case of industrial districts) or people (in cities) are able to generate. Marshall coined the concepts of internal and external economies, where he saw industrial districts generating 'extra' returns outside the firm due to its

---

needed infrastructure. On the role of the China Development Bank in this process, see Sanderson and Forsythe (2013).

9. Michael Batty in his *New Science of Cities* (2013) fashions such a principle which he calls 'Brand's law' after Stewart Brand's observations in his 2010 work *Whole Earth Discipline: An EcoPragmatist Manifesto*. Batty states (p. 40): 'As cities get bigger, they get "greener", in the sense of becoming more sustainable. This is, of course, a recent finding, and it is exactly the opposite of what happened as cities grew during the Western Industrial Revolution and as some but not all cities are still growing in the developing world. This we will call *Brand's Law* after Brand (2010), whose observations on the growth of cities and sustainability suggest that to maintain the quality of life that cities seek, higher densities are necessary for good social interaction ..' Lower density sprawl is in this sense the enemy of greening.

co-location with other firms. The richer the cluster, the more intensive are the interactions, leading to greater specialization of labour – which results in superior efficiencies. Marshall used the memorable phrase that knowledge in such locations is 'in the air' – or what economists would more prosaically term today knowledge spill overs. Adam Smith was wrestling with the same phenomenon when he declared that the 'division of labour is limited by the extent of the market' – meaning that labour efficiency due to specialization increases with the size of the market.

Scholars are now starting to find ways to quantify just how these knowledge spill overs are generated and how they provide that 'extra' that cities and clusters benefit from. Luis Bettencourt and Geoffrey West at the Santa Fe Institute in New Mexico have been utilizing large data sets susceptible to computer analysis to generate what they modestly call 'a unified theory of urban living'. They are able to demonstrate that for every doubling of the size of a city, its infrastructure costs (like roads, telecommunications networks, water pipes) reduce – by 15 per cent less than would be expected – a saving that they equate with economies of scale. Even more interestingly they quantify the superior achievements of cities in terms of knowledge and innovation, where again there is a scaling of 15 per cent over and above what would be expected if the relationship were linear. In their words, cities deliver superlinear performance – or what Marshall referred to as external economies, or others refer to as synergies and systemic effects.

Non-linearities or what are referred to as 'increasing returns' are fundamental to the success of cities. Economic productivity (measured in terms of value-added in manufacturing, GDP, wages, or personal income) all increase on a per capita basis by ~15 per cent with every doubling of a city's population, regardless of the city's starting size. This is a result that holds across a wide variety of cities in all parts of the world (in the US as much as in China). Bettencourt et al. refer to this as 'a continuous and systematic acceleration of socioeconomic processes with increasing numbers of people' (2010: 2). The result is that 'larger cities produce and spend wealth faster, create new ideas more frequently and – the dark side of the process of urbanization – 'suffer from greater incidence of crime' – all to more or less the same degree.[10] Other

---

10. Bettencourt, West and colleagues generalize this finding in their analysis of 'scaling and universality in urban economic diversification' (Youn et al. 2016).

scholars such as the group assembled by Michael Batty at UCL in London are constructing scaling laws for cities based on complexity analysis and the availability of large data sets.[11]

Bettencourt and West introduce three 'laws' of city growth, namely that (1) space required per capita shrinks (economies of greater density); (2) the pace of socioeconomic activity accelerates, leading to higher productivity (e.g., in income, or patents awarded); and (3) economic and social activities diversify and become more interdependent. The third feature is most interesting; it means that cities generate new forms of economic specialization and cultural expression. The history of cities delivers ample evidence of this process at work.[12]

By the year 2000, more than 70 per cent of the population in developed countries lived in cities, while the proportion urbanized in developing countries was only around 40 per cent. By 2030 the urban population in developing countries is anticipated to more than double to reach around 4 billion (occupying a threefold increase in land). Moreover the pace of urbanization in the developing world is picking up. In China for example the urban population in 2000 was around 450 million, representing 37 per cent of the total population; yet by 2015 it had reached 770 million, by which time the proportion of urban dwellers had risen to 56 per cent – the fastest urbanization in history.

Cities may be viewed as a kind of 'enclosed environment' for economic interaction, where it is not the weather or soil fertility that is being controlled, but the infrastructure on which human interactivity is nourished. We see that there has been an enormous uptick in urbanization in recent decades, as people flock to the cities from the countryside – with highly beneficial effects in terms of productivity, income generation and innovation, and negative effects in terms of proliferating crime, disease and growth of slums. People in the developed world are around 80 per cent urbanized – expressing a clear preference for city living – and this proportion is expected to apply to everyone by the year 2050. That will mean that around 2 billion people will be moving into cities in China, Africa, India and Southeast Asia.

---

11. See Batty (2012; 2013) for an outline of a future 'science of cities' and Arcaute et al. (2015) for a demonstration of the power of analysis of large data sets in 'constructing cities, deconstructing scaling laws'.

12. See Bettencourt and West 2010: 912.

Contrary to widespread expectations, the current trend towards urbanization, with more people in the world today living in cities than in the countryside (an historic transition), is associated with a diminishing impact of humans on the planet. The trend is for us as a species to be concentrated in cities (urban agglomerations) which by mid-century should see up to 80 per cent of people engaged in urban activities, and living in cleaner circumstances – with enormous benefits for the global population as a whole. We generalize this as a trend towards eco-cities, discussed in the penultimate chapter.

An earlier generation viewed the expansion of cities and the agglomeration of cities into a monstrous megalopolis as fearsome developments. But now the same phenomenon occurring at even greater scale in China puts the whole issue into some perspective.[13] In China there are three emergent megalopolis developments – the Yangtze River delta around Shanghai (92 million inhabitants), the Pearl River Delta in the south (accounting for over 100 million people) and the emergent northeast JingJinJi megalopolis encompassing the cities of Beijing and Tianjin and the province of Hubei (accounting for 110 million). These developments are viewed, in China and without, as major drivers of greening rather than as sources of degradation. Indeed the greening of the world's industrial processes can be expected to start in the cities themselves. Cities are already the drivers of wealth generation and innovation, and this is likely to carry over now to the greening of the world's industry – the next Great Transformation. This transformation has to start with energy – because it was with energy that the first industrial revolution began.

---

13. See Mumford (1961) and Gottmann (1961) as prominent examples.

CHAPTER 11

ENERGY THAT IS CLEAN, CHEAP, ABUNDANT – AND SAFE

The only reason I'm optimistic about this problem [of global warming] is because of innovation. And innovation is a very uncertain process. [...] I want to tilt the odds in our favor by driving innovation at an unnaturally high pace, or more than its current business-as-usual course. I see that as the only thing. I want to call up India someday and say, 'Here's a source of energy that is cheaper than your coal plants, and by the way, from a global-pollution and local-pollution point of view, it's also better.'

BILL GATES, 'WE NEED AN ENERGY
MIRACLE', *THE ATLANTIC*, 2015

Thought leaders like Bill Gates argue that we have to wait for an 'energy miracle' that will allow renewables to take over from fossil fuels – meaning that the conventional renewables (such as first generation solar PV cells) are not going to be able to drive the transition – in his view.[1] But Bill, there is no need to wait for a miracle. The evidence is already to hand that it is falling costs that are the fundamental drivers of the global energy transition. The 'miracle' is already here. Take first generation solar photovoltaic cells as exemplary. The most recent analyses find that new solar photovoltaic (PV) installations are comparable in cost to fossil-fuelled power plants, and falling at a rate of 16 per cent for every doubling of capacity.[2] The evidence is provided in Figure 11.1.

---

1. See Bill Gates's comments, 'We need an energy miracle', *The Atlantic*, November 2015, at: http://www.theatlantic.com/magazine/archive/2015/11/we-need-an-energy-miracle/407881/.

2. For discussion of the falling costs of renewables generation by UN-affiliated agencies, see UNIDO-GGGI (2015) and IRENA (2014).

FIGURE 11.1. Solar PV module experience curve, 1976–2013.

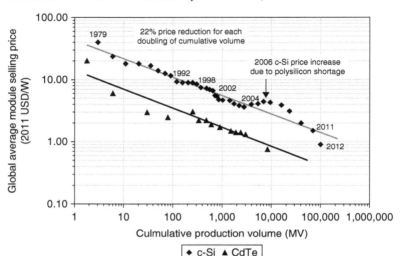

SOURCE: IRENA.

How low can costs of first generation solar go before the second generation and subsequent generations kick in? The cost of solar PV power can be expected to continue its plunge, and to reach well below the costs associated with burning of fossil fuels for electric power by 2020 or earlier.[3] At this point an industrializing country would be well advised to study closely its options regarding energy, and evaluate the costs of going with renewables as opposed to fossil fuels and nuclear. The world could pass the 1000 GW mark of solar PV power (the first terawatt) in less than a decade from now, that is, before 2025. This is entirely plausible. Already China has an official goal of 160 GW by 2020, and India has come close to matching that goal with its National Solar Mission target of 100 GW by 2022. There are extensive rooftop solar programs in Europe and the USA, and Japan seems poised to join the process.

Indeed the solar energy revolution is proceeding much faster than most people have anticipated. Cumulative solar PV capacity has been doubling every

---

3. For one view on this, see Ramez Naam, 'How cheap can solar get? Very cheap indeed', *Energy Post*, 21 August 2015, at: http://www.energypost.eu/cheap-can-solar-get-cheap-indeed/.

two years or so – and continues at such a prime exponential rate today.[4] So the 1 TW mark for the world as a whole is actually likely to be passed by around 2020 or even earlier. By then the generating cost of new solar PV installations should be somewhere between 4 and 6 cents per kWh (or $40 to $60 per MWh) – a *lower cost than generating power using even the cheapest brown coal*. This is how fast the renewables revolution is unfolding. Of course there will be innovations that continue to disrupt the evolution of solar PV power (as I discuss in a moment). But the fundamental revolution is already here.

A similar story can be told for wind power. Consider the learning curve for wind power, which demonstrates a clear cost reduction potential out to 100,000 MW (or 100 GW – a level already achieved by China). The levelized cost of wind power has been falling at a rate of 14 per cent per year as cumulative production experience and the scale of the market grows. And a further incredible story is being told for energy storage – which has until now been the 'reverse salient' of the renewables energy game, holding back the diffusion of the new renewables systems. A paper published in *Nature Climate Change* reviewed the situation, and found that costs had been falling at the rate of 14 per cent per year between the years 2007 and 2014, with a learning rate of 6 to 9 per cent – typical of manufacturing experience curves.[5]

We show that industry-wide cost estimates declined by approximately 14 per cent annually between 2007 and 2014, from above US$1,000 per kWh to around US$410 per kWh, and that the cost of battery packs used by market-leading BEV manufacturers are even lower, at US$300 per kWh, and has declined by 8 per cent annually. Learning rate, the cost reduction following a cumulative doubling of production, is found to be between 6 and 9 per cent, in line with earlier studies on vehicle battery technology.

We see in Figure 11.2 how fast the costs of lithium-ion battery technology are falling (measured as battery price index).

---

4. Few energy scholars have been alive to these exponential trends. One exception is the futurist Ray Kurzweil, who in successive interventions has pointed to the doubling rate of solar PV, and to the few doublings needed to make solar the world's dominant source of power. See the report by David Morris in *Fortune*, 'Ray Kurzweil: Here's why solar will dominate energy within 12 years', 16 April 2016, at: http://fortune.com/2016/04/16/ray-kurzweil-solar-will-dominate-energy-within-12-years/.

5. See Nykvist and Nilsson (2015).

FIGURE 11.2. Lithium-ion battery costs.

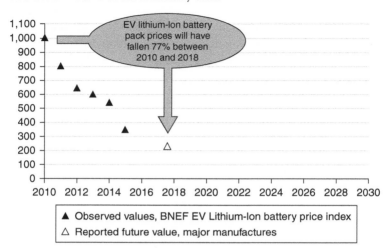

SOURCE: BNEF.

It is the rapidly declining costs of renewables that is the fundamental feature of the greening process. There can no longer be any doubt that clean and renewable energy technologies are now, or will shortly be, lower in cost than the fossil fuels that they replacing. This amounts to a fundamental sociotechnical shift – as argued in Chapter 4 above – that will have widespread social, technical and economic repercussions. It challenges countries to revise their developmental strategies and challenges companies to craft new business models that take advantage of the plunging costs of renewables.

MANUFACTURING ENERGY

There are important reasons for this shift that go beyond the contingencies of one technology or another. All renewable energy devices – wind turbines, solar PV cells, CSP lenses and mirrors – share the characteristic that they are all the products of manufacturing. And this is what connects renewables fundamentally to industrial strategy. As Hao Tan and I put it in our article published in 2014 in *Nature*:

> […] unlike oil, coal and gas, the supplies of which are limited and subject to geopolitical tensions, renewable-energy devices can be built anywhere and implemented wherever there is sufficient water, wind and sun. (2014: 166)

What we meant by this is that manufacturing is the very special process where increasing returns (reducing costs) can be generated: as the scale of production increases, so the unit costs decline. This has been understood by every mass production entrepreneur, from Henry Ford onwards.[6] It is now understood by Chinese, Indian, and Brazilian entrepreneurs who are scaling up production of renewables devices and installing them at ever higher capacities, to reduce costs and drive market expansion. In this way, *renewables are becoming central to the industrialization process*, because they involve manufacturing, learning curves and market expansion linked to cost reduction.

These features are not found in fossil fuel extraction and utilization. On the contrary, all fossil fuel extraction, from coal mining to oil and gas drilling and now right up to extraction of coal seam gas via hydraulic fracturing, involves a relentless process of diminishing returns (or long-run increasing costs).

As for the famed 'energy revolution' that has gripped the United States, with so much enthusiasm being shown for extending the life of fossil fuels via hydraulic fracturing ('fracking') for shale oil and coal seam gas, this too will pass. There is nothing remotely 'ecomodernist' in continuing to drill for fossil fuels – even if the drilling is done horizontally and around bends. And if reports of a 2014 meeting between the US Secretary of State John Kerry and King Abdullah of Saudi Arabia are true, even the US government has been willing to sacrifice its own shale oil industry in the name of securing lower oil prices that are aimed at crippling the Russian and Iranian oil industries.[7]

So the case for renewables as agents of industrialization in the twenty-first century does not rest so much on climate change concerns or oil price concerns as on the capacity of renewables to build energy security for the countries that promote them – based on the central fact that they are manufactured. As such they can be utilized to generate energy across a dispersed landscape, as well as generating local employment and exports for the future.[8]

---

6. Between 1909 and 1916, Henry Ford reduced the cost of his Model T Ford from $950 to $360, a 266 per cent drop over seven years. Each year, sales doubled – from just below 6,000 in 1908 to over 800,000 in 1917. The drop in prices was connected directly with the expansion of the market and the sales made by Ford himself.

7. See reports such as Andrew Topf, 'Did the Saudis and the US collude in dropping oil prices?', 23 December 2014, *OilPrice*, at: http://oilprice.com/Energy/Oil-Prices/Did-The-Saudis-And-The-US-Collude-In-Dropping-Oil-Prices.html.

8. These points are emphasized in my various articles including Mathews 2008a; 2009; 2011; 2012; 2013a,b; 2015; and Mathews and Tan 2011; 2014; 2015; 2016; and Mathews, Hu, and Wu 2011.

Because renewables devices are always the products of manufacturing, they can in-principle be produced anywhere. This is fundamentally why renewables provide energy security – because a country can enhance its energy security through building manufacturing systems that can operate independently of the vagaries of supplies (and prices) of fossil fuels. No wonder China, India et al. are turning to renewables as fast as is technically and economically possible. And as they do so, they expand the scale of production and so drive down costs even more, providing further incentives for market expansion and entry by presently underdeveloped countries into the industrialization process.

This virtuous cycle was discovered in its original form around 400 years ago in Europe by the Italian scholar Antonio Serra, who first recognized how manufacturing could make a state wealthy – even if the state had no mines or mineral resources. He was comparing Naples, which as part of the Spanish monarchy could call on the vast mineral resources of the New World but remained poor, with Venice, which had no such resources but was growing to be the richest city-state in Europe at the beginning of the seventeenth century. Now the same argument can be used, this time in connection with renewables.[9]

The transition to energy wealth has been blocked by fossil fuels and their vast infrastructure controlled by the developed world, creating a barrier to industrial development for everyone else. But greening processes unblock the process. That is why it is so fruitful – and why green development is the culmination and likely next chapter in a process of global industrialization.

RENEWABLES – A MOVING TECHNOLOGICAL FRONTIER

One of the key advantages that renewables have over their fossil-fuelled competitors is that the renewables are evolving rapidly along several fronts – encompassing electric energy generation, energy storage and energy distribution. Power generation by solar PV devices for example has already moved through several generations, with thin-film conductors raising efficiencies and reducing costs. Now the next step promises to be cells fashioned from perovskite materials, which are cheap and abundant and could remove

9. See the Anthem Press publication of the book by Antonio Serra, 1611, *A Short Treatise on the Wealth and Poverty of Nations*, edited and introduced by Sophus Reinert, at: http://www.anthempress.com/a-short-treatise-on-the-wealth-and-poverty-of-nations-1613. I have developed this argument with Erik Reinert in our paper published in *Futures* (Mathews and Reinert 2014).

the barriers to diffusion of solar cells due to materials shortages and costs.[10] There are technical barriers to overcome, such as creating perovskite cells with greater stability – but these are technical problems, not fundamental conceptual problems, and therefore susceptible to being resolved by concentrated R&D. There are advances in silicon solar cells manufacturing, such as the Pluto cells that have been scaled up by Suntech in China, based on passivated emitter with rear locally diffused (PERL) cell technology developed by the UNSW School of Photovoltaic and Renewable Energy Engineering in Sydney.[11] This all promises further advances in both efficiency and productivity of solar cells.

Energy storage, which has been the key reverse salient holding back diffusion of renewables, is finally being addressed by several advances. Tesla once again set the field ablaze with interest when it released its Powerwall energy storage system in 2015. Powerwall offers elegant and cost-efficient wall-based systems for both domestic and commercial/industrial applications. While these products are based on lithium-ion batteries, there are also advances in battery technologies themselves, such as the zinc-bromide version of a liquid battery that can be scaled up by simply enlarging the scale of the tank. New companies like Redflow are emerging to promote these technical advances.[12]

Energy distribution through IT-enhanced electric grids is also receiving increasing attention – particularly in China where the construction of a national IT-enhanced 'strong and smart grid' is viewed as a major twenty-first century infrastructure project, led by the State Grid Corporation of China. Not only is the SGC championing new high-voltage Direct Current (HVDC) power lines linking western provinces with eastern seaboard cities like Shanghai, and the industrial value chains that are developing the products for such infrastructure, but it is advancing ideas for international cooperation such as its proposed Global Energy Interconnection (GEI). Under the GEI renewable power generated in one country (e.g., Mongolia) would be exported to another country such as China or Japan.[13] The GEI as a concept provides the infrastructure needed to support

---

10. On perovskite cells see the article in *Science* by Gary Hodes (2013), at: http://science. sciencemag.org/content/342/6156/317.

11. See the account of PERL cells and Pluto technology at: http://www.pveducation.org/ pvcdrom/manufacturing/high-efficiency.

12. See the description of a zinc-bromide battery at the Redflow website: http://redflow. com/products/.

13. See the book-length exposition of the Global Energy Interconnection composed by the then-President of China's State Grid Corporation, Liu Zhenya (Liu 2015), at: http:// store.elsevier.com/Global-Energy-Interconnection/Zhenya-Liu/isbn-9780128044056/.

trade in renewable power – thus extending the reach of the previously proposed
Asia Super Grid, advanced by the Japan Renewable Energy Foundation and its
founder, Masayoshi Son. The GEI as concept is backed (at this point unofficially)
by the IEA, and promises to drive diffusion of renewable energy systems as
effectively as the Internet of Things promoted by futurists like Jeremy Rifkin. In
these ways, renewable energy systems are advancing along technical fronts, to
become the energy option of choice for countries everywhere.

PRODUCTION/GENERATION OF ENERGY THAT IS CLEAN, CHEAP, ABUNDANT – AND SAFE

I would love to have been a fly on the wall at the meetings of the group producing the *Ecomodernist Manifesto*, when they decided to change their call for
energy that is 'cheap, clean and abundant' to energy that is 'cheap, clean, *dense*
and abundant'. What a difference a word makes! Adding density as a requirement opens the door to all things nuclear and (apparently) closes the door on
conventional renewables – wind and solar power in particular are considered
much less power-dense than nuclear. And yet the *Ecomodernist Manifesto* is also
careful to endorse solar power, which is seen as having huge potential (trillions
of watts). There is surely a glaring contradiction here.

How much better it would have been had the authors chosen to add the
word 'safe' instead of 'dense'. Safe implies that the technology in use does not
constitute a major hazard to present or future populations; that it not be subject to catastrophic failure modes like the process that created the Fukushima
disaster in Japan, and that the technology not constitute a terrorist target that
calls for excessive security measures to control the threat. All these conditions
constitute the principal arguments against persevering with nuclear power.

And these conditions – cheap, clean, abundant and safe – all support
the production/generation of power utilizing artificially produced means
for harvesting renewable sources like wind and sun – that is, manufactured
technologies. So while it is undoubtedly the case that nuclear power sources
offer energy abundance, because of their superior power density, they do so
under conditions that otherwise rule them out.

Emphasis on the density of power supplies is the hallmark of the thinking
of some scholars who focus on the twin notions of *decarbonization* and *power density* as guiding energy transitions.[14] Now density is closely linked to the idea

---

14. See for example works by Ausubel, Nakicenovic, or Gruebler which in their different
ways make use of the concept of density of power generation. I critique these views in
Mathews (2016a).

of yield, and this is certainly one of the defining features of what I am calling 'sixth wave' technology transitions. Open air agriculture is giving way in cities to closed environment growing of plants, often without any soil at all (hydroponics and aeroponics) in totally enclosed vertical stacks of plants kept in optimal growing and harvesting conditions. The fact that manufacturing lies at the base of this kind of farming (termed by some 'skyfarming') is what may be seen as its central or principal feature – giving such an approach to obtaining food the advantage of falling costs due to manufacturing learning curves. It is scalable as well as cheap, clean and (potentially) abundant.

Sixth wave technology transitions all follow the principles of technology substituting for natural systems, where the technology is cheap, clean and abundant – and superior in yield. In *food production*, for example, technologies like aeroponics utilized in enclosed spaces (e.g., vertical greenhouses) provide the possibility of breaking with traditional open air agriculture with its extreme land requirements, run-off pollution and water inefficiency. In fresh *water production*, new methods of desalination (e.g., multiple effect distillation) provide possibilities of securing abundant supplies of potable water in place of naturally supplied rainwater and ground water, making cities utilizing desalination processes water-secure – particularly when they link desalination to renewable energy for its power supply. In *energy production* itself, manufactured devices like wind turbines and solar cells make it possible to generate power that is cheap, clean and abundant, liberating humanity from dependence on extracting and burning fossil fuels from the earth with all the geopolitical and global pollution consequences involved.[15] In resource 'production' or *regeneration of resources*, accessing the resources needed in the range of manufacturing activities that industrial societies need, again technologically recirculated resources increasingly provide the source ('urban mining') through circular economy initiatives; in effect the circular economy is the means for decoupling resource use from natural supplies.

The *Ecomodernist Manifesto* is quite correct to argue that these processes of substituting the technological (artificial) for the natural provide us with the only known method for reducing our damaging impact on the earth, and for creating the possibility of 'rewilding' the earth, that is, for protecting nature itself. This

---

15. I am using the term 'energy production' here as synonym for 'energy generation' in order to emphasize the parallels with fresh water production, food production and resources 'production' via regeneration and recirculation. Of course strictly speaking energy is simply transformed from one kind to another (e.g., chemical energy transformed into electrical energy via a battery) but some device is needed and in that sense we may describe energy as being 'produced'.

is a profound argument. It is pro-Gaia in that it looks towards the possibility of our reducing our destructive impact and allowing Gaia herself to reclaim the management of the earth. But the argument does not have to be carried across to all 6W transitions as a defining feature that necessarily applies to all of them.

What a pity then that the authors added 'density' to the canonical list of qualifications – that technologies (e.g., energy technologies) be cheap, clean and abundant. Adding density simply opens the door to highly centralized power sources like giga-scale nuclear technologies which most people would see as contributing to the problem rather than to the solution. Yes, new nuclear technologies like thorium reactors and mini-reactors are not nearly as dangerous as first generation versions (such as light water reactors, heavy water reactors etc.). But they still make extraordinary demands on human capacities to safeguard current operations as well as stored radioactive waste for thousands of years – something that no sixth wave technology should demand. They still pose an ever-present threat of conversion from civil to military operation, and pose an attractive target for terrorists intent on getting their hands on fissile material. None of these descriptors apply to conventional renewable power generation nor to other 6W technologies like water desalination or vertical urban farming.

Yes, increasing yield is one of the hallmarks of urban, vertical crop production. (Let's not call it agriculture because of the association of the term with open fields – ager.) It is the superior yields of skyfarming (vertical farming, sky gardens) that will undoubtedly drive its adoption and ensure its success while traditional open field agriculture can be expected to decline. But the benefits of tapping enhanced yields in producing food, water and resources should not be taken as necessarily requiring such improved yields in energy production as well. The fact is that there is no global trend towards energy systems with rising power density – just as there is no global trend of decarbonization of energy sources that has been viewed as a process leading inevitably towards the hydrogen economy. These technological tendencies are intellectual traps that obscure clear strategic vision.

Adding the word 'density' appears designed to rule out conventional renewables like wind and solar power, which in their first generation state do not offer higher levels of power density than, say, nuclear reactors. Yet these are fundamental 6W technologies that are liberating the world from dependence on fossil fuels. Density is actually irrelevant to energy issues, particularly when considered as contributing to diffuse power generation by villagers who have no access to the grid but would benefit immediately from having solar or wind powered energy sources for lighting, heating and cooking without polluting their environment by using traditional fuels. India has a vast programme to bring such energy-poor villagers into the twenty-first century with 'diffuse' renewable power sources – and should be applauded for doing so.

By contrast, I have no objection when nuclear advocates promote new generations of nuclear power like thorium reactors, provided they give the same consideration to the need to scale up conventional renewables. I have no objection because I do not see nuclear having much chance of catching up with renewables – given the cost advantages that renewables already enjoy. Nuclear power is already being beaten in the market place. And I welcome any advances in wind and solar power created by innovations, particularly in the field of energy storage which remains the major 'reverse salient' holding back widespread diffusion of renewables and their complete substitution of fossil fuelled and nuclear power generation. But that of course does not call for postponing making investments in renewables today – as argued by observers like Bill Gates.

It is necessary to 'unpack' these energy processes and debates because they have been postulated as constituting a necessary or unavoidable technological trend that we cannot change. This is technological determinism with a vengeance – something to be strenuously avoided. Let us evaluate renewables from a different perspective, as open-ended contributors to energy security rather than solely as initiatives making a perceived contribution to reducing carbon emissions and thereby helping to mitigate climate change. This broader perspective is what we explore in the next chapter.

CHAPTER 12

REFRAMING RENEWABLES AS ENHANCING ENERGY SECURITY

Energy security continues to be a dominant theme in the energy policy literature. Ever since in 1913 Winston Churchill deemed Britain's national security to be tied closely to energy security in terms of oil supplies from Iran and the Middle East, switching away from coal as fuel of choice in the Royal Navy, oil supply and energy security have been two closely intertwined concepts. In the wake of the OPEC oil embargo and the dramatic rise in price of oil in 1973, Western nations founded the International Energy Agency (IEA) as an adjunct to the OECD, essentially as a body responsible for keeping a watching brief over Western energy (oil) security. Security of oil supply (in terms of physical deliveries and maintenance of essential infrastructure) has been expanded conceptually to cover the issue of supply at a reasonable price. Despite the proliferation of competing dimensions in the definition of energy security, the notion remains wedded to issues of oil and fossil-fuel supply.[1]

The most recent round of discussion concerns energy (oil) security and claimed energy independence with the rise of hydraulic fracturing and 'alternative' fossil fuel supplies, such as coal seam gas and shale oil. Energy security issues have been emphasized by the oil majors in framing the prolonged debate over the extension of the Keystone oil supply pipeline to the US, from Canadian tar sands to US oil refineries on the Gulf coast. 'Energy independence' and enhancement of energy security were the watchwords in this debate.[2]

This framing of the debate over the future of a pipeline assumes that 'energy security' is a matter that concerns primarily continuing access to fossil fuel

---

1. See for example Sovacool and Brown 2010; or Cherp and Jewell 2011.

2. See for example 'The new politics of energy' by Daniel Yergin, *New York Times* magazine, 9 June 2012, available at: http://www.nytimes.com/2012/06/10/opinion/sunday/the-new-politics-of-energy.html?pagewanted=all and _r=0.

supplies. Yet a moment's reflection reveals that there can be a quite different construction of the concept of energy security. There exists an alternative means of securing energy, which is available to all – and that is through the manufacture of renewable energy devices and their utilization to tap renewable sources of energy. This provides security in the sense that manufacturing is available to all, and supplies of power from renewable sources do not involve geopolitical calculations and the global projection of armed might to protect long fossil fuel supply lines.

Much of the debate over renewables is framed as a debate over mitigation of carbon emissions and impact on global warming. A *reframing* of the debate around issues of energy security provides a fresh impetus for policies on renewable energy. If energy security (or reduction of insecurity) is the prime consideration – as it clearly is for many newly industrializing countries that turn to renewables as a means of avoiding power interruptions and the geopolitics associated with fossil fuels – then issues to do with continuity of manufacturing and trade, and the maintenance of competition, start to loom large. The contribution to mitigation of global warming can be viewed, from such a perspective, as a convenient side-effect. In this Chapter I explore the implications of such a switch in perspective.

ENERGY SECURITY AND FOSSIL FUEL GEOPOLITICS

Energy security is by definition a somewhat vague concept that nevertheless has clear geopolitical origins. It is not surprising that scholars have had difficulty in coming to grips with such a nebulous notion.[3] Their difficulty is understandable. If the focus is exclusively on security of fossil fuel supplies (as is normally the case) then the goal is actually impossible to achieve. There is no such thing as 'security' of oil supplies, given all the geopolitical complications in which they are embedded; the mitigation of energy 'insecurity' is the best that can be hoped for in the context of fossil fuel dependence. Fossil fuel dependence, and in particular dependence on oil imports, thus lies at the core of a complementary notion of 'energy insecurity'.[4]

---

3. See Kruyt et al. 2009.

4. Leung (2011) notes that China's concerns over energy security focus mainly on rising dependence on oil imports, while Boyd (2012) notes also that the concept of energy security has expanded in Chinese debates to cover matters of security of pricing of energy and reliable provision of electric power (such as guarding against blackouts).

Daniel Yergin, 'godfather' of oil business debates in the US, defines energy security as driven by the need 'to assure adequate, reliable supplies of energy at reasonable prices and in ways that do not jeopardize major national values and objectives' (Yergin 1988: 111). Yergin, like most commentators, has in mind here the role of oil as being central to a country's energy security. But if we turn things on their head, and reframe energy security in terms of the manufacture of renewables devices and their installation to capture freely available renewable energy sources, then interestingly enough the same definition applies. Renewables can be said to provide assurance to a country of 'adequate, reliable supplies of energy at reasonable prices and in ways that do not jeopardize national values and objectives'. Specifically, renewables uphold the social and economic structure of a country – consistent with its 'national values and objectives' – better than do fossil fuels, particularly when the fuels have to be imported. Renewables as manufactured items promise a revival for a national manufacturing centre in the US like Detroit, whereas continued reliance on fossil fuels (traditional or alternatives) promises only further decline for such centres.

Many developing countries are now starting to use the language of energy security in building their renewable energy systems. Take the case of Malaysia, and in particular its Sarawak Corridor of Renewable Energy (SCORE) project, which involves construction of 20GW of hydroelectric power along a 320-km riverine corridor, and calling for investment of US$105 billion by 2030. SCORE is viewed by Malaysia's planners as a developmental project of the highest priority, an important component of both the 9th and 10th Malaysia Plan (respectively covering the years 2006–2010 and 2011–2015).[5] One of the key drivers of the SCORE development is energy security, namely to get Sarawak off its current near 100 per cent dependence on fossil fuels (gas and oil) and move instead to a portfolio of energy sources, with hydropower anticipated to rise from a 10 per cent share in 2006 to more than a 70 per cent share by 2030. Part of the energy security aspect of SCORE is reliability of power supplies. The point of this example is that it demonstrates that developing countries can enhance their energy security by making intelligent use of renewable energy sources and focusing on the multiple developmental advantages that such sources offer.[6]

---

5. A specific development agency has been created for SCORE: the Regional Corridor Development Authority (RECODA), which is vested with responsibility for attracting and coordinating the investment. For the latest developments, see the project's website at: http://www.recoda.com.my/.

6. In their analysis of SCORE, Sovacool and Bulan (2012) identify four features or national goals that are met by the project – industrialization, energy security, inclusive development and spillover effects. Mitigation of climate change is viewed then as an ancillary (albeit convenient) effect – not the central goal.

ENERGY SECURITY BASED ON MANUFACTURING
OF RENEWABLES

The argument so far has avoided the issue as to whether renewables can provide 100 per cent of our energy needs. There is of course great debate over this very issue. Some scholars are dubious. The IPCC itself has gone on the record to state that by 2050 up to 80 per cent of global energy supplies could be coming from renewables (IPCC 2011).

The attraction of formulating energy security as a matter of manufacturing power devices rather than fossil fuel extraction is that we don't have to reach a judgment on the question as to whether renewables can adequately generate power sufficient for the needs of an industrialized society.[7] All that matters is that we reframe the consideration of the renewables option, from one that is burdened with the resolution of the entire global warming problem, to one that is concerned much more narrowly with securing reliable and economic power supplies. If renewables cannot provide the entire power needs of a country (and few countries would be able to boast that they could, as of now) then fossil fuels will perforce have to continue in use – with all their associated insecurities (political, economic, environmental, social). From the perspective of energy security, and amelioration of electrical blackouts, most countries with access to their own domestic renewable sources of energy would see their levels of energy insecurity fall insofar as they resort to manufacturing (or importing) of renewable power devices.

I propose that the notion of energy security be reframed as one that is tied not exclusively to fossil fuels' accessibility but more broadly to availability of renewable sources of power.[8] This is a perspective that views energy security as emanating from a country's capacity to generate power through accessing renewable resources, utilizing manufactured equipment (wind turbines, solar PV cells, CSP lenses and mirrors etc.) that is either produced in the country concerned, or is imported from another manufacturing country. This alternative perspective is closely linked to the notion of declining costs for manufactured products, as embodied in the learning curve. Predictability of

---

7. Some scholars (e.g., Jacobson and Delucchi 2011) have argued that a renewables programme based solely on water, wind and solar could be powering large industrial countries by the year 2030.

8. The IEA has been engaging in studies of renewable energy systems from the perspective of energy security ever since the landmark report of 2007 (IEA 2007). It is anticipated that the 2016 edition of the IEA's flagship *World Energy Outlook* will be focused on the role to be played by renewables in the coming energy transition.

costs (and their decline) and hence of prices, is central to any notion of energy security through manufacturing.

Indeed we can extend this line of argument. Yergin (2006) develops a framework of five principles that he argues provide the setting for any discussion of energy security. These are: 1) diversification of supply; 2) resilience (maintaining a 'security margin'); 3) recognition of the reality of (economic) integration; 4) information (to facilitate rapid market adjustments); and 5) globalization of the energy security system with the need for military protection along global supply pathways. While clearly framed by Yergin to provide a setting for fossil fuel (principally oil) security, nevertheless it is interesting that we may frame our notion of 'security through renewables manufacturing' in exactly the same terms. Let me demonstrate.

Diversification: Renewable energies (REs) are typically discussed as a portfolio of sources, including wind power, solar PV, concentrated solar power (CSP), direct water heating, as well as geothermal and bioenergy. No country aware of energy security would put all its eggs in a single RE basket. Diversity is integral to renewables generation and diffusion.

Resilience: REs are by their very nature diffuse and decentralized, favouring local supply over centralized generation. For this reason they are resilient, and a country's optimal means of guarding against blackouts and other supply disruptions. REs are by their very nature resilient.

Economic integration: Renewables devices such as wind turbines and solar PV cells are manufactured products, and traded internationally. They are becoming important components of the globally integrated business system – while some countries, such as China, see them becoming a pillar industry, contributing more and more to national wealth generation.[9]

Information access: RE devices and systems are heavily traded products and as such, their prices and costs are available for all to see. There is no source of information insecurity such as government suppression of oil supplies and reserves data (still practised as national policy by Saudi Arabia). As RE devices are increasingly integrated into grids, so the demand for 'smartening' grids through IT will make information more and more accessible.

---

9. China is focused on building a set of renewable energy and environmental industries that would become a 'pillar' of the economy by 2015 – and be expected to grow at a rate of 15 per cent per year (twice the level of the economy overall) and provide an export platform for the future.

Globalization: Fossil fuels are undoubtedly a global economic phenomenon, with pipelines and shipping lanes spanning the globe – but this creates a global problem for countries looking to reduce the insecurity of these global supply lines. By contrast, RE systems are globally manufactured and traded in a peaceful manner, without the need for overt military protection.

Thus renewables contribute directly to promotion of energy security (or rather reduction of insecurity) even when evaluated in terms devised to discuss security in terms of fossil fuel supplies. Accordingly, renewables may be considered fundamentally as a source of energy security – in that they are associated with manufacturing activities that generate increasing returns and declining costs. As recognized over centuries, manufacturing activities are superior in terms of wealth generation to agricultural and extractive activities because they embody increasing returns, as opposed to diminishing returns for activities that are dependent on land as a resource.[10]

By contrast with the fossil fuel focus of energy security, and its emphasis on diversity of fossil fuel supplies and their economic feasibility, the emphasis in energy security through manufacturing (ESM) is on ensuring the viability of manufacturing value chains and the prosperity of manufacturing firms, where competition will ensure that prices are reasonably predictable. This is a perspective that focuses on the real advantages of renewables, as manufactured products. The processes of creating manufacturing value chains will build on each other, creating multiple interconnections and increasing returns as they do so. This may be described as a chain reaction of value creation that can benefit all countries that have some level of renewable energy resources. The contrast with the prospect of diminishing returns from extractive activities is striking.

FROM OIL SECURITY TO ENERGY SECURITY

The reduction of energy insecurity through the addition of renewables to an energy portfolio does not call for the overnight replacement of a fossil fuel system with one based on renewables. It calls instead for evaluation of energy options at the margin, where choices are being made. Seen from the

---

10. Erik Reinert has made this point forcefully in many writings; see his book Reinert (2007) for a summary exposition.

perspective outlined in this book, renewables offer energy security along several dimensions – economic, environmental, and social – which lend themselves to new policy formulation, irrespective of climate change effects.

Renewables that are manufactured offer economic security in that the costs of devices (turbines, PV cells, lenses, mirrors) can be expected to fall, continuously, while the efficiency of power generating systems (wind farms, solar PV farms, CSP plants) can be expected to improve. This is a dynamic that is fundamental to renewables, contrasted with the essential insecurity associated with both availability of fossil fuels (even new sources such as coal seam gas and shale oil) and their cost.[11]

Renewables offer environmental security in terms of their ability to generate power without associated pollution, either in terms of particulates associated with the burning of fossil fuels (coal, diesel, gasoline, aviation fuel) or in terms of carbon emissions now associated with climate change and global warming. While some aspects of manufacturing renewables devices are associated with use of toxic materials (e.g., use of cadmium in Cd-Te solar PV cells), these are amenable to control through existing laws and regulations. In any case, countries moving towards the use of solar PV as primary energy source would be expected to be looking beyond cadmium-tellurium cells towards less toxic alternatives.

Renewables offer potential social security in terms of the resilience of re-newable power generating systems. They offer security in social terms through their diffuse character, providing rural employment and the potential to re-vive declining manufacturing regions. Energy policies aimed at enhancing these different aspects of energy security – economic, environmental and so-cial – clearly need to register the contribution to be made by renewable energy systems even if expanding power requirements also call for continued use of fossil fuels. The conclusion to this argument is that energy security in driving industrialization is to be found in the manufacture of energy devices (such as wind turbines or solar cells) rather than in extracting fossil fuels from the earth in increasingly dangerous, inhospitable and inaccessible parts of the world.

---

11. This point that renewables generate energy self-sufficiency is emphasized by Seth Shonkoff and colleagues in correspondence with *Nature*, 540 (15 December 2016): 341.

CHAPTER 13

THE MYTHS OF 'RENEWISTAN'

[...] the land area dedicated to renewable energy ('Renewistan') would occupy a space about the size of Australia to keep the carbon dioxide level at 450 ppm. To get to Hanson's goal of 350 ppm of carbon dioxide, fossil fuel burning would have to be cut to ZERO, which means another 3 terawatts would have to come from renewables, expanding the size of Renewistan further by 26 percent.

SAUL GRIFFITH, THE LONG NOW SEMINAR, 2008[1]

RIDICULOUS 'RENEWISTAN'

Authors and scholars associated with the Breakthrough Institute have been fond of ridiculing the land and resource demands of a global conversion to renewable power (WWS or wind, water and solar) by mockingly claiming that a new country, labelled 'Renewistan' would be needed. The implication is that the land and resource costs of conventional renewables would prove to be impossibly large. In this spirit the Australian-American inventor Saul Griffith gave a presentation at Stewart Brand's 'Long Now' seminar series in 2008, in a talk championed and propagated by Brand himself. But it is Renewistan itself that is ridiculous.

The essence of Griffith's contribution, which as it stands would condemn the world to inactivity over renewables, is as follows. Between 'now' (2008) and 2033, that is, over 25 years, Griffith postulates that the world needs to build 12.5 trillion watts of zero-carbon power sources. He distributes them liberally – 2 TW solar PV, 2 TW solar thermal (mirrors and lenses), 2 TW wind, 2 TW geothermal, 3 TW nuclear and 0.5 TW biofuels. (I will return to these postulated goals in a

---

1. See the seminar text, available at: http://longnow.org/seminars/02009/jan/16/climate-change-recalculated/.

moment.) He then outlines what he calls the engineering challenges of building these systems. For 2 TW of solar PV, the world would have to build 100 square meters of solar cells every second, for the next 25 years, where the cells are rated at 15 per cent efficiency and have good siting. For wind power, the world would have to build 12 wind turbines rated at 3MW every hour for the next 25 years. For 2 TW solar thermal the world would have to build 50 square meters of mirrors every second for the next 25 years, at efficiency rating of 30 per cent. These totals are clearly framed to sound impossibly large.

But it is the land areas that Griffith proposes that are the deadliest of his miscalculations. Positing a size for Renewistan as being comparable to Australia (with its 7.6 million km² area) is bad enough; adding a further 26 per cent by reducing use of fossil fuels to zero (which is, after all, the goal), would add a further 2 million km², to bring the total to 9.6 million km² – which, if the figures were true, would be so large as to condemn renewables to irrelevancy.

But they are not true – and I propose to show why. Whatever gloss Griffith chooses to give this contribution, its major impact is undoubtedly to discourage anyone from viewing conventional renewables as real alternatives to the fossil fuels status quo.

Hao Tan and I evaluated such claims (indirectly) by examining the real resource and materials requirements needed to meet a 100 per cent conversion of energy systems to renewables. We met the task of reviewing what would be the manufacturing and power generation challenge in a paper we published in the *Journal of Sustainable Energy Engineering*, in 2014. Instead of trying to estimate likely power levels needed in 25 years and working backwards from there, we instead posed the 10 TW challenge as a means of substituting for most of the world's fossil fuel energy systems. At realistic rating assumptions, this 10 TW nominal target translates into actual installed capacity of 31.4 TW. Using the same terminology as Griffith (and reproduced by Brand) we may engage with the challenges of meeting the resource requirements of a country called *Renewistan*.

Hao Tan and I took actual examples of operating renewable power systems as providing benchmarks for wind, solar PV and CSP systems. Updating this work, we may take actual examples of renewable energy projects as our benchmarks. For solar PV we may take as best practice case the Montalto di Castro solar PV park in Italy, completed by the contractor SunPower in 2010, and operating at 84 MW from an area of 1.7 km² – or at a land 'cost' of 50 MW per km². For wind power let us take the Shepherds Flat wind farm in the US as typical of recent installations, operating at 845 MW out of an area of 78 km² or a land 'cost' of a little over 10 MW per km². For CSP we may take the Noor I plant in Morocco as world's best practice for CSP, generating power at 160 MW at a land 'cost' of 16 km² for 1 GW of power, or 62.5 MW per km² (the project is described in Chapter 7 above). We thus have increasing densities of power generation:

Wind	10 MW/km^2
Solar PV	50 MW/km^2
CSP	62 MW/km^2

Hao Tan and I then sketched the land and physical resources required to reach a 10 TW goal of installed capacity, and a plausible pathway through which this might be achieved. Rather than replicate exactly what we did, let me take some examples that are closer to the Griffith calculations, and closer to the immediate concerns of China and India. Let us start with Griffith's notional distribution of renewable power requirements as being 2 TW wind, 2 TW solar PV, and 2 TW CSP. If we take him at his word and ignore the capacity factors, this would translate into a land requirement for wind (at 10 MW/km^2) of 200,000 km^2; for solar PV (at a land 'cost' of 50 MW/km^2) of 40,000 km^2; and for CSP (at 62 MW/km^2) of 33,000 km^2 – or a total land area for 'Renewistan' of 273,000 km^2. This is large certainly – but less than one sixth the size of Mongolia (in fact 16 per cent of Mongolia). I choose Mongolia as point of comparison because it is adjacent to China and has already demonstrated a willingness to convert some of its abundant renewable resources to facilities to generate electric power that can be exported to China. It is also the least densely populated country on the planet and thus an ideal candidate to embark on a large-scale renewable power programme. So Renewistan could easily fit into Mongolia, a country with a strong policy of exploiting its land and renewable resources to generate renewable power – for itself, and for export to neighbouring China.

If we take a different approach and specify a straightforward 10 TW 'Big Push' made up from a mix of wind, solar PV and CSP (say, 2 TW wind, 5 TW solar PV and 3 TW CSP) then this would translate into land requirements for wind of 200,000 km^2, for solar PV of 100,000 km^2 and for CSP of 50,000 km^2, or a total of 350,000 km^2 – in this case less than a quarter the size of Mongolia.[2] Again an estimate of the size of 'Renewistan' is that it would fit comfortably within an existing country like Mongolia.

---

2. The land area of Mongolia is 1,553,000 km^2. If we introduce capacity factors and set all sources at a rating equivalent to 100 per cent then these would result in nominal power ratings of 4 TW for wind, 10 TW for solar PV and 15 TW for CSP, based on capacity factors of 0.33 for wind; a capacity factor of 0.20 for solar PV; and for CSP a capacity factor of 0.32 (based on the Moroccan Noor I plant, as described below in Chapter 15). These estimates of capacity required, which already exceed capacity of present power systems, would result in larger land requirements.

So much then for the claim that Renewistan would need a land area of 9.6 million km² if the world is to move to zero fossil fuels. This is a completely erroneous claim, wildly out by a factor of 30 or 40 depending on how the calculations using real experiences are done. It is long overdue that these erroneous calculations be taken down from the web where they continue to do much mischief.

As for the manufacturing requirements of the 10 TW Big Push, Hao Tan and I calculated these as being considerable but again well within the bounds of the feasible. For wind power the total material requirements each year would be 29 million tons iron, 90 million tons steel and 580 million tons concrete each year over the 20 year period. These are relatively small quantities when compared with the world's yearly output of 1.1 billion tons iron, 1.4 billion tons steel and 3.4 billion tons cement (all for the year 2011). As point of comparison with the present scale of manufacturing output, we pointed to the automobile industry that churns out 84 million cars and commercial vehicles every year (or 2,300 vehicles globally every day); this allows us to view the production of 3 million wind turbines over 20 years in a fresh light. Likewise Nokia and other companies build around 1.75 billion mobile phones every year – or around 5 million every day. This again sets the task of producing solar calls and reflective mirrors at the scale required in an appropriate light.

These calculations that Hao Tan and I have been publishing are all hypothetical calculations, designed to show the technical and resource feasibility of a 100 per cent renewables global energy strategy. In practice over the next 20 years there will doubtless be improvements in efficiency, in capacity factors, and in yield (e.g., as the size of wind turbines increases, or the scale of CSP plants improves), while there will be further cost reductions as the scaling-up of these benign energy sources is enhanced.

It turns out that the scary targets like 100 square meters of solar cells having to be manufactured every second for 25 years, and land areas comparable to that of Australia, are in fact very wide of the mark. Renewistan is in fact easily accessible, and (depending on the approach to the calculation) could fit within one sixth to one quarter of a country like Mongolia, without disturbing present herding activities. The power generated would be available to drive the country's own industrialization and export the surplus to next-door neighbour China.

Of course India does not have such large, sparsely populated countries adjacent to it. India's best candidate would be Kazakhstan, a huge country nearly twice the size of Mongolia (at 2.7 million km²). The issue is that power from Kazakhstan would have to pass through either Pakistan or China to reach India; this is a geopolitical complication. India would be best served by pursuing its own domestic renewable power developments (as it is doing through its National Solar and National Wind Missions) and working to promote international initiatives (like the East Asian Super Grid and the Global Energy Interconnection) to supplement its domestic resources.

The upshot of this analysis, based on scaling up from current wind power, solar and CSP installations, and utilizing known material and land requirements, is that the task of providing the world with 10 trillion watts of renewable power at 100 per cent capacity (or 30 trillion watts nominal capacity) is certainly a manufacturing challenge – but one that could be met with sufficient resources and coordination. And this is of course exactly what China is doing with its Five Year Plan targets for renewables and its channelling of finance towards investments needed to achieve the targets, and what India is starting to do with its National Solar and Wind Missions.

REBUTTING THE ARGUMENTS RAISED AGAINST RENEWABLES

While the case 'against' renewables is widely canvassed (that they are fluctuating, unreliable, and not centralized), and heavily publicized, the case for them – that they are reliable in aggregate, secure, and capable of generating power at close to zero marginal cost – is seldom spelled out in detail. So let me do so in this chapter.

The fundamental advantages of renewables, as revealed by practical experience in China as well as in industrialized countries like Germany (e.g., Morris and Pehnt 2012), are these. They are *clean* (low to zero-carbon); they are *non-polluting* (important in China and India with their high levels of particulate pollution derived from coal). They tap into *inexhaustible* energy sources. They have *close-to-zero running costs* since they do not need fuel. All of these advantages are self-evident. Moreover they are *diffuse*. Rather than being endlessly characterized as a defect, this needs to be viewed instead as a fundamental advantage, since this means that renewable sources are *decentralized*, and can be harvested by both large and by small operations wherever they may be found. If they matched the power density of a nuclear power plant this would have to be seen as a defect. These are all obvious advantages.

Some advantages of renewables are not at all obvious and need to be made explicit. Fundamentally, renewables are *scalable*. They can operate at a power level of 1 kW, to 1 MW, to 100 MW or 1000 MW (1 GW) – all the way up to 1 TW, or 10 TW. They are scalable because they can be built in modular fashion – one solar panel, 100 solar panels, 1000 solar panels. As they are replicated in this fashion so their power ratings continue to rise, without complexity cutting back on efficiency. This cannot be said of nuclear reactors, which have an optimal operational size – below which or above which the plant under-performs

Moreover as renewables scale they do not present greater and greater hazards. Instead they are relatively *benign technologies*, without serious risks other than the risks inherent in any complex piece of equipment that needs to be fabricated and erected. When they utilize hazardous materials, like the cadmium in Cd-Te solar cells, there is a ready solution: it is to recycle materials in order to minimize the use and waste of virgin materials.

Because renewables devices are always the products of manufacturing, they can in-principle be produced anywhere. This is fundamentally why renewables provide energy security – because a country can build its energy security through building manufacturing systems that can operate independently of the vagaries of supplies (and prices) of fossil fuels. No wonder China, India and Brazil are turning to renewables as fast as is technically and economically possible. And as they do so, they drive down costs even more, and provide further incentives for market expansion and entry by presently underdeveloped countries into the industrialization process. This is a virtuous cycle. It was blocked by fossil fuels and their infrastructure controlled by the developed world. But greening processes unblock the process. That is why it is so fruitful – and why green development is the culmination and likely next chapter in a process of global industrialization.

Another advantage is their close-to-zero running costs. This is the issue that is used by techno-optimist writers such as Jeremy Rifkin to make an implausible case for renewables as providing the means for prosumers to exchange energy directly in peer-to-peer networks that bypass markets. On this flimsy basis Rifkin speculates that renewables will undermine the foundations of capitalism.[3] The fact that renewables have close-to-zero running costs is a material factor in making them so attractive for developing countries in particular, given that such countries do not have to bear the burden of fuel payments in generating power. But no feature of renewables has given rise to such needless controversy, because these close-to-zero running costs undermine the business model of large, centralized power generation utilities.

All kinds of strange arguments are fashioned in relation to this question. Some claim that by being used to generate baseload power in the middle

---

3. Rifkin makes the case in his two recent books (Rifkin 2013, 2014) and in his four-part blog posting at *The World Post*, Nov 2015, available at: http://www.huffingtonpost.com/jeremy-rifkin/third-industrial-revolution-green-economy_b_8286142.html.

of the day, when sunshine and wind tend to be abundant, renewables power imposes greater costs on the grid – to the disbenefit of all power consumers. Here we see arguments that are desperately grappling with the fact that there is indeed an energy transition under way. Yes, the transition is undermining existing business models based on the capacity to earn extra profits by supplying baseload power at average prices when in fact the marginal costs of generating in the middle of the day are lower. The entrenched power utilities that persevere with such arguments are unlikely to survive the transition.

SUPERIORITY OF RENEWABLES

Fundamentally, the superiority of conventional renewables lies in their being always the products of *manufacturing* – and mass production manufacturing, where economies of scale really play a role.[4] This means that they offer genuine *energy security* in so far as manufacturing can in principle be conducted anywhere. There are no geopolitical pressures stemming from accidents of chance where one country has deposits of a fossil fuel but another does not. Manufactured devices promise an end to the era in which energy security remains closely tied to geopolitics and the projection of armed force (Klare 2012). Unless nuclear can be moved off its dependence on uranium, it will by contrast be subject to endless geopolitical uncertainty.

Manufacturing is characterized by improving efficiencies as experience is accumulated – with consequent cost reductions captured in the *learning* or *experience curve*. Manufacturing generates increasing returns; it can be a source of rising incomes and wealth without imposing further stresses on the earth.

Add to these advantages that renewables promise *economic advantages* of the first importance: they offer rural employment as well as urban employment in manufacturing industry; they offer an innovative and competitive energy sector; and they offer an export platform. From this perspective, renewables would seem to be good business – as India and China well understand.

This is to list the advantages of renewables without even having to mention their low and *diminishing carbon emissions*. Indeed they offer the only real long-term solution to the problem of cleaning up energy systems. They offer real decarbonization – without assuming that this process has to pass through the hydrogen stage.

---

4. The argument is outlined in my paper co-authored with Erik Reinert and published in *Futures* in 2014.

With all these advantages, it is little wonder that China and now India are throwing so much effort into building renewable energy systems at scale. These are not exercises undertaken for ethical or decorative purposes, but as national development strategies of the highest priority.

Clean and non-polluting

As compared with the particulate pollution from the burning of fossil fuels (and it forms a particularly toxic soup in China's cities, where what is combined is emissions from factories, power stations, cars, and trucks) and the pollution from the mining and transport of uranium in the use of nuclear power, the use of renewables is remarkably pollution free. Insofar as renewables devices utilize real technologies and real materials (like cadmium in Cd-Te thin film solar cells) they can pose environmental threats. And the production of silicon ingots as source for crystalline silicon solar cells in China is also prone to pollution from the carbon tetrachloride production process. These are all real environmental hazards (they would not be real-world processes if they had none) – but once identified then there can be substantial efforts devoted to finding substitutes that are less toxic.

The main point is that the use of renewables to generate power – sunlight falling on solar cells and wind blowing turbines – is pollution-free. There can be no getting around this fundamental point.

Tap into inexhaustible renewable resources

Unlike fossil fuels power sources and nuclear power with its dependence on uranium reserves, renewables pose no risks of exhaustion of resources. The wind will blow and the sun will shine – no matter what.

Through all these debates, the fact is that REs are complex technologies. The debate over the case for or against them has been shaped since the 1970s by Lovins' famous article on 'soft paths' vs 'hard paths'.[5] And these terms still help to shape the debate today. For example, the fact that renewables have a benign failure mode is a strong element of the case for them, as opposed to a 'hard' failure mode in the case of nuclear power.

The REs option is essentially a technology option. Anyone who has visited a wind turbine factory in China cannot escape that impression. Building wind turbines is every bit as technologically demanding as building ships – in scale

---

5. See Lovins (1976).

and complexity and technological sophistication. These are technology options and technological choices. My argument is that China and India are now making their technology choices – and these will have long-term repercussions that will be to the advantage of these countries. Their beneficial effects in terms of lower carbon emissions are fortunate side-effects.

Practicable, scalable, replicable

The world does not have to wait for an 'energy miracle' to enjoy the benefits of renewables – the technologies underpinning solar PV and wind power are already mature and well developed. Emerging improvements are well attested – such as improvements in conversion efficiency of solar cells. The costs are reasonable, and declining. In other words, renewables are a supremely *practicable* energy option. They are *scalable* in the sense that they can be rolled out almost without limit, and in the sense that they are modular and easily expanded – unlike nuclear power stations which grow more complex the bigger they get. And renewables are *replicable* in the sense that a solar PV system installed in one city can be replicated in 100 cities, or 1000 cities – because such systems are based on manufacturing and on controlled conditions of production rather than on the vagaries of mining, drilling and extraction. We shall refer to these properties of practicability, scalability and replicability again as we work through sixth wave eco-innovations, and particularly in our discussion of eco-cities in the penultimate chapter.

CHAPTER 14

RECIRCULATION AND REGENERATION OF RESOURCES (CIRCULAR ECONOMY)

There is a story that every school child in Australia is familiar with – Norman Lindsay's *Magic Pudding*. The thing about the magic pudding is that no matter how often it is eaten, it always re-forms to be whole again. The pudding itself is a character in the story, along with heroes Bunyip Bluegum the koala, Bill Barnacle the sailor, and Sam Sawnoff the penguin. The heroes have to battle pudding thieves who are out to acquire the wonderful culinary creation for themselves.

There is something of the 'magic pudding' about the circular economy, where the issues of note are not limits to growth (as highlighted in the famed Club of Rome report of 1972) but the regeneration of resources, either as such (recycling or reusing) or more significantly as extracted from a flow of waste materials. Through 'urban mining' the resources can be extracted and utilized once again in manufacturing processes – and then again, and again – for as long as the material sustains such reuse and regeneration.

The central idea of the 'Limits to Growth' with its insistence that the only known source of resources would be virgin deposits that are increasingly exploited until the limits are reached, is one that has held sway for decades. This is not the way the world is moving however. Instead the world is moving towards a view of resources that sees them as being regenerated via closed loops, or circular flows, through such practices as 'urban mining'. These processes of urban mining are instances of manufacturing where again scale economies can be reaped as efficiencies improve through learning curves. Enhancement of resource security is the driver, where manufacturing processes take over from minerals extraction. It is a way of turning resources into an industrialized 'magic pudding'.

ENHANCING RESOURCE SECURITY

For countries like China and India the task of building energy security is one important aspect of their creation of a new kind of industrial economy. The other important aspect concerns resources. Here too we find a critical situation emerging that can only be resolved by radical measures – in this case a restructuring of the economy along circular lines. Again, we find that China presents the biggest problem and the most radical solution.

China, by the second decade of the twenty-first century, has become the world's largest producer of industrial commodities and world's largest consumer of resources, which are sourced from all around the world. China already produces 46 per cent, 50 per cent and no less than 60 per cent of the world's aluminium, steel and cement, respectively.[1] This gives it an enormous resource appetite and footprint. At the same time China is growing its waste output, leading many scientists to assert that waste production must peak within a few short years.[2] These problems have arisen, and are now reaching crisis point, because China adopted at first the linear model of industrial production – the one perfected by the West and now passed on to emulators in the East. In the linear model resources are sourced at one end of a chain of production and wastes accumulate at the other end. Resources are mined (extracted) from the earth at one end, and wastes are dumped at the other end. The linear model assumes the existence of a planet of infinite proportions that can go on supplying virgin resources at one end and absorb wastes dumped at the other end, seemingly without limit. This is not a very realistic assumption.

Of course the limits are now being reached. China cannot afford to breach geopolitical constraints on resource extraction around the world; it cannot afford to indulge in wholesale plunder of continents like Africa or South America in search of endless quantities of raw materials. It has to find a way to 'internalize' its quest for the materials needed by its gigantic industrial system. So it is in China – where the limits are being felt acutely in the form of resource dependence and waste disposal pollution of crisis proportions – that the most radical solution is being sought in the form of the *circular economy*. Indeed, the solution is simplicity itself – just as the solution to energy issues lies in the simple expedient of shifting to renewable sources that are manufactured. The circular economy proposes to turn outputs into inputs – just as in natural cycles the wastes of one organism are turned into food by another organism.

---

1. See Mathews and Tan 2015, Table 3-6, p. 68.

2. See Hoornweg, Bhada-Tata and Kennedy (31 October 2013). *Nature* 502: 615–617.

But turning the simple idea into practical examples proves to be exceedingly difficult – for the reason that it calls for companies to cooperate in sharing resources and discovering resource loops that can be closed. This is as difficult in China as it is anywhere else.

China's appetite for resources is immense. Its overall consumption of commodities rose fivefold over the two decades 1990 to 2010, from 5.4 billion tons to 25.2 billion tons (according to the OECD). That means that China's consumption by 2010 exceeded that of all the countries that are members of the OECD. Yet China's efficiency in utilizing resources is low. OECD countries consume half a kilogram of material resources for every dollar generated (that is they have a material intensity of around 0.5kg per US$ GDP). But China's material intensity is five times worse, at around 2.6 kg per US$ GDP.[3] The target under the twelfth five-year plan (FYP) was to reach around 2.2 kg per US$ – better than the current level, but still far from the average for the OECD (Figure 14.1).

China's economic boom of the past decade and a half means that it has already had a big resource impact on other countries, particularly in Africa and Latin America. Copper from Chile, or soybeans from Argentina, or iron ore and processed pig iron from Brazil now flow to China in vast quantities, causing great material destruction. Kevin Gallagher in his new book *The China Triangle* documents much of this destruction being wrought in Latin America by Chinese resource interests. In a review of the book, Margaret Myers describes a 'path of environmental destruction and social conflict' traced throughout Latin America on account of the rise of China.[4]

China's treatment of wastes is likewise a source of growing problems. In 2014 the country generated 3.2 billion tons of industrial solid waste alone, of which just over 2 billion tons were recovered, by recycling, composting, incineration, or reuse. By contrast the total waste generated by economic activities and households in the 28 EU countries accounted for 2.5 billion tons in 2012, in which almost 1 billion tons was recycled or used for energy recovery.[5] China's municipal solid waste is expected to reach 23 per cent of the world total in 2025

---

3. China requires 2.5 kg of materials to produce one US$ of GDP (in 2005 US$ adjusted for Purchasing Power Parity) compared with 0.54 kg in OECD countries (http://stats.oecd.org/viewhtml.aspx?datasetcode=MATERIAL_RESOURCESandlang=en).

4. Margaret Myers (10 March 2016). China in the new world (review of *The China Triangle*, by Kevin Gallagher), *Nature*, 531: 109–110.

5. See http://ec.europa.eu/eurostat/statistics-explained/index.php/Waste_statistics#Further_Eurostat_information.

FIGURE 14.1. China: Material intensity trends, 1990–2015.

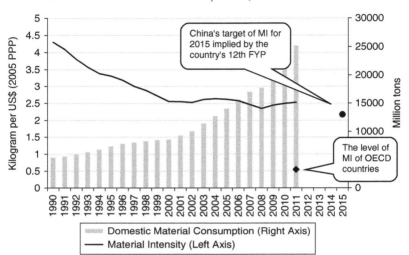

SOURCE: Mathews and Tan 2016; Source of primary data: UNEP (2015). http://www.unep.org/roap/Activities/ResourceEfficiency/IndicatorsforaResourceEfficient/tabid/1060186/Default.aspx

(Hoornweg et al. 2013) – in line with its share of world manufacturing activity. The municipal solid waste going to landfills or incinerators more than doubled in China during the period between 2004 and 2014, from 73 million tons to 160 million tons. But there are significant limits to such disposal solutions, as illustrated by the landslide in a waste disposal site in Shenzhen which killed no less than 69 people (and led to the official involved taking his own life), as well as a number of protests turning into riots by local residents over enforcement of waste incineration projects during recent years.[6]

The toll of this extreme dependence on mined and extracted raw materials at one end of the linear economy, and of waste generation and disposal at the other, is extreme. Tragedies continue to occur, underlining through their toll on human life that minerals extraction cannot cope with this surging level of demand for commodities from China, India and elsewhere. A recent calamity involved the collapse of a tailings dam in Brazil in an iron ore mine

6. On the Shenzhen incident and its aftermath, see: http://www.scmp.com/news/china/society/article/1895516/shenzhen-landslide-aftermath-official-who-rubber-stamped-waste.

in 2015, resulting in flooded villages and the loss of many lives.[7] Conservative news outlets like the *Wall Street Journal* are now pointing to the alarming risks associated with vast mining operations and the unstable structures being created to hold the 'tailings' or mining wastes.[8] There are also soaring costs of waste disposal and the terrible environmental consequences that flow from these practices. Clearly this kind of situation of rising depredations and rising risks leading to a regular succession of calamities cannot be allowed to continue.

CHINA'S CIRCULAR ECONOMY INITIATIVES

China feels the brunt of rising levels of waste being accumulated and the social resistance to measures taken to deal with it, such as incineration. And it is not surprising then that China is taking radical action to deal with these enormous problems of resource insecurity created by growing dependence on imports of resources from dangerously unsafe operations in sometimes dangerous parts of the world. China's efforts to create an alternative in the form of a Circular Economy (CE) date back at least to the release of the 2005 'white paper' from the ND&RC, on 'Opinions on Accelerating the Development of the Circular Economy'. This paper advanced a number of taxation, fiscal, pricing and industrial policy measures that have since been enacted to support the diffusion of circular flows of materials (or closed loops). The 2005 document also signalled that carriage of the issue at national level would be moved from the State Environment Bureau to the ND & RC – a considerable upgrading in political influence, and marking the shift in China to the promotion of the Circular Economy (CE)as a national development strategy.[9] This shift was followed by further developments, including targets for the shift to a Circular Economy in the 11th FYP (covering the years 2006 to 2010) and a whole chapter devoted to the CE in the 12th FYP (covering the years 2011 to 2015). The 2005 policy statement was followed by the passage of the Circular Economy Promotion Law of 2008, which called on local and provincial governments to take resource circulation issues into consideration in their development

---

7. See the news report at: http://www.theaustralian.com.au/business/news/brazil-community-flooded-after-dam-burst-at-bhp-and-valeowned-iron-ore-mine/news-story/ed5795af50d455eb3a76d2d5a02c90c1.

8. See the *WSJ* article at: http://www.wsj.com/articles/brazils-samarco-disaster-mining-dams-grow-to-colossal-heights-and-so-do-the-risks-1459782411.

9. On this strategy, see Mathews et al. (2011).

strategies. There were also sectoral targets enacted for the electronic and IT sectors as well as the chemical and petrochemical sector.

Financial measures have been taken in China to accelerate the uptake of Circular Economy initiatives. Pilot CE projects all around the country are being promoted, particularly in existing industrial parks and export processing zones where companies are already operating next door to each other and are able to see where they might have interests in common in sharing resources such as heat, water or steam.

According to a policy jointly issued by the ND&RC in 2010, the Central Bank of the PRC, the China Banking Regulatory Commission, the China Securities Regulatory Commission as well as state-owned banks are being encouraged to provide loans for CE projects. It is notable that CE-related industrial parks and enterprises are being given priority for their financing needs in the capital markets (e.g., the stock and bond markets) as well as through contingent loan facilities from state-owned banks. This has been an important financial underpinning of moves towards a Circular Economy, complemented by similar moves to utilize green bonds as tools for greening the Chinese economy.

During the decade from 2005 to 2015, there have thus been numerous attempts in China to upgrade the significance of the Circular Economy as a national development goal, involving tax policy, bank lending policy as well as specific measures to accelerate the conversion of traditional industrial parks (clusters of related activities) to eco-industrial parks with an emphasis on greening. The case of the *Suzhou New District* as an exemplary such conversion is discussed below. In the 12th FYP several objectives were set for achievement by 2015, including reaching a comprehensive resource utilization rate of 72 per cent for industrial solid waste, and an improvement in resource productivity of 15 per cent. The 12th FYP laid out a three-pronged 10/100/1000 strategy (applying to 10 major CE programs, 100 CE demonstration sites and cities, and 1000 CE demonstration enterprises or industrial parks) for accelerating the shift to a Circular Economy.

URBAN MINING

The great urban futurist Jane Jacobs argued in her classic work *The Economy of Cities* that instead of viewing cities as sources of increasing mountains of waste they should instead be viewed as sources of materials in themselves: cities should be viewed as the new mines. As an example she cites a coal-burning power plant in Pennsylvania where a trial was run to capture sulphur dioxide from the smokestacks and convert it to sulfuric acid. Based on the facts that costs of extraction were $7 a ton while the market price for the delivered material was $8 to $10 a ton, she reasoned that 'the process amounts to a new way of mining sulphur for sulfuric acid' (1969: 109). This simple but far-reaching insight is the basis for a vast new industry – urban mining.

Jacobs was heavily criticized in her time as being naïve and unduly technologically optimistic, for example, by Stein Weissenberger in his response to Richard Sennett in the *New York Review of Books* (12 March 1970) where her proposals for 'mining' cities to recover valuable materials in wastes, and simultaneously eliminating heat pollution and conserving fuel by recycling the hot water from power plants, not only reveal her characteristic combination of self-confidence and naiveté [...] but also 'demonstrate an implicit and unwarranted faith in the ability of technology to solve all possible problems'.[10] But Richard Sennett's reply buttresses Jane Jacobs' point that cities and countryside complement each other. Cities support efforts to reconcentrate and cluster productive and exchange activities – exactly as called for by Jacobs. The Chinese megalopolises of today are the logical end result of this process. But they need complementary policies designed to recycle and rechannel the flows of materials that threaten cities' well-being.

As supplies of resources come under increasing strain (at one end of the linear economy) and waste generation accumulates to unsustainable levels (at the other end) the traditional model of linear resource throughput is coming up against physical and geopolitical limits. Urban mining presents itself as a viable solution – one that goes back to the industrial recycling practices of the nineteenth century and the growing concentration of manufacturing activities in cities in the twentieth century.

Consider the case of electrical and electronic waste – or e-waste. Just in China new statistics reveal that upwards of 30 million cell phones are discarded each year, along with 4 million refrigerators and 5 million TV sets – along with PCs, printers, scanners, fax machines and microwave ovens. It adds up to around 3,000 tons of e-waste alone.[11] And then the e-waste from the Western world also finds its way to China, where southern towns like Guiyu in Guangdong province have become centres for 'informal' recycling – that

---

10. See Stein Weissenberger, with reply by Richard Sennett, 'How cities grow', *New York Review of Books*, 12 March 1970, at: http://www.nybooks.com/articles/1970/03/12/how-cities-grow/.

11. These data are cited in 'The problem of e-waste', *China.org.cn*, 8 January 2008, at: http://www.china.org.cn/english/China/238544.htm.

is to say, unregulated dismantling and recycling that ignores environmental hazards. But the rewards of recognizing this increasingly gargantuan flow are themselves large.

As an illustration of the power of urban mining, in China a ton of discarded mobile phones can yield as much as *280 grams of gold*; by contrast only about 4 grams can be extracted from a ton of ore in South Africa. The concentration of valuable metals in e-waste is such that 'mining' these waste flows is becoming a sound business proposition – especially if there are government incentives provided in the form of subsidies on recycled materials and taxes on virgin materials or unused waste. That same 1 ton of mobile/cell phones will yield also 140 grams platinum and palladium – not to mention as much as 140 kilograms copper. The plastic and glass in the phone can be extracted and processed into pure forms of the materials.[12] This is what is meant by *urban mining* – the extraction and processing of metals from streams of waste such as e-waste in an urban setting, where the recovery rates are superior to those obtained in the extraction and processing of virgin ores. Jane Jacobs was prescient in her vision of cities being the mines of the future.

A visit to the Chinese e-waste processor Huaxin Environmental is an eye-opener. This Beijing firm is one of 49 national demonstration sites for e-waste recycling and metal recovery – or 'urban mining'.[13] Huaxin runs a website that means literally 'banana peel' as a means of encouraging consumers to re-cycle their mobile phones, PCs, printers and even household white goods like cookers, microwaves and refrigerators. Consumers can log on to the 'banana peel' website and have the discarded items collected, to be channelled to the disassembly lines at Huaxin's Beijing plant. China is now reaching the point that it has large flows of electrical and electronic goods being discarded – so-called EEW (electrical and electronic waste) or e-waste. Huaxin has long lines for disassembly of all electrical and electronic goods, followed by sophisticated processes involving magnetic separation, chemical dissolution to produce the mined raw materials in various levels of purity.

Of course it is not just recently that such urban mining prospects have become apparent. The nineteenth century industrial leaders in both Europe and the United States enjoyed plenty of 'waste recycling' as spontaneous industrial initiative. The volumes involved were impressive – and it is a shock

---

12. See the estimates provided by 'Cell phone recycling – the gold in your cell phone', 12 June 2008, at: http://www.pacebutler.com/blog/cell-phone-recycling-gold/.

13. I visited the Huaxin e-waste recovery plant in Beijing in October 2016; my thanks to Professor Jinhui Li of Tsinghua University for organizing the event.

for observers in places like China where waste flows are greatest today to rediscover the inter-firm recycling linkages that knitted together the industrial districts of former times. Industrial ecology was alive and well in these past industrial districts – a long time before the concept was developed in the late twentieth century.[14]

Indeed it is arguably environmental regulation that has prevented spontaneous creation of inter-firm waste disposal linkages. Under this kind of regulation, 'waste' became identified with 'pollution' and came to be viewed as something to be controlled in itself. Emissions standards, which are the hallmark of environmental standards in the linear economy, actively dissuade firms from viewing their waste streams as sources of profit – even if alternative uses for the 'waste' can be found. It is in places like China where the waste flows are becoming unsustainable and unmanageable that a circular approach makes abundant sense, and is being implemented rigorously. The theme of urban mining as an essential aspect of the Circular Economy has been taken up by Chinese scholars themselves; Li Jinhui for example argues that 'wastes could be resources and cities could be mines'.[15]

So the idea behind urban mining is one that overturns traditional attitudes towards 'waste' and its control. Early essays in industrial ecology tended to see the built environment itself as source of metals and materials; this was doubtless what Jane Jacobs herself had in mind when referring to 'cities as mines'.[16] It is now instead the flows of recycled electronic and electrical goods that provide the main source for urban mining – one that needs to be recognized in policy prescriptions that reward recycling and punish supplies of virgin materials through subsidies and taxes. This is all an essential aspect of the green shift – a reshaping of what Paul Brunner calls the urban metabolism.[17]

---

14. For scholarly investigation of the prevalence of inter-firm industrial recycling linkages, see Desrochers (2002a; 2002b).

15. See the exposition by Li and his Tsinghua University colleagues in Li et al. (2015).

16. Scholars today likewise tend to favour the built environment as primary source for urban mining, not recognizing the scale of the flows of 'waste materials' in manufacturing centres like China. Krook and Baas (2013) for example refer to 'mining the technosphere' as a generalization of urban mining – but they seem to have in mind stocks of materials and landfill as the target, rather than waste flows themselves.

17. Paul Brunner is widely regarded as founder of the discipline of material flow analysis (MFA) which underpins activities such as urban mining. See his summary expositions in Brunner (2007; 2011).

WHAT HOLDS BACK THE DIFFUSION
OF THE CIRCULAR ECONOMY?

Despite discussion of the need to switch away from the linear economy, with all its resource insecurity and waste disposal problems, it has proven to be extremely difficult to make progress in the West. There have been isolated examples of best practice, such as Kalundborg in Denmark, Yokohama in Japan, Ulsan in Korea and Kwinana in Australia.[18] But they are all limited in their scope and have not sparked much emulation. The difficulty is getting individual firms to cooperate along supply chains, so that one firm could discover that it could share resources (e.g., energy, water, heat) with other firms in the same supply chain – particularly if they are co-located in the same industrial zone or city.

China has been able to break through this 'reverse salient' (to use Thomas Hughes' graphic phrase) by focusing its CE efforts on existing industrial parks and export processing zones. It is a telling fact that over half of China's manufacturing activities are concentrated in industrial parks and export processing zones (an example of the power of industrial clustering); these then constitute an obvious target for CE initiatives.

In our article published in *Nature* in March 2016, Hao Tan and I referred to this issue and gave the example of the *Suzhou New District* (SND) as a case in point. This new industrial agglomeration is a vast complex with around 16,000 firms engaging with each other, of which around 4,000 are manufacturing firms. Many of these are involved in high-tech activities such as IT and electronics, as well as advanced machinery and biotechnology. There are waste flows generated by all these activities which, in a traditional linear economy, would constitute a big problem and call for undesirable 'solutions' such as incineration. Instead, through its local CE initiatives, instigated under the auspices of the SND administration, the firms in the Suzhou park are enabled to find common cause and thereby turn outputs into inputs. In the terms utilized in the discipline of industrial symbiosis, this is known as 'closing the loop'.

Take the recirculation of copper. Many of the IT and electronics firms in the SND produce printed circuit boards, where connections between transistors are laid out by printing with copper rather than linking them with wires. In the traditional linear economy, the copper would have to be sourced from virgin materials, mined somewhere on the planet by a large mining concern like BHP-Billiton or China Minmetals. This creates a strain on existing resources and

18. See my paper co-authored with Hao Tan published in the *Journal of Industrial Ecology* (Mathews and Tan 2011) for details.

triggers potential geopolitical conflict. (The shocking war in Katanga in the then Belgian Congo comes to mind, where controlling copper was a principal driver of the breakaway province.) It also creates a major waste disposal problem when the PCBs are discarded along with their IT products. Recycling components and seeking to build them into remanufactured IT products can only go so far in resolving the waste generation problem, and the firms that pursue such a business inevitably remain as marginal producers earning paper-thin profits.

Instead, in the CE initiatives instigated by the SND administration, the issue of copper extraction from waste flows is viewed as a major problem (reverse salient) and action is taken to 'plug the gap' in the *copper regeneration loop.* An initiative was taken resulting in the formation of a venture involving Dowa Metal in Japan in forming an advanced metal recycling business in Suzhou. As described by Hao Tan and myself, waste etching solution generated in copper laminating and PCB manufacturing is treated chemically and returned to other firms in the SND park. The role of firms like Dowa is to reclaim the copper and water from sludge and recirculate it; it is literally 'urban mining' where the mining is performed not in a virgin location but on industrial waste flows. Based on work reported by Wen and Meng, we pictured the process as in Figure 14.2 (while space considerations precluded

FIGURE 14.2. Copper regeneration in Suzhou New District.

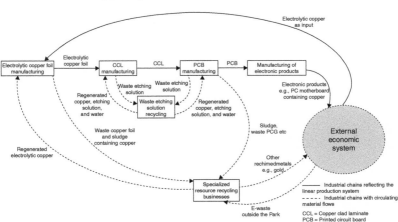

SOURCE: Mathews and Tan, based on Wen and Meng (2015) and the websites of companies involved.

its being carried in our *Nature* article, it is carried here with permission of my co-author Hao Tan).

These initiatives of closing loops like that involving copper recirculation in the SND are now being taken all across China. Clearly there are moves afoot to shift from a linear industrial economy, with its costs to the earth in terms of extracting virgin resources at one end and dumping wastes at the other end, to a circular economy with its closed loops. Again the driver is going to be reducing costs – as the cost of virgin resources rises and waste disposal becomes more expensive financially and in terms of land, while the costs of 'urban mined' resources can only be expected to fall, given their foundation in manufacturing processes and their learning curves. In this way, resource re-generation is emerging as a central feature of ecomodernization – with China as a principal player. It is the country with the biggest resource insecurity problems and the country with strong state agencies that are prepared to in-tervene in the economy to make the changes needed. This is a powerful driver of the green shift.

CHAPTER 15

FOOD AND FRESH WATER
PRODUCTION

*In my view, vertical farming represents one of the few new opportunities that
we should fully explore over the next 10–20 years, especially if we are serious about living our lives in balance with the rest of the life forms on Earth
without further endangering both theirs, and ultimately ours.*

JACKSON DESPOMMIER, 'FARMING UP
THE CITY' (2013)

As the world's population continues to grow, traditional agriculture puts increasing pressure on our planet's finite resources and environment. More and
more of the world's water is used in growing crops and watering livestock;
chemical runoff is increasingly contaminating these water supplies and poi-
soning soils. The challenge is to decouple food and water production from
those resources by relying on nature's abundance (e.g., in sun and seawater) to
grow the world's food industry – sustainably as well as profitably.

Agriculture was one of the great innovations of *Homo sapiens* – but it has
barely changed in its fundamentals ever since it emerged in the fertile river
valleys around 10,000 to 12,000 years ago. It continues to be dependent on soil
quality (which is rapidly eroded under intensive cultivation), on seasonal rain,
and now on chemical inputs of fertilizers, herbicides and pesticides, and more
recently on mechanization and innovations in seed via genetic engineering
or genetic modification. All of these approaches are running into limits as
the world population expands and the land available for cultivation shrinks,
while exploitation of water tables is reaching critical levels through wasteful
irrigation practices. The raising of livestock for meat production consumes
an increasing share of arable land as well as of grain crops for animal feed.
Chemical runoff from fertilizers, herbicides, pesticides and animal wastes is
degrading soils themselves and having serious wider repercussions including

such horrors as the mass die-off of bee populations ('colony collapse disorder') which is widely attributed to these same chemical incursions. Something clearly has to be done.

Various ameliorative approaches are being tried. There is organic farming with its minimal use of chemicals; there is low-impact seed drilling ('no till farming') and methods of biological control in place of chemical zapping. But these are limited in their impact and cannot easily be scaled up to have a global impact – while they remain outside the scope of urban developments. Within cities themselves there have been various attempts to utilize wasteland as sources for local vegetables growing and urban farms (sometimes as educational facilities rather than commercial operations), to promote rooftop growing and to green buildings with vegetation – all with positive but limited impact. Again, something more substantial needs to be done.

Controlled environment agriculture (CEA) has emerged as a response to these pressures and demands. Indoor farming has flourished in many settings, and is growing in sophistication with addition of key new features. For vegetables, these include use of stackable vertical structures for holding and rotating rows of plants through light and water spray containing nutrients; or the use of LED lighting which can be adjusted in wavelength to be tuned to the needs of growing vegetables and other plants; and further developments in controlling the environment of the growing plants in terms of nutrients, acid–base balance, humidity, temperature, airflow and other parameters. As CEA initiatives have flourished, most have of necessity been located away from cities where land is cheaper – but this means that transport costs are high and the food is less fresh on arrival. Locating the high-tech greenhouses within the city is thus the final step in this evolutionary process, which is where 'vertical farming' makes its entry.[1] The most adventurous solutions addressing the issue of food security involve complete abandonment of traditional horticulture, even in its greenhouse version, in favour of vertical farms or what are known in Singapore as 'sky gardens'.[2]

Meanwhile for meat and its expanding grip on the world's water, grain supplies and land resources, the solution lies in manufacturing meat and dairy products, utilizing artificial culturing of meat and proteins. The direction of the technological developments is clear: these food products would be produced in vast vats or bioreactors that resemble nothing so much as a

---

1. See the discussion in Despommier 2013.

2. See Germer et al. (2011).

brewery. There will be inputs of nutrients and water and outputs of tissues that are grown to resemble meat and dairy products like milk that promise to be indistinguishable from the originals.

Alternatives to traditional farming/open air agriculture are known under many names, including 'vegetable factory' methods, or 'plant factory' more generally (names that are not very inspiring);[3] or 'controlled environment' farming, which originated with space research and is technically accurate but again not very inspiring; and spatially-oriented terms like 'vertical farming'. The most generic version of the trend is 'urban farming' to indicate that the food production is taking place in an urban setting – a feature captured best in the terms skyfarming and vertical farming. Skyfarming (Germer et al. 2011) is an excellent term that captures the spirit of enclosed space vertical farming suitable for production of vegetables in urban regions. Clean meat or cultured meat are other excellent terms that capture the production of artificial meat and clearly distinguish it as a product from the kind of meat secured through slaughtering animals where disease and fecal spoliation are rife, not to mention the cruelty of the whole process. I propose to bring all these approaches together under the term 'Sixth Wave' (6W) food production, with the clear intention of placing them on the same footing as the shift towards renewable energies, towards a circular economy and towards water regeneration via desalination and recovery.

URBAN VEGGIES: VERTICAL FARMING INITIATIVES

Cities turn out be ideal candidates for sixth wave food production – as demonstrated by vegetables grown in vertical farms in urban centres around the world. Let me illustrate with examples from Singapore, Japan and North America.

Sky Greens, Singapore

One of the brightest, clean and sustainable food initiatives within Singapore (itself a world-class green city) is *Sky Greens*, a venture founded by local entrepreneur Jack Ng. It is a case of vertical farming to produce a variety of fresh green vegetables, such as the popular bok choy (Chinese cabbage) and lettuce for salads. The distinctive feature of the Sky Greens approach is that it builds modules of 9-metre

---

3. See for example Dong et al. (2015) on comparison of 'plant factory' systems with other methods; or Hu et al. (2014) specifically for 'plant factories' in Taiwan.

tall vertical towers (equivalent to two and a half storeys of a city building) with stacked tiers of planting troughs that constantly move the growing plants around to catch the sun and dip into the hydroponic water baths – as on a Ferris wheel. The plants thus grow in a contained space, with controlled nutrients delivered by the water at the base of the module, while the growing plants receive abundant sunlight as the trays rotate through the upper levels of the tower.[4]

Sky Greens is based at a 3.6 hectare vertical farm at Lim Chu Kang in Singapore. It is geared to urban life and to supplying supermarket chains: Sky Greens started supplying fresh vegetables to the FairPrice supermarket chain in Singapore in 2012. The most popular greens are nai bai (milk cabbage), spinach, chye sim, kangkung and lettuce. The vegetables are vacuum packed and stored immediately in cool containers prior to transport; the proximity means that consumers receive the greens super-fresh.

The biggest advantage of Sky Greens over traditional gardening and over artificially-lit vertical farming initiatives is cost. The Sky Greens growing towers are built in transparent buildings that are flooded with natural light, so that costs imposed by artificial lighting are slashed. In Japan LED-lit vertical farms use 20 to 25 kW of power to produce 1 kg of vegetables. But in Singapore Sky Greens use just 0.3 kW, where energy savings come from using natural light and from rotating the tiered trays using gravity-fed water wheels (exploiting an ancient technology in a new way).[5]

Jack Ng has ambitious plans for a sophisticated *Agripolis* which from a 20-hectare plot of land and buildings would be able to produce no less than 30 per cent of Singapore's green leafy consumption. Mr Ng envisages a high-tech production and research facility that would have different vegetation zones, producing up to 15,000 tons of leafy veggies per year (a total comparable to the output of Sundrop Farms rated at 15,000 tons per year from 20-hectare greenhouse complex).[6] Mr Ng envisages separate zones to house even fisheries and humane egg production facilities as well as recycling facilities and support services (e.g., packaging, logistics and food processing).[7]

---

4. See 'Building vertical "houses" for plants', by Wong Siew Ying, December 16 2015, *The Straits Times* (Singapore), at: http://www.straitstimes.com/business/building-vertical-houses-for-plants

5. At the end of 2015 Sky Greens had 1,000 towers in operation, with plans to double the scale to 2000. At full scale Sky Greens would be able to produce 5 to 10 tons of fresh vegetables per day – or up to 3,500 tons per year.

6. See the discussion of Sundrop Farms in the next chapter.

7. See the company's website, at: http://www.skygreens.com/sky-urbans-sg100-agripolis-of-the-future-2/

The Mirai Initiative in Japan

An exemplar of 6W food production would have to be the urban farm operated by Mirai Company in Japan, championed tirelessly by Shigeharu Shimamura, the company president. Mirai (which means 'future' in Japanese) was founded by Shimamura in 2004. Food shortages at the time of the Fukushima disaster (when an earthquake followed by a tsunami crippled the Fukushima nuclear plant) prompted Shimamura into action, taking advantage of government subsidies to take over a semiconductor factory that was shut down, in order to produce vegetables – 'factory produced' vegetables. Initial efforts to grow vegetables in hydroponic trays illuminated by fluorescent lights proved disappointing, since the power costs exceeded the potential revenues from lettuces. Shimamura was then able to take Mirai into a joint venture with General Electric to take advantage of GE's LED lights, tuning the light output of the lamps to the needs of the growing lettuce plants. The result has been such a significant productivity improvement that the Mirai plant now produces lettuces at 100 times the productivity of traditional farms. Mirai is using the 1,260 sq. meter factory at Kashiwanoha, in Chiba Prefecture, as a totally enclosed farming environment that has a rosy glow because of the LED lighting with its specific waveband output. It is one of many Japanese initiatives to produce enclosed vegetable farms in former factories – some undertaken by IT companies themselves in their own former plants, like Fujitsu and Toshiba.

Mirai not only produces vegetables like clean lettuces grown under LED lighting, but is selling the technology itself and building the racks needed for vegetable factories to be sold throughout Japan. The factories have rows of vegetables stacked on top of each other, beneath LED lighting and grown within a mist of water that contains nutrients – eliminating soil altogether. The factory can be kept clean and sealed off from external air, and so is pest-free and pesticide free. The best vegetables for this kind of aeroponic cultivation, according to Shimamura, are leafy types like lettuces, because they contain high levels of water in themselves. It is possible in principle to produce other crops like tomatoes and even staples like rice, but they do better in a more open environment and with sunlight, according to Shimamura.[8]

The growing environment is carefully controlled – encompassing factors such as water, humidity, lighting and carbon dioxide levels. Fertilizers are also an important component, and a trade secret deployed by Mirai. The vegetable

---

8. See the report in *Japan Times*, at: http://www.japantimes.co.jp/news/2014/08/11/business/tech/future-appears-bright-indoor-veggie-farms/.

production system is increasingly automated, with racks moved regularly in accordance with measured physiological conditions of the plants. Shimamura has stated that he expects robots to take over much of the running as the system diffuses. The Kashiwanoha factory was opened in June 2014 and can produce up to 10,000 heads of lettuce per day. The factory uses lots of power, and at the moment this is sourced from the local electric utility, making the costs high – and adding to consumption of non-renewable electric power. Clearly this is an angle that Mirai would need to address in the future.

Shimamura sees scaling up production as the key to becoming a stronger competitor with traditional vegetable producers. As the scale of production increases, so costs can be expected to decrease – as per standard mass production principles. These are very different from the diminishing returns that prevail in conventional agriculture where natural resources like soil fertility constitute a barrier to endless improvement. Mirai is increasingly selling its technology as well as lettuces themselves. For example, the Mirai system has been licensed to firms in Russia and Hong Kong and even Mongolia where vegetables can be grown year-round (in very cold conditions during the winter or hot conditions during the summer) because they are cultivated in a controlled environment.

How do the Mirai lettuces taste? Actually they are extremely popular in Tokyo. They are pesticide-free and clean, not having to be washed before being eaten. The first time that the lettuce comes into contact with external air is when a consumer opens the packet containing the lettuce. With stable taste and production the vegetables are particularly suited to supermarkets and commercial users such as restaurants.

Vertical vegetable farming in the United States and Europe

There are already emulators of Sky Greens and Mirai Farms in the US and Europe.[9] There is the case of AeroFarms, for example, with its initial operation in New Jersey producing leafy green vegetables 'without sunlight, soil or pesticides'. The methods used to achieve these desirable results are based on vertical stacking of rows of growing plants in enclosed spaces, with lighting from LEDs and hydroponic growing environment using closed loop irrigation that reduces water

---

9. A prominent article in the *NY Times* in May 2016 provided a critical engagement with vertical farming). See the report 'Farms that rise to the challenge', 17 May 2016 at: http://www.nytimes.com/2016/05/18/business/energy-environment/farms-that-rise-to-the-challenge.html?_r=0.

requirements by 95 per cent.[10] The company claims that it achieves drastic gains over conventional agriculture (termed 'flat earth farming') and utilizes 95 per cent less water. The growing cycle takes around two weeks, allowing for up to 25 harvests per year. If replicated internationally this would indeed revolutionize traditional food production. AeroFarms has ambitious plans to have 25 facilities similar to its New Jersey operation located around the world by 2021.

By contrast, the Berlin venture *Infarm* is based on an indoor modular farming concept, where vertical stacks of leafy vegetables are watered hydroponically and lit by LEDs. In 2015 the company built Europe's first in-store farm at the Metro Cash & Carry supermarket in Berlin. The idea is that consumers have access to a perpetual supply of ultra-fresh produce produced in-store from non-GMO organic seeds and using pesticide-free culture. This is yet another way forward for green veggies farming in the city.[11] A different European business model has been developed by the Swedish company *Plantagon International*, which uses natural lighting in order to reduce energy costs. A pilot green-house has been built in the Swedish town of Linkoping, where heat supplies are shared with the local power company (an important factor in a cold climate). No doubt these examples will multiply in the next few years.

While these various forms of 6W food production have proven themselves for leafy vegetables and salad ingredients such as cucumbers and tomatoes, and can clearly be extended to other horticultural activities and fruit growing, the capacity of this model of food production to be extended to broad acre farming of grains and cereals remains open to doubt. There seem to be no successful cases of 6W food production techniques involving a closed environment with sun and seawater as sources for inputs in growing wheat, rice or other staple crops – as yet. This is clearly an activity that would repay intensive R&D – inspired by 6W principles rather than genetic modification to adapt cereals to our present very limited sources of innovation in broad-acre farming.[12]

MEAT – WITHOUT TORTURING AND MURDERING ANIMALS

The soaring demand for meat, exacerbated by the rise of a new middle-class in China and India that wish to expand their meat consumption, is driving

---

10. See the AeroFarms website for further details: http://aerofarms.com/.

11. See the Infarm company website at: https://infarm.de/#what-we-do

12. For some advances in rice cultivation, see: http://www.biogeosciences.net/11/6221/2014/.

the animal husbandry industry to new levels (depths) of maltreatment that shock and dismay anyone who becomes aware of them. Animals like cows and pigs are confined in feedlots, frequently for the whole of their short lives, and treated like cogs in a vast and expanding meat-producing machine. They are subjected to fear and stress by cutting and cauterizing; they are cramped and deprived of their natural environment and social interaction; and finally they are summarily slaughtered – in a manner that grossly offends their own animal rights and our own ethical dignity.

While vegetarianism and its extreme version in the form of veganism is an alternative that is growing in popularity as details of animal rights abuses become more widely known, this does not seem to be the optimal way to improve food supplies for a growing world population. A superior approach would promise genuine substitutes for animal products in the form of meat, milk and eggs. How is this to be done?

A sixth wave technology that cannot arrive too quickly is the one that promises to transform our abuse of animals to provide us with meat, milk and eggs produced synthetically, without the cruelties perpetrated by the animal husbandry, dairy and chicken industries. The big breakthrough that is now coming online is the culturing of animal muscle cells in huge vats that produce real meat – without slaughtering any animal or keeping them penned up in detestable conditions in feedlots. A first burger created in this manner was publicly cooked and tasted by a panel in London in 2013 – setting a start date for one of the most significant revolutions promising to overturn traditional food production.[13] Now what is being called 'lab meat' or 'clean meat' or just 'cultured meat' is being produced by start-ups such as Memphis Meats and promoted by NGOs like New Harvest or the Modern Agriculture Foundation. Real milk products are being offered by Perfect Day, who craft 'animal-free dairy products that taste like the real thing' and egg whites created by proteins produced by genetically modified yeast.[14]

Cultured meat is the real thing. It is grown from stem cells collected from live and healthy animals, so that as the cells grow in a culturing medium they

---

13. This public demonstration of the practicability of cultured meat was financed by Google co-founder Sergey Brin. See the report 'Google's Sergey Brin bankrolled world's first synthetic beef hamburger' by Alok Jha, *The Guardian*, 5 August 2013, at: https://www.theguardian.com/science/2013/aug/05/google-sergey-brin-synthetic-beef-hamburger.

14. See the Perfect Day website for background: http://www.perfectdayfoods.com/our-story/. For an overview of prospects for cultured meat (or 'in vitro meat'), see Bhat, Kumar and Bhat (2016).

form tissues that are the same as muscle tissues that we call 'meat'. This is not a meat substitute like soy-derived veggie patties that are marketed as meat look-alikes (sometimes with suspicious ingredients and almost always derived from genetically modified soy beans).[15] The early cultured products are looking to present as substitutes for burgers and frankfurters – offering meat patties and sausages that are clean, that have none of the growth hormones and antibiotics that are fed to animals in feedlots and are transferred to their meat, and of course that avoid the nasty organisms like *E. coli* that come from slaughtered meat that is contaminated with animal fecal matter.

It is difficult to overstate the significance of this breakthrough. It resolves the ethical dilemmas raised by animal slaughtering and the cruelties involved in raising cows, pigs and chickens in the confined conditions made notorious by videos released by animal welfare NGOs.[16] And just as significantly it avoids the need to divert grain flows to feed the rising numbers of animals kept in feedlots – now estimated by FAO as representing 40 per cent of world grain supplies, and rising.

Milk that is produced not from lactating cows but artificially, from bioengineered yeast, is now too becoming a reality. The company Perfect Day, for example, has bioengineered yeast to produce not ethanol but milk proteins, to which can be added vitamins and minerals found in cow's milk as well as vegetable derived fat – to make the synthetic product as close to the real thing as possible. Two young Indians founded the company (then known as Muufri – meaning 'moo-free' or no live animals) in 2014 and it is now growing rapidly while producing a range of dairy alternatives. The founders argue that milk is easier to synthesize than meat because it has fewer than 20 components which can be produced and blended in a way that actively biomimics what cows themselves do.

The bioengineered yeast produces the milk proteins in large vats that look much more like breweries than dairies. And there are prospects for producing milk and milk products without the specific proteins and sugars like lactose that provoke lactose-intolerance in many people. As in the case of real meat substitutes, these synthetic milk products promise to revolutionize the dairy industry, making dairy feedlots unnecessary and producing a product

---

15. See the warnings at: http://www.onegreenplanet.org/natural-health/veggie-burgers-ingredients-health/.

16. See videos like 'Food industry animal slaughter: Now go and enjoy your burger' February 2016, available at *YouTube*: https://www.youtube.com/watch?v=rGfJQveYFKo.

uncontaminated by the hormones and antibiotics utilized in the traditional industry, and relieving the ethical dilemmas we face in forcing animals to become simply machines for producing the desired product.

The meat industry leaves a huge environmental footprint. Animal husbandry takes a rising share of arable land, and diverts feed, water and fuel supplies. Two statistics can serve for many: in the US, the livestock population consumes seven times as much grain as people. The FAO predicts a near doubling of worldwide meat production by 2050.[17] To produce 1 kg of animal protein calls for 100 times as much water as 1 kg of grain protein. These are utterly unsustainable levels if they were to be scaled up to encompass the growing middle classes in countries like China and India.[18]

The principal advantages of these new sixth wave developments – apart from an end to the suffering of millions of animals subjected to the torture and slaughter that we as a species so callously inflict on them – are the environmental gains and (eventually) the cost benefits. It is worth spelling out the advantages that would be expected to flow from large-scale production of cultured meat. The first and obvious advantages concern cost and time to market; cultured meat produced at scale will be able to undercut the price demanded for traditional meat, and will doubtless be grown in time spans much shorter than with traditional processes. This in turn means that resource and energy costs of cultured meat production will be greatly diminished. Bioreactors for producing cultured meat and dairy proteins will of course make possible enormous savings in terms of land required – particularly when they are stacked on top of each other as may be envisaged for urban meat culture.

The pollution associated with traditional livestock raising, such as runoff of manure and slurry from feedlots and methane production from herbivores like cattle, promises to become a thing of the past. In a paper published as early as 2011, based on life cycle analysis, Tuomisto and Teixeira de Mattos estimated that cultured meat would utilize 7–45 per cent less energy than conventionally produced meat, 99 per cent lower land use, and 82–96 per cent reduced water usage.[19] Not the least of cultured meat's advantages would be

---

17. The projection is that global meat production would rise from 270 million tons to 470 million tons by 2050 – see the report of the 'How to feed the world 2050' conference organized in Rome by FAO, available at: http://www.fao.org/fileadmin/templates/wsfs/docs/Issues_papers/HLEF2050_Global_Agriculture.pdf.

18. On the challenges that cultured meat presents specifically for China, see Sun et al. (2015).

19. See the paper by Tuomisto and de Mattos (2011).

the land it liberates from existing intense usage by livestock raising – bringing forward the real possibility of rewilding and reforestation, viewed as central goals of ecomodernization.

What would large-scale culturing of meat look like? Actually we already know the answer – it would look like the brewing industry today. Large vats or bioreactors would be employed to produce cultured meat, grown as muscle tissue on lattices in the vats to produce the structure that characterizes muscle fibres. There would also be production of artificially cultured blood and fat that lends the 'feel' and 'savour' of meat. The raw materials needed at scale would be nutrients utilized by the biotech industry, not the fetal calf serum that is currently used (and which would not scale up to the levels needed for industrial meat culture). I wonder whether this might be an opportunity for a company to supply a nutrient material such as corn steep liquor, available in abundance, possibly fortified with salts and minerals – more or less as supplied originally for production of antibiotics like penicillin.

Anticipated evolution of the market for cultured meat

How might the market for cultured meat evolve, assuming that it takes off rapidly in the next five years as techniques for savoury meat production and protein production (for dairy products) develop? The costs can be anticipated to fall dramatically, as the scale of production increases – making these cultured products increasingly attractive as substitutes for traditional meat products derived from animal slaughter. Cultured meats may take over the bulk of the market, because of low cost, and force traditional meat products into a premium upper level in the market; those who want their steaks bloody and authentic will have to pay a premium price.[20]

But many of the advantages to be derived from cultured meat could be nullified by outdated (or hostile) regulation. In the US setting, is enforcement of quality standards in production of cultured meat to be the responsibility of the Department of Health or of the FDA or of the Department of Agriculture – with their radically different regulatory and enforcement cultures? In many countries the production of cultured meat is seen as so improbable (or dangerous) that it is illegal. So there are extensive regulatory reforms needed to clear the way for this most pressing of sixth wave developments.

---

20. See the discussion of this possibility in Bonny et al. (2015).

CLEAN, FRESH WATER

Agriculture uses 60–80 per cent of the planet's scarce fresh water, so food production systems are being re-examined to reduce their fresh water footprint. But what about the pressures on water sources themselves – can they be reduced through the trends towards city living and dematerialization? Can fresh water be 'produced' at will?

One place to look for a guide to the future is Singapore – where water pressures loom large, even in this tropical island state. It is a small city-state, of 5 million people, occupying an island of 716 km^2 and surrounded by seawater. It has to import fresh food and water each day from neighbouring Malaysia – creating a tense relationship of dependence. Singapore has built water desalination plants and water regeneration plants with the explicit aim of reducing its water dependence. Two water desalination plants have now been built, by the water projects firm Hyflux, supplying Singapore with 100 million gallons (380 ML) of fresh water per day. This meets 25 per cent of Singapore's water needs, with a further desal plant to be completed in 2017 and a fourth being commissioned – supplying a further 60 million gallons of water per day. Then a further 30 per cent is supplied by NEWater (i.e., recycled 'grey' water) while the balance comes from reservoirs fed by rainwater and some imported water by pipeline from Malaysia.[21] Hyflux operates Singapore's two desalination plants using its own Membrane Distillation technology, while the technology itself has been developed by the Singaporean partly government-owned enterprise Keppel-Seghers.[22]

So an obvious solution to water production at scale that is quite independent of natural cycles, rain water supplies and traditional methods like irrigation, is to tap into the enormous resource of seawater and circulating waste water – preferably using solar power to drive the desalination and purification processes. Technologies are readily available such as 'multiple effect distillation' (MED) and new forms of membrane-based desalination via forced osmosis sources from seawater. These innovations liberate cities from traditional water supply sources and open up new possibilities of recycling water, decoupling the

21. See 'New desalination plant brings Singapore closer to self-sufficiency', by Woo Sian Boon, *Today Singapore*, 19 Sep 2013, at: http://www.todayonline.com/singapore/new-desalination-plant-brings-spore-closer-self-sufficiency.

22. See the public-private partnership document available at: http://www.cdia.asia/wp-content/uploads/PPP-Case-Example-11-Mar-2011.pdf. On the two plants now operated by Hyflux, see: http://www.hyflux.com/biz_desalination.html.

process from dependence on natural water cycles. Sources of power to drive the desalination processes can increasingly be derived from renewable sources including sun and wind, so reducing the costs of desalination and facilitating its wider adoption through the power of the learning curve. Let me provide some examples.

CSP-desalination

Linking concentrated solar power production with desalination of water is now under active investigation and commercial development – particularly in isolated and arid parts of the world. The *Almeria Solar Platform* in Spain has been actively researching and demonstrating the use of hybrid CSP-desalination systems, evaluating different technical combinations. Likewise the Multiple Effect Distillation – CSP project financed by the EU has been conducting controlled feasibility studies through comparable sites around the Mediterranean.[23] The World Bank is actively promoting linkage between solar thermal power projects and water desalination in North Africa and the Middle East.[24] Both Saudi Arabia and the United Arab Emirates have major solar desalination projects under way. The UAE project, backed by the Gulf Cooperation Council, is being built at Ras Al Khaimah; it is planned to generate 20 MW power and produce 83 ML fresh water per day.[25] Of course other renewable energy–desalination combinations are possible.

CSP-greenhouse ventilation

Worldwide, greenhouse-based horticulture is expanding rapidly, driven by pressures of urbanization and the higher yields obtainable in greenhouse food production. Renewable energy systems and in particular various forms of

---

23. See for example Moser, Trieb and Kern 2010; or Trieb et al. 2009. The Almeria Solar Platform research group in Spain have investigated many CSP+D combinations, including one described by Palenzuela et al. (2011), and earlier combinations discussed by Zaragoza et al. (2007). For a general recent review of solar water desalination, see Shatat et al. (2013).

24. See the comprehensive World Bank report on *Renewable Energy Desalination* (World Bank 2012).

25. See 'UAE to set up world's largest solar desalination plant', *Zeenews*, 27 November 2013, at: http://zeenews.india.com/news/eco-news/uae-to-set-up-world-s-largest-solar-desalination-plant_892791.html.

concentrating solar radiation are being investigated as a means of enhancing the performance and lowering the costs of greenhouse operation in temperate climates, as well as in cooling greenhouses in arid climates (e.g., Sonneveld et al. 2010). We shall see a powerful demonstration of this idea in the Sundrop Farms model to be discussed in the next chapter.

While we have considered widely divergent food and water technologies in this chapter – from enclosed vertical farming of vegetables, to culturing meat in reactors and producing clean, fresh water through desalination and regeneration, they all share the features that they are products of manufacturing – in the sense of clean, controllable inputs and clean, controlled environment. They all share the properties that they are *practicable* (the technologies already exist), *scalable* and *replicable* – and hence can be utilized to meet the world's pressing energy, resources, water and food problems. They co-exist with cities – reinforcing the argument that cities are the major drivers of greening, and will save on land and resources constraints as they incorporate these basic elements of survival in the future urban fabric. Again we can view China as the lead player in this process because its cities are emerging as the fastest growing concentrations of population on the planet. These cities and their sixth wave technologies are the only known solution to the otherwise insoluble problems of energy, water and food security.

Considered on their own, the issues of generating power, finding water and growing food for an ever-expanding global population appear insuperable. *Power systems* developed through the course of the industrial era rely on fossil fuels and centralized generating plants, but these are now known to cause serious damage through global warming and particulate pollution, and are vulnerable to blackouts and brownouts as they become stressed. Renewable energy alternatives are making slow headway against the combined industrial inertia of these established systems. *Water systems* are based largely on relying on rainfall and extracting ground water, which is lowering water tables to dangerous levels, while one way-flow irrigation systems and hydropower systems are denuding once-fertile river valleys. Solutions in the form of water desalination are limited by the intensive energy demands usually involving fossil fuels. *Food production systems* in the form of irrigated open field cultivation, supplemented by greenhouse production for fresh vegetables and mariculture for seafood, is subject to severe water replenishment problems and pollution through runoff of fertilizers, herbicides, and pesticides. Urban-based solutions like vertical farms as yet make only a small dent in these problems because of associated power and water needs.

There is debate on each of these separate problem areas of power production and the rise of renewables; water usage and the impact of desalination; and urban food production and the potential contribution of hydroponics. Considered individually, on their own, solutions to these separate problems face obstacles that become even greater as they are encountered together. This is what is known in the literature as the *triple nexus* – the exacerbation of water, energy, and food problems each contributing to the severity of the others.[26] Something has to be done to break this logjam. We consider a leading candidate for providing a solution in the next chapter.

---

26. See for example Scott, Kurian and Westcoat 2014.

CHAPTER 16

ENERGY, WATER, FOOD FOR CITIES: DEPLOYING A POSITIVE TRIPLE NEXUS

Scholars are pointing to ways in which problems of energy security, water security, and food security interact, each exacerbating the effects of the others in what is called the Triple Nexus. But few examine the same issue from the perspective of the three fundamental drivers – energy, water, and food – systemically interacting to enhance and support each other's contributions. In this text we are concerned not so much with the problems as with solutions. So turning things on their head, we can see how solutions to the individual power, water, and food problems might be able to reinforce each other so that solutions that are not economically or technologically feasible on their own *become feasible when considered together.* The way forward has already been identified in the form of proposals for combining production of power, water, and food in various ways that draw on renewable and replenishable resources.

In arid areas, for example, concentrated solar power and desalination systems can be developed that share a common heat-transfer fluid that is used both for desalination and for power production via concentrated solar power. The costs of each system taken on its own are considered uncompetitive, but if combined these costs are reduced so that the joint production of power and fresh water becomes feasible. Urban production of fresh produce such as vegetables can be reframed using specially designed greenhouses powered by renewable sources such as urban waste, turning cost disadvantages on their head. Clean food can thereby be produced from clean energy in a way that generates advantages over traditional horticultural methods. These are the clear directions of change in the evolution of the industrial system.

When an industrial ecological perspective is applied, the three problems are tackled simultaneously, thereby generating multiple synergies or shared benefits. I propose to call this *hydrosolar gardening*, which produces power, water, and fresh food through joint production, with each activity supporting and enhancing the others. When you think of it, traditional agriculture can be called hydrosolar farming, since it depends on nature's inputs of sun and rain. But calling it gardening adds the element that it is farming within an enclosed, controlled environment. It can be applied at micro-scale at local level as well as at a macro-scale global level.

HYDROSOLAR GARDENS: SYSTEMIC INTERCONNECTIONS

Let us call the interconnected production of food, fresh water and energy from renewable sources hydrosolar gardening. The fascination of the concept is that it liberates food production from the soil and the weather – and even from a fixed location. Hydrosolar gardens could be floating gardens on board a vessel that is moored in a convenient location – and which comes back to base once a month (say) for harvesting.

The core of the hydrosolar gardening system is the greenhouse, which receives inputs of fresh air and fresh water and heat from the ancillary systems. Nothing is supplied in the form of utilities other than a stand-by generator. The heat (for heating and cooling) is supplied from the storage tanks, where the fluid is held at a constant temperature, linked to the solar thermal system using (for example) parabolic mirror arrays and a pipeline containing the heated fluid. The water is supplied by the desalination unit, which would use heat and power generated from the solar system. The interconnected system can be depicted as shown in Figure 16.1.

FIGURE 16.1. Schematic of the Hydrosolar Garden system.

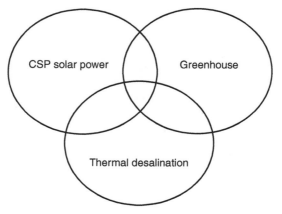

SOURCE: Author.

The hydrosolar garden consists of parts that individually are well tried and tested, but which in combination deliver new and undiscovered efficiencies, or synergies. This is the essence of the concept of a system, viewed as an integrated entity, where the whole is greater than the sum of the parts. There is already a commercial exemplar of this approach – the *Sundrop Farms* concept.

SUNDROP FARMS

The Sundrop Farms model is a scalable and modular version of renewable farming that utilizes only clean and sustainable inputs. The first instance of the model, created at Port Augusta in South Australia, started full production in September 2016. The venture consists of four huge greenhouses, each 5 hectares in area, making a total of 20 hectare under cover in which trussed tomatoes are flourishing. The farm is producing tomatoes at a rate of 15,000 tons per year, all supplied to the national retail chain Coles, under a ten-year exclusive supply agreement.[1]

The power that runs the whole facility is supplied by a Power Tower system utilizing a field of mirrors, deploying Concentrated Solar Power (CSP) technology supplied by the Danish firm Aalborg CSP. The mirrors are computer-controlled to follow the sun, and reflect concentrated solar energy to the top of the tower, where water is heated and passed to both a huge storage tank and to a turbine system to generate electric power. Seawater is pumped in from the nearby Spencer Gulf and transformed to fresh water, at a rate of 450 million litres per year, using a Multiple Effect Distillation (MED) system. The MED water desalination process mimics nature in heating the seawater and capturing it as it condenses as fresh water – just as the water cycle uses evaporation from the sea to create rainclouds which then provide precipitation over land.

The fresh water is then pumped to the 20 hectare greenhouses, to provide the medium in which to grow the plants (initially tomatoes) enriched with nutrients. Because everything is so clean there is no need to use herbicides or pesticides or any other nasty chemicals. The few pests that are encountered are dealt with biologically, by introducing predators for any identified insects. In winter the plants are warmed by the heated water pumped to the heat tanks

---

1. See details at: http://2015.sustainability.wesfarmers.com.au/case-studies/environment/coles-enters-10-year-contract-for-tomatoes-powered-by-sun-and-seawater/.

direct from the Power Tower. In summer the plants are cooled by another simple technology involving wet cardboard grills cooled by evaporation as seawater is pumped through them.

The whole farm is designed to be 100 per cent based on renewable energy and unlimited supplies of seawater. At the moment, in this very early phase, there is still some reserve pumping from diesel-powered generators – but it is planned to eliminate this remnant of the fossil fuels economy as soon as possible.

As a high-tech business venture, the project has been driven by accessing the best technology – advanced greenhouses, advanced hydroponics, CSP power system and MED desalination unit – as well as smart finance. The venture attracted early financing from Australia's Clean Energy Finance Corporation.[2] After the 10-year exclusive supply agreement was reached with the supermarket chain Coles (what could be called a 'production purchase agreement' or PPA, by analogy with comparable power purchase agreements for renewable power ventures), the global venture capital firm KKR was attracted and agreed to invest $100 million. So the whole project is up and running with total investment of $200 million – or $10 million per greenhouse hectare.

The entrepreneur behind all this is Philipp Saumweber, a former merchant banker and graduate of Harvard Business School. He started out partnering with the founder of Seawater Greenhouse but quickly went his own way with high-tech CSP and MED technologies while Seawater Greenhouse insisted on staying at a low-tech level. He has designed Sundrop Farms as a modular and scalable solution to the global agricultural dilemma, where it is clear that expanding global population cannot possibly be fed by traditional methods, even with more and more fossil fuel inputs. Saumweber is talking up the possibility of extending the Sundrop Farms concept to other sites in Australia and to other parts of the world as well, such as the US (Tennessee) and Odemira in Portugal. China is the obvious candidate for the Sundrop farms approach to growing fruits, vegetables and berries – all at scale, in sustainable fashion, and near the burgeoning cities.

There are some limitations of course. The concept does not seem to be suitable for broad-acre farming of grains, which still remain a major sink for fossil fuel use and greenhouse gas emissions. And the concept is still not completely clean while the brine left after desalination is simply pumped back

---

2. See. details. at:. https://www.cleanenergyfinancecorp.com.au/media/65410/cefc_factsheet_sundropfarms_lr.pdf.

to the Spencer Gulf. This one farm is obviously not going to make a difference to the salinity of the Southern Ocean. But scaled up to a global level there could be concerns, and so 100 per cent recycling is obviously the eventual goal.

The essence of the Sundrop Farms System (SFS) is that it is modular, scalable and can be located anywhere in the world, with preference for arid coastal areas that would otherwise be quite unsuitable for any form of agriculture, let alone horticulture. It turns the two most abundant resources of the planet – sunlight and seawater – into food, energy and fresh water. There are literally no limits to its application.

WIDER ECONOMIC SIGNIFICANCE OF THE SUNDROP FARMS CONCEPT

The idea of triple-benefit projects like Sundrop Farms comes into its own when scaled to the levels needed by China that is urbanizing as well as industrializing rapidly. From a basically rural country at the time of the Revolution, China achieved 20 per cent urbanization by 1980, then 30 per cent by 1996, 40 per cent by 2002 and 50 per cent (or majority city-based) by 2011. Over the decade from 2005 to 2015, China's urban population increased from 560 million to 770 million, or 210 million over the decade – meaning on average 21 million people moving to the cities each year. The task of providing adequate fresh food and water to these vast urban populations would appear to be insuperable without radical changes such as those suggested by the triple-benefit version of the triple nexus concept (or what I am calling hydrosolar gardening).

Sundrop Farms seen as an economic entity captures increasing returns as its output grows and sufficiently advanced customers (e.g., supermarket chains) can absorb its output. In this way Sundrop is replicating the same issues encountered by the Ford Motor Company as it invented the mass market for the automobile early in the twentieth century – a management challenge of finding adequate distribution outlets that was solved by the development of car dealerships as specialized retail outlets that could expand the market and operate at scale.

In effect Sundrop represents the application of mass market industrialization to the production of fresh food, utilizing manufactured components (greenhouse with irrigation and pumping systems; power generation and heat from the concentrated power system; desalination unit) that liberate production of food from environmental conditions (soil, weather, water). All the components interact with each other and produce synergies. Desalination plants or CSP plants on their own would not be economical in arid parts of the world, but when combined with greenhouse production of fresh food they become an attractive proposition. Moreover the food is virtually pest-free because the environment in which it is grown is controlled (and the few pests that penetrate can be controlled biologically).

This is mass-market industrialization in a sustainable manner, where the inputs are the two most abundant resources on the planet – sunshine and seawater. There would appear to be no limits to the scalability of the SFS, which can be replicated around the world and can be broadened to encompass different vegetable crops and then beyond vegetables to seedlings and flowers (floriculture), and eventually to protein produce such as fish and seafood (via mariculture) or production of algae. In fact in principle all forms of nurtured living entities (fruits, berries, vegetables, flowers, seedlings, seafood) can be raised according to the principles of the SFS.[3]

Since the world's fresh water resources are under great stress, with irrigated agriculture taking up to 70 per cent of available resources (according to FAO), projects like the Sundrop Farms version of sustainably industrialized horticulture has vast promise. It promises not just clean food in virtually unlimited quantities but also great development potential for poor countries, since all the elements of the Sundrop farms module have to be manufactured and constructed – which can provide business opportunities for local entrepreneurs and employment for local, rural communities. And manufacturing activities are able to exploit improved productivities to capture increasing returns as markets for mass produced goods expand. By contrast, traditional agriculture with its dependence on soil and climate is subject to diminishing returns.

---

3. Mention should also be made of the Sahara Forest Project, which likewise grew out of the Seawater Greenhouse concept, and is operating a quasi-commercial facility in Qatar.

CHAPTER 17

ECO-CITIES OF THE FUTURE

Now we bring all these sixth wave initiatives together to discuss their integration in the creation of new eco-cities. There is no difficulty in describing the features or elements needed to define an eco-city: it is one where energy is as renewable as possible; resources are regenerated and waste disposal approaches zero; where water is regenerated from waste flows or produced via renewable desalination; where food is grown in enclosed spaces again powered by renewable energy; and where there is as much green open space as is physically compatible with a city. Even more simply, the eco-city is itself a *sixth wave innovation* drawing on all the other sixth wave advances.

The key to comprehending the emergence of eco-cities is to view these features as working off each other, capturing synergies that truly make the whole greater than the sum of the parts. Water regeneration utilizing renewable energies sparks creative ways of providing renewable power; renewable solar energy and desalinated water enable urban food production to be conducted on a grand scale. Resource regeneration through urban mining promotes initiatives in energy and resource efficiency enhancement. And what captures all these features and brings them together is eco-imagination. It is the eco-imagination of local entrepreneurial talent that is the real driver of the emergence of eco-cities, and that defines them – better than any particular set of features or elements. And it is worth noting that this approach to defining an eco-city is perfectly consistent with the view of cities as generators of wealth through synergies captured, based on density of development. In this case, the 'wealth' generated is a green economy, one that brings economic and ecological forces and systems closer together.

There are advanced eco-cities approximating this description found around the world – with mixed success so far. There is Masdar City in the UAE, which is planned as an eco-sphere or eco-garden in the middle of the desert. But by late 2016 it was struggling to get started, with only the students at the

Masdar Institute being permanent residents. There is Songdo, an advanced international business district created at Incheon, Korea. Here the airport is closely linked to the city through a 7-mile bridge spanning the beautiful waters off the Korean coast, and making a ride to or from the airport simply a 10-minute affair through breath-taking vistas. Songdo enjoys facilities such as an advanced waste collection system operating underground and driven by compressed air. It is certainly more successful at this stage than Masdar.

As befits a country looking to leapfrog to a new twenty-first century industrial civilization, China has figured prominently on the eco-city front. There have been many projects proposed – and not a few failures. The proposed eco-city of Dongtan on Chongming eco-island, at the mouth of the Yangtze river near Shanghai, was heavily promoted in the first decade of the twenty-first century as a completely new kind of eco-city; it has since floundered and come to nought.[1] In its wake have come a legion of new cities that have badged themselves 'eco-cities' as a means of putting an acceptable face on otherwise naked property speculation ventures.[2]

But there are three outstanding Sino–Singapore joint ventures that are genuinely raising the bar on future urban eco-developments in China. These ventures are creating new eco-cities in Suzhou, in Tianjin and in Guangzhou. Others are likely to follow – sparking emulation around the world.[3] The first of these was the joint venture known as the Suzhou Industrial Park (SIP), which was begun as a joint venture between the governments of Singapore and China at central state level and at provincial level. There were grand ambitions on the part of Singapore, led by former PM Lee Kwan Yew, to create a genuine replica of Singapore in China, focusing more on the 'software' of good administration and legal procedures than the hardware of buildings and land development. But there were well known hiccups encountered along the way, and while private sector players were involved at every step, the whole Suzhou development never made a profit until Singapore had handed over 65 per cent of the equity to local provincial and municipal interests in China. Once the new ownership arrangements were in place the venture began to attract investment on a large scale and it started to return a profit – so much

1. Dongtan figures prominently in the Julie Sze's account of Chinese 'eco-fantasies' (Sze 2015). For other comprehensive and critical accounts, see for example Chang and Sheppard (2013).

2. See the useful analysis by Taiwanese geographer Shiuhshen Chien in Chien (2013).

3. See the exposition and historical analysis in Chien et al. (2015). The point is that the Sino-Singapore eco-city joint ventures are viewed in China as candidates for replication – not as the last word in eco-cities themselves.

so that the SIP is one of the largest and most successful of green developments in China today.

The next initiative came from Singaporean Senior Minister Goh Chok Tong and Chinese Premier Wen Jiabao in April 2007, culminating in a government-to-government agreement of November 2007 to create a new eco-city. Here the lessons learned by both sides in the Suzhou development were put to good use. The China side insisted that the Tianjin development was not to take up valuable arable land, and would have to be sited on degraded land that could be improved by eco-urbanization. In the event, the site chosen was salt pans and land ruined by toxic waste discharges on the Bohai Bay industrial region. This had the indirect advantage that it would make the Sino-Singapore Tianjin Eco-city a model of land regeneration: if it could be achieved in such an unpromising setting, then it could be achieved anywhere. For its part the Singapore side insisted that there had to be real business opportunities for Singaporean firms as well as other foreign investors, with a formula developed to frame this approach – private sector driven and government facilitated.[4] In this second initiative, the Singaporean side learned the importance of involving the local Chinese provincial and municipal authorities at the outset, and calling for no more than 50 per cent of the equity in the SSTEC joint venture administrative entity. In this joint venture, the Singaporean side provided the capital, while the Chinese side provided the land.

The latest of these involves a new city built in a beautiful location featuring a lake and mountains in the southern Guangdong province, just a few kilometres from the city of Guangzhou (the former Canton, now a small pocket of colonial history in a booming megalopolis). This venture, the Sino-Singapore Guangzhou Knowledge City (SSGKC), is framed within a government to government agreement (the province of Guangdong and the city-state of Singapore) that gives it political credibility and clout. Within this framework it has a private sector driven strategy (once again) involving an overall government-to-government coordinating committee and consortia of corporations on both the Singapore and the China sides. This pattern of private–public cooperation between two countries has been found by experience to be the most practicable means of driving genuine eco-city

---

4. For a study of the Tianjin eco-city project as compared with other Asian and European developments, as the next stage in the evolution of clean production systems, see Hu et al. (2016). I visited the Tianjin eco-city in October 2016 to see the development at first hand; my thanks to Professors Jinhui Li and Xianlai Zeng at Tsinghua University for their arranging the visit and to Professor Zeng for accompanying me.

development. It builds on earlier experiences firstly in Suzhou and then in Tianjin.

While the Tianjin-based eco-city has been relatively slow to take off, with few large international companies stepping forward as yet to invest in the venture, the Guangdong-based development promises to be up and running almost as soon as the basic infrastructure (transport, communications, water and waste services) is completed and initial housing is constructed.[5] The reason is that there is a clear economic imperative to the Guangdong initiative, which is designed to house not only the first intellectual property office in China outside Beijing (for activities such as patent application and examination, and copyright registration) but also the first Intellectual Property Office of Singapore to be built outside the city-state. Thus the plan to develop a 'knowledge city' is being taken quite literally in this case, where knowledge assets (IPRs) and the services that go with them (such as training in IP activities), universities and patent and copyright-based legal services, together with courts for hearing cases, promise to provide specialist employment that will in turn spark accelerated development of the city. This will be expected to create the demand for advanced social services encompassing education and health, including child care, and entertainment and leisure services, so that the city would be expected to transition to a real city with the 'buzz' of an existing metropolis like Hong Kong, Shanghai and Guangzhou itself.

THE ECO-CITY INFRASTRUCTURE

Drilling down into the details of the Sino–Singaporean eco-city projects, what emerges is an approach that may be viewed as consistently practicable, replicable, and scalable – as stated explicitly by the Tianjin eco-city plans. The implementation of waste collection, recycling and waste-to-energy systems is eminently practicable, based as it is on technology for underground movement of wastes via pneumatic traction and their capture at central sorting locations built entirely under cover. This is a commercially available (practicable) technology, marketed assiduously for example by the Swedish firm Envac – and yet in China's eco-cities developed by Chinese–Singaporean interests the

5. I visited the site of the SSGKC in September 2016 and saw the progress being achieved in building the infrastructure, as well as landscaping around the central lake. I am grateful to Mr Jason Tay of the SSGKC administrative office and Professor Zheng Yongnian for facilitating this visit.

technology is being scaled up and thereby made replicable for all cities and not just for a handful of affluent estates.

Likewise for energy matters, we find in the Tianjin eco-city that whole industrial 'parks' like the National Animation Facility are now served by their own energy centres, which provide shared power supplies and shared heating and cooling flows – in what is technically known as a trigeneration facility. If you look up trigeneration on Wikipedia you find that it is a technically abstruse development confined to a few experimental locations, particularly in Scandinavia. But in the Tianjin eco-city it is being scaled up so that all firms involved in the animation 'park' are provided with shared power (largely sourced from renewables), stores of hot water for heating in winter and of cold water for cooling in summer – all delivered via a self-contained, modular, energy centre that can be scaled up to any dimension, from that of a neighbourhood to an entire city.

Central underground pneumatic waste collection systems with conversion of waste-to-energy, and localized trigeneration energy centres serving whole city modules, are just two of the 'hardware' features found in these Sino-Singaporean eco-city projects. Others include water regeneration and recycling; green building codes and green transport; green open spaces and modular development around 'eco-cells' that retain a human scale everywhere. The 'software' involved includes administrative procedures, 'one-stop' facilities for opening businesses, and the tax collection procedures introduced by the Singaporean organizations. These features are eminently practicable, utilizing technologies and social practices that are commercially available – and the Sino-Singaporean ventures scale them up so that they become replicable, as models for the rapid urbanization of the whole of China. The fact that they are being pursued at such scale protects them from the charge that they are merely fiddling at the edges. And the fact that they are based on Singaporean administrative and business capabilities protects them from the charge that they are utopian. But the question remains: can they really be scaled up in time throughout China – and then in other countries beyond – to meet the demands of exploding urbanization?

CHINESE ECO-FANTASIES?

There is a prominent stream of argument that holds that China's eco-imagination is running ahead of itself, and that plans for eco-cities and eco-islands like Dongtan (near Shanghai, now defunct) have been driven by Western fears of China's rise. Julie Sze (2015), for example, argues that

Dongtan (and by extension other eco-projects) are mere eco-fantasies; they need to be viewed (she says) as part of a discourse of an 'ecological Shanghai' that insists that development and environmental responsibility proceed hand in hand – rather than development first and ecology second. She argues that Dongtan promoted a grand ecological vision that in the end outran itself: 'Dongtan was evoked as a new phase of development, one that took ecology seriously, and which foretold a different pathway for the Chinese nation' (2015: 9). The Arup design company, the British master planner of Dongtan chosen by the Shanghai Industrial Investment Corporation, described the projected eco-city as 'the quest to create a new world'. That this world came crashing down is beyond dispute. But was it because of excessive and over-ambitious ecological dreaming?

There is another, more prosaic explanation for these failures. The Chinese state authorities have been mindful of food security, and correspondingly wary of conversion of farmland to city development. So they have imposed quotas on such farmland conversion on municipal authorities – and career paths are shaped by officials' ability to work within these quotas. In the case of Dongtan it seems that the eco-city was promulgated with the last remaining quota of farmland conversion – and that land speculation away from Dongtan reduced the quota available – which in turn led to the demise of Dongtan itself.[6] By this argument, Shanghai municipal authorities simply failed to provide for the land needed by Dongtan despite all the international publicity, and the proposed city languished as a result. One would like to see more research on an issue as pressing and fundamental as this.

Sze's argument is beguiling. She sees Dongtan, even if it had been successful as a business and technological development, as irrelevant – as artificial as Thames Town, the UK replica built as a fantasy in the precincts of Shanghai, and which today serves merely as a backdrop for wedding photos.[7] She is right that eco-cities sometimes can be nothing more than glorified real estate speculations. But they can be so much more – as demonstrated emphatically by the Sino–Singaporean joint ventures in Suzhou, Tianjin and Guangzhou and possible further locations. These ventures all involve new creations – since it is clearly so much easier to create new infrastructure as

6. The Taiwan economic geographer Shiuh-Shen Chien has an argument along these lines (see Chien 2013), as do Chang and Sheppard (2013).

7. See the review of Sze's book by Fred Pearce in *New Scientist*, 'Eco-city dreams vs real eco-activism', 21 January 2015, at: https://www.newscientist.com/article/mg22530050-900-eco-city-dreams-vs-real-eco-activism.

an investment project rather than through retro-fitting an existing city. They do not call for specific innovations; rather they bring together best practices and 'package' them in a new system or combination that is scalable and replicable.

Above all these eco-cities are exercises in imagination – and it is imagination that the world needs in creating cities that will prove to be economically and ecologically successful – at scale. While the West plays with mini-projects and fashionable inner-city conversions, it is China that is imagining green cities at scale, as real prospects for a rapidly urbanizing world. This is the significance of the eco-city projects that promise a model of the green future that is practicable, scalable and replicable.[8]

---

8. These are the descriptors utilized by the planners of the Tianjin eco-city development – and they apply to all such eco-city developments and indeed to sixth wave innovations generally.

CHAPTER 18

WHEN CERES MEETS GAIA

In this closing chapter I wish to review the trends that at are driving the world economy in order to take a stance on where these trends are leading us. It is the role of responsible analysts/commentators to identify the major trends and forces at work, seeking to place them in the 'big picture' – and that is what I propose to do.

The big picture in this case is the reconciliation between the economic and ecological, located in the setting where the industrializing processes through which China and India, then others like Brazil et al., are brought within the ambit of the 'moderately wealthy' world – without destroying that world through ecological murder, or ecocide. Such a big picture is not one generated by the world of investors in London, Tokyo or New York – the readers of the *Financial Times* or the *Wall Street Journal*. They are comfortable in their present circumstances, and we cannot expect sacrifices from them. But in the case of China and India the imperative of development, to be delivered through industrialization centred on manufacturing as the only known pathway to wealth and rising incomes, is paramount – and constitutes the cutting edge of the reconciliation between economics and ecology that we all wish to see. This will need to be a reconciliation for everyone, *for all nine billion on the planet* – given the strong probability that there will be a 'demographic transition' where countries with high birth rates today will moderate them voluntarily tomorrow as they move up the development and wealth enhancement ladder.

The argument presented in this book is this. The biggest issue of our time is the industrialization of China and India. This is their pathway to modernization, to the ending of age-old prejudices and to the defeat of anti-modernizing religions/ideologies like militant Islamic jihad against – against what? modernity? – and to rising incomes and wealth. But can such a process be made compatible with our new understanding of the limits to fossil fuelled expansion of linear processes, trampling over the earth in search of fuels and resources and dumping wastes onto the same planet. This anti-systemic approach is clearly incompatible with the evident finite character of our beautiful planet.

That does *not* translate into a call for zero growth – as is so often heard now in radical circles in the West. In response to concerns over the future of the planet, many are calling for an end to economic growth – in the name of respecting ecological limits and finite planetary resources.[1] The problem is that this concern is based on a misunderstanding of the character of economic growth. If it is a case of extensive growth, that is, where the growth is based on increasing resource throughput, then it is clear that it must one day come to a halt and be succeeded by a stationary state – if humans and life in general are to survive. But it is perfectly possible to have *intensive* growth, that is, growth that is generated through improvements in productivity, where incomes can grow without a corresponding growth in resource throughput. This is what is meant, in fact, by increasing returns – getting more than before out of a given set of inputs. So capturing increasing returns means, essentially, embarking on a process of intensive growth, or growth that is decoupled from resource throughput. When based on renewable energies (that are always available) and resource recirculation and regeneration, this can be called accurately 'green growth'

The reasons for China's success so far in the greening of its economy are hotly debated. There are those who see it as simply a product of cheating, or using low-cost labour as a means of undermining producers of green goods in the West. This is the position of trade associations like the Solar Energy Industries Association in the US or SolarWorld in the EU, which have lobbied hard for trade sanctions to be imposed unilaterally by the US and EU against Chinese imports of products like solar PV cells. Such sanctions have certainly curbed Chinese production and exports of green goods – but they have not killed off the industry, since cost reductions continue irrespective of trade issues, and smart producers are able to find ways around such sanctions, for example by relocating their sources of supply to the US and EU, and even by relocating investments to produce their goods behind the tariff barriers, within the US or EU. And of course such sanctions carry dubious political baggage, in that they run flatly against aspirations to decarbonize the world's energy system, expressed in other forums such as Paris Climate Conference meeting in December 2015. There are others who see China's success as all being the

---

1. See for example Jackson 2009.

result of unfair competition attributed to the power and omniscience of the Chinese government, which is viewed as intervening unfairly through subsidies and tax breaks to tilt the playing field towards Chinese producers.

I wish to offer another perspective on these matters. China's success in expanding the green sectors in its economy surely has to do with its ability to implement industrial policy with determination, and to focus its strategies at the point of investment, where there is already change under way. It is at the point of investment – before things become fixed on the ground – that change can best be effected, in whatever field of inquiry. It works in related fields like protection of occupational health and safety, where (say) some new finding that a chemical has serious health effects can best be accommodated not by requiring existing firms to make changes to their existing operations to curb the chemical's use (expensive and disruptive) but by requiring firms to adjust their investment strategies to delete the offending chemical from their operations. It is far easier for a company to change an investment schedule than it is to change plant design and operations in facilities that are already built and operating. We have seen a prominent case of this principle in operation in the new eco-cities being proposed (and built) in China.

MANAGING CHANGE: THE DIFFERENTIAL PRINCIPLE

One could give a name to this approach, calling it the Differential Principle, after the mathematical insight that a system's rate of change is captured most effectively by its differential, and most comprehensively by a set of differential equations. Mathematically the differential may be viewed as the slope of the tangent drawn to a curve at any point, and so intuitively as expressing the degree of change at that point. So a public policy targeted at the differential of a system – at the point where change is being driven by new investments – is the one most likely to be effective.

It seems that China has discovered that the most effective way to green its economy – driven (as I have argued) by considerations of energy and resource efficiency – is to drive investment towards specified green targets. This is the purpose of the successive Five Year Plans, with their targets for increasing investment in renewable power systems (led by power generation from water, wind and sun) and in circular economy initiatives (led by closing loops in existing manufacturing agglomerations). Such plans provide clear incentives (in the form of low-interest loans from state development banks) as well as assistance from local and provincial governments in the form of housing, land grants and local tax breaks to entrepreneurs who are prepared to run the risks of investing in the targeted sectors. Banks that raise green bonds on the capital markets are able to disburse the funds raised towards firms that have investment goals consistent with the overall greening targets.

The Chinese approach to steering its economy towards green goals is thus to set clear targets as part of the rolling five-year planning process and then to utilize all available means to drive investment towards fulfilment of the targets adopted. This is arguably a more sensible and effective approach than the practice discussed in the West of imposing carbon taxes, which raise costs for carbon polluters and thereby give a nominal advantage to firms operating with low carbon emissions (such as generators of renewable energy). Environmental taxes more generally raise costs for polluters as compared with firms that have low impact on the resource environment through closing industrial loops to create a circular economy. These carbon and environmental taxes are resisted so strongly for the reason that they alter the cost environment for firms once they have already committed to projects at a certain cost level and face potential disadvantages if they are required to change their cost structures as a result of the imposition of the carbon tax. Of course carbon taxes (and environmental taxes more generally) can help to shape the investment environment and frame investment decisions by firms, once the economy is on a new, greening trajectory. But can they do the 'heavy lifting' in shifting an economy from a fossil-fuelled 'business as usual' trajectory to a new, greening trajectory? The evidence is now in – they cannot. There is no alternative to state intervention and industrial policy, captured through the setting of investment targets and then utilizing the financial system to drive investment towards the specified targets.

Such an approach does not have to be heavy-handed, with the state issuing commands that have to be followed by the private sector subject to sanctions being imposed if the targets are not met. The system works best through incentives being offered, usually in the form of lower interest rates on loans utilized to invest in greening projects, or various forms of state aid such as tax breaks and subsidies offered to firms that make the desired investments. In this sense what China is building is a performance-driven system, where firms that meet the targets are rewarded and firms that don't are not so rewarded. This was the system 'discovered' by East Asian industrializing countries such as Korea and Taiwan in the post-war period, particularly the 1970s and 1980s when what the World Bank called the 'East Asian Miracle' was in full swing. Most commentators see the 'developmental state' era as being defined by the rise of these East Asian countries and closing with the Asian financial crisis of

1997. But this is to miss two important features: 1) the extent to which China has been following the East Asian model very closely (but with the important qualification that it is doing so with a 'two-level' state system, involving both the central (national) state coordinating the actions of provincial-level governments; and 2) the extent to which China is applying the developmental state machinery to the greening of its economy.[2]

In fact the successful cases of greening so far all involve strong state intervention, in the name of industrial policy, through the setting of targets and the mobilizing of finance to drive investment towards these targets. This is what may be observed in the case of China, at multiple levels, and in cases such as Korea and now in the case of India as well. India is utilizing all these tools, with strong national government leadership in setting grand targets (such as the National Solar Mission to build 100 GW of solar power by 2022 and the National Wind Mission to build 60 GW of wind power by the same date) and then utilizing developmental banks to direct loans at preferential rates towards firms that are explicitly seeking to invest in activities that would meet the specified targets. The advantage of industrial policy utilizing greening targets is that the targets can guide the investment behaviour of players at multiple levels – from provincial and local governments, to eco-park administrations, to corporate headquarters and to local firms and subsidiaries that are actually making the changes required.

Targets, as well as other state-mediated incentives like public procurement, have the positive effect of coordinating the actions of the various players at different levels.[3] Taxes by contrast have no such impact, and merely shift the cost environment for everyone. Again I hasten to add that such a shift (e.g., raising the cost of polluting with carbon emissions) can help in driving an economy along a new, greening trajectory – but cannot be expected to do the 'heavy lifting' involved in shifting from one (brown) trajectory to another (green) pathway. The only reason that mainstream neoclassical economists oppose targets and support taxes is ideological; support for targets would carry with it the implication that the economy is evolving and developing along paths

---

2. My colleagues Dr Elizabeth Thurbon and Dr Sung-Young Kim call this 'developmental environmentalism' (Kim and Thurbon 2015) or a 'developmental mindset' with a focus on green growth (Thurbon 2016) and an emphasis on cases of successful application such as Korea.

3. It is not just the East Asian countries that have mastered these state-mediated interventions. See Weiss (2014) for a scholarly account of the role of the US state in driving innovation.

that can be shaped by government intervention. This is not how neoclassical economists wish to view the economy! But reality consistently proves their models (with all their equilibrium-based assumptions) wrong. Now the greening of the economy, with success associated with industrial targets rather than carbon taxes, is providing yet another example of the failure of the neoclassical economic vision. One has to ask: how many failures does a certain approach have to incur before it is judged invalid and abandoned?

There are further points to be made before we leave this discussion. First, the issue is one of 'greening' rather than defining some 'green' end point. In fact there will never be a defined 'green economy' (or at least not before mid-century or so) partly because the criteria will be shifting as the economy itself evolves and grows closer to ecological balance, and partly because the focus of policy will need to be on the greening process rather than on any putative end point. The end point may be a 'steady state' where inputs are balanced by outputs – but in order to arrive at such a state what is needed is a greening of the present processes of growth. Economic growth has to be a feature of the industrialization of the new giants like China and India – but it needs to be green growth, that is growth that tempers its use of fossil fuels with the problems of energy insecurity they generate, and tempers its use of virgin resources and waste dumping (at either end of the linear economy) through recirculating resources via the circular economy.

So green growth – under whatever convenient name a government calls it, like the 'creative economy' terminology used by the Korean administration – is the watchword, guiding state intervention in the economy to drive investment towards green targets. The major carriers of this shift are renewable energy systems on the one hand (needed to enhance energy security), and circular economy initiatives on the other (to enhance resource security), both facilitated and shaped by the greening of finance. With green targets that drive investments towards renewables and circular economy initiatives, set by a state that is prepared to engage in the industrial policy needed to shift an economy's direction, a process that we can describe as 'greening' will inevitably be getting under way. This is a process with such profound repercussions for the economy that it is best characterized as a technoeconomic transition – indeed the sixth such transition since the advent of the industrial era – and now the one that promises to enrich China and India before diffusing to the rest of the industrializing world.

The utility of the approach outlined here is that it delivers the reduced carbon emissions and reduced resource impact (global footprint) that are widely viewed as desirable or necessary – without imposing draconian measures to achieve such reductions. The reduced carbon emissions flow from the emphasis on installing renewable energy systems – not putative systems created by 'innovation' (as per Bill Gates) but the solar and wind power systems that are currently being installed and whose growing scale of usage has led to such dramatic cost reductions.[4] When we maintain clear focus on these core ideas, the 'chatter' that accompanies debates over the future of the green economy fades away.

A 'MODERATE' ECOMODERNISM: IN DEFENCE OF CONVENTIONAL RENEWABLES

I find it distressing that otherwise superb scientists like James Lovelock (to whom we are forever indebted for his creation and championing of Gaia theory) go out of their way to diminish the contribution that conventional renewable sources might make to resolving the world's energy problems. Renewables are given zero credit by Lovelock for solving the world's greenhouse gas (global warming) problem and for solving the energy security problems of emerging industrial giants like China and India. Indeed Lovelock never mentions the complementary changes occurring in terms of resource flows, as China moves from a linear to a circular economy. In fact Lovelock never mentions China and India as serious industrializers at all, other than as sources of carbon-based pollution. They are mentioned only indirectly when he asserts that the world will have to live with 1 billion or fewer inhabitants, leaving unanswered the question as to where the culling is expected to start.

I will come to the potential culling of billions of people in a moment. But just think what it would mean if China were indeed able to meet the terawatt challenge within less than a decade, say by 2025. First, it would mean for China that a 1 TW renewable energy capacity system would provide the much sought after energy security that fossil fuels could never and would never provide. The savings in terms of oil and gas imports provided by the generation of a trillion watts of power from domestic, manufactured sources would amount to trillions of dollars each year. Second, the land areas required would easily be accommodated in the country's western arid and semi-arid regions – without visual impairment of the western seaboard and cities like Shanghai

---

4. The reference here is to Bill Gates's promotion of renewable energies' R & D but his refusal to countenance support for diffusion of existing solar PV and wind power technologies in industrializing countries. See for example see his blog posting 'We need energy miracles', 25 June 2014, at: https://www.gatesnotes.com/Energy/Energy-Miracles, as discussed above in Chapter 11.

or Tianjin. Third, China would be driving not just the industries that produce wind turbines and solar PV cells, becoming world leaders in these sectors, but also in the technologies of smart grid development, high-voltage power cables and the internet of energy, as well as energy storage (solid state and liquid batteries). Fourth, China would be driving down the costs of all these energy-related technologies to the point where they would be producing power at costs well below those of fossil fuelled electricity generation – with a corresponding huge shift in the competitiveness of fossil fuel industries, starting with coal and then moving through the phases of oil and gas. So China's adoption of conventional renewables would have the impact of basically finishing off the fossil fuel industries globally – something that the West has been unable to do on its own through all the debates over global warming and the operation of the Kyoto process lasting for decades.

And the shift to conventional renewables need not interfere with the natural landscape in a country like Britain – the apparent primary concern of critics such as Lovelock. A relatively small producer of electric power like Britain would be able to ride on the coat-tails of China's adoption of renewables, benefiting from the cost reductions that would enable countries in North Africa to become mainstream generators of renewable power that could then be exported to Britain and Europe generally. This would solve the problem completely satisfactorily, giving the European countries a stable and reliable source of renewable power while contributing materially to the industrialization of the North African countries. It would not result in over-dependence on a single country (and perhaps one dominated by Muslim extremists) because there would be competition between various countries for the export market of Europe. No doubt there would be further developments in costs of nuclear power, which again because of China's involvement in Gen III reactors might become available for countries like Britain at less outrageous costs than those experienced in recent years. Unlike Lovelock, whose support for nuclear power leads him to oppose all forms of wind power (and conventional renewables generally), I have no problem with allowing the nuclear industry to flourish alongside the wind and solar industries. I have no problem with this because I see wind and solar firmly winning the battle for supremacy in the marketplace. I would like to see Jim Lovelock be able to leave this earth (he is now in his late 90s) content that his beloved rural walks in England are preserved – because the real battle for supremacy between fossil fuels and alternatives like renewables and nuclear is going to be fought in China and to some extent in India, not in Britain.

I am not making predictions here as to what is likely to happen or not happen in China. No one knows what is going to happen. I am simply saying that it might be reasonable to assume that present trends in China will continue for another decade, particularly the trends towards greater and greater dependence on conventional renewables and less and less dependence on fossil fuels. What then would be the anticipated outcome? I think this is a question worth asking – first, because the current trends are strong, and are very likely to continue for at least another decade (up to the mid-2020s) and beyond. Second, because China would be the largest adopter of an increasingly renewables-based electric power system, with global repercussions of major import. Third, because China's adoption of renewables at scale would have a major impact on the fossil fuel industry, dismantling and disarming it to remove all remaining opposition to cleaning the world's carbon economy.

The argument advanced here does not depend on making a case for or against climate change. Whatever my personal position regarding global warming (and I am a Gaian supporter so view the changes unleashed by fossil fuels as planetary in impact and not just involving climate) I am simply discussing the developments in China in terms of their impact on the country's energy security and resource security. I see China's shift towards renewables as wholly positive because it makes the country less dependent on fossil fuels, which would increasingly be sourced from geopolitical hotspots. China's strategy as I see it is to build up renewables as a way of warding off the threat of war, revolution, and terror induced by increasing dependence on fossil fuels. This turns out to be a stronger driver for action in building renewables than is fear of climate change. And it applies with much greater force in China (and likewise in India) than in Europe, or in a small island like Britain where energy security rates lower in the scale of national priorities.

A HOT PLANET

In this book I do not attempt to answer the unanswerable. Lovelock may be right that a hot planet forced by our fossil fuel burning industrial civilization into a hot state might not be able to support more than 1 billion people. Our agricultural capacity would be reduced and with it our food supplies and eventually our population would shift to accommodate these new circumstances. In his final book Lovelock envisages a new industrial civilization emerging with cities as the key units or modules, where humans could dwell in relative air-conditioned comfort (rather like Singapore in the tropics) growing food industrially either within their boundaries or tightly linked to the city and leaving the rest of the land and the oceans to get along best as Gaia intends.[5] The most savage way

---

5. See Lovelock (2015).

of culling the human population would be though war, disease and famine. A less violent way would be through women taking charge of their own fertility (as they do in the West and increasingly in the industrializing East) and adjusting their birth-rate to the circumstances of the time – which could see the birth-rate decline within a generation to effect something like the required population reduction. All it takes is for girls to be educated – not an impossible demand – and for the urbanization revolution to continue unabated. There are grounds for optimism here.

Of course Jim Lovelock cannot know for sure how things will turn out, and will not be around to see whether the anticipated global shift to a hot planet comes to pass or not. Neither will I. So the best we can offer is to foresee how well and how fast we as a species can liberate ourselves from the present dependence on fossil fuels that is clearly killing us and much of the planet. Here is where the argument comes back to China. For China seems to be doing the job of liberating itself from fossil fuels better than any other industrial country – albeit from a very high carbon-based starting point (i.e., a black coal–fired economy). China's dependence on coal in electricity production currently stands at 73 per cent and – if present trends continue – will be expected to fall well below 70 per cent by 2020 and rapidly thereafter to below 50 per cent, at which point the electric power system would be described as green rather than black. At the same time China's reliance on renewables in the form of WWS can be expected to be increasing, and is likely to exceed 1 trillion watts of power from WWS sources by 2025 (again, if present trends continue) together with perhaps 100 GW from nuclear sources – itself the largest commitment to nuclear power of any country on the planet. So by halfway through the twenty-first century China can be expected to have shifted from coal-powered electricity to renewably powered energy sources, at enormous scale. This will have knock-on effects as the entire grid is modernized and energy storage increases (via battery technology) so that electric mobility will become the norm (EVs with charging infrastructure, high speed rail). There could also be further changes that we cannot yet anticipate such as artificial photosynthesis, solar fuels and possibly electric powered aircraft.

I have made the point earlier that as China drives through this energy industrial revolution, away from fossil fuels towards a renewably powered system, it can be anticipated that costs would continue to fall dramatically and would encourage (in stronger terms, force) other countries to move in the same direction, for reasons of competitive emulation and national energy security. This is how we may envisage the global energy system being transformed in the first half of the century from one based largely on fossil fuels to one based largely on renewables (with some nuclear as well). This shift would be driven by China's initial adoption of renewables for immediate reasons to do with energy security and curbing of particulate pollution. But of course it would be expected also to have profound effects on carbon emissions and hence on the symptoms of a sick planet such as global warming.

The huge question that is quite unanswerable today is whether these changes will occur fast enough, and be deep enough, to forestall a shift by Gaia to the hot state foreseen by Jim Lovelock and by many other planetary scientists such as Jim Hansen. I cannot think of a scientific question of greater significance – nor one deserving of greater financial support from the world's foundations. I have depicted the changes unleashed by China's renewables revolution as a first 'cut' at answering the question. Just how fast is China able to decarbonize? From the evidence of the twenty-first century it would seem that our best estimate is that China is transitioning its energy system from one based on fossil fuels to one based on manufactured renewables at a rate of around 1 per cent per year – and that China is doing this as fast as is physically, technically and economically feasible. As other countries take up the challenge they can add to the momentum, through propagating diminishing costs and technology enhancements. Note that change of 1 per cent a year amounts to a 10 per cent per decade change – which means that the system can shift from being dependent on coal and thermal sources for 80 per cent of its generating capacity in 2010 down to less than 50 per cent within just three decades – or within the 2030s. That is an extremely rapid rate of change for such a huge and complex system – the largest and most complex on the planet.

TWILIGHT OF THE GODS: GAIA, VULCAN AND CERES

Richard Wagner's last opera is the grandly named *Götterdämmerung*, or *Twilight of the Gods*. It was the final instalment in Wagner's cycle of musical dramas that he called *Der Ring des Niebelungen* (*The Ring of the Niebelungen*), which enjoyed its premier at Bayreuth in 1876 – and has become one of the most beloved of musical compositions ever since. I wish to end this account of the global green shift with a similar appeal to a drama at the level of the Gods. In the case of this book we have the drama of Gaia, the queen of the gods in the Greek pantheon, personifying the living earth, being pitted against Vulcan, the god of fire and metal (and proxy for fossil fuels), while Ceres the goddess of fertility guides us as a species in our choice of a sustainable technoeconomic system. A happy ending for this drama would be our development of a capacity to build a technoeconomic system based on circularity and renewables that is compatible with, and complements, Gaia's natural cycles. A tragic outcome would be our failure to do so, with Vulcan emerging triumphant and destroying the balances that Gaia has fashioned. But this is not a tragedy foretold; it is in our power to restore Ceres to her rightful place as nurturer of humankind.

BIBLIOGRAPHY

Allen, R. C. 2009. *The Industrial Revolution in Global Perspective*. Cambridge, UK: Cambridge University Press.

Arcaute, E., Hatna, E., Ferguson, P., Youn, H., Johansson, A. and Batty, M. 2015. Constructing cities, deconstructing scaling laws, *Interface (Journal of the Royal Society)*, 12: 20140745. http://dx.doi.org/10.1098/rsif.2014.0745.

Asafu-Adjaye, J., Blomqvist, L., Brand, S., Brook, B., DeFries, R., Ellis, E., Foreman, C., Keith, D., Lewis, M., Lynas, M., Nordhaus, T., Pielke, R., Pritzker, R., Roy, J., Sagoff, M., Shellenberger, M., Stone, R. and Teague, P. 2015. *An Ecomodernist Manifesto*, available at: www.ecomodernism.org.

Ausubel, J. H. 2007. Renewable and nuclear heresies, *International Journal of Nuclear Governance, Economy and Ecology*, 1 (3): 229–243.

Ayres, R. U. 2008. Sustainability economics: Where do we stand? *Ecological Economics*, 67: 281–310.

Ayres, R. U. and Ayres, E. H. 2010. *Crossing the Energy Divide: Moving from Fossil Fuel Dependence to a Clean-Energy Future*. Upper Saddle River, NJ: Wharton School Publishing.

Barnes, W. and Gilman, N. 2011. Green Social Democracy or Barbarism: Climate change and the end of high modernism. In C. Calhoun and G. Derluguian (eds), *The Deepening Crisis: Governance Challenges after Neoliberalism*. New York: Social Science Council.

Barrett, S. 2011. Rethinking climate change governance and its relationship to the world trading system, *The World Economy* doi 10.1111/j.1467-9701.2011.01420.x.

Batty, M. 2012. Building a science of cities, *Cities*, 29: S9–S16.

Batty, M. 2013. *The New Science of Cities*. Cambridge, MA: MIT Press.

Bettencourt, L. and West, G. 2010. A unified theory of urban living, *Nature*, 467 (21 October 2010): 912–913.

Bettencourt, L. M. A. 2013. The origins of scaling in cities, *Science*, 340 (21 June 2013): 1438–1441.

Bettencourt, L. M. A., Lobo, J., Strumsky, D. and West, G. B. 2010. Urban scaling and its deviations: Revealing the structure of wealth, innovation and crime across cities, *Proceedings of the National Academy of Sciences* (10 November 2010), doi http://dx.doi.org/10.1371/journal.pone.0013541.

Bhat, Z. F., Kumar, S. and Bhat, H. 2016. In-vitro meat: A future animal-free harvest? *Critical Reviews in Food Science and Nutrition*, 57(4): 782–789.

Bigdeli, S. Z. 2014. Clash of rationalities: Revisiting the trade and environment debate in light of WTO disputes over green industrial policy, *Trade, Law and Development*, 6 (1): 177–209.

Bonny, S. P. F., Gardner, G. E., Pethick, D. W. and Hocquette, J.-F. 2015. What is artificial meat and what does it mean for the future of the meat industry? *Journal of Integrative Agriculture*, 14 (2): 255–263.

Boulding, K. E. 1966. The economics of the coming Spaceship Earth. In H. E. Jarrett (ed.), *Environmental Quality in a Growing Economy*. Baltimore, MD: Johns Hopkins Press.

Boyd, O. T. 2012. China's energy reform and climate policy: The ideas motivating change, CCEP Working Paper 1205, Crawford School of Public Policy. Canberra: ANU.

Brand, S. 2010. *Whole Earth Discipline: An EcoPragmatist Manifesto*. New York: Viking-Penguin.

Bruckner, P. 2013a. *The Fanaticism of the Apocalypse: Save the Earth, Punish Human Beings*. Cambridge, UK: Polity Press.

——— 2013b. Against environmental panic, *The Chronicle of Higher Education*, 17 June 2013.

Brunner, P. 2007. Reshaping urban metabolism, *Journal of Industrial Ecology*, 11 (2): 11–13.

Brunner, P. 2011. Urban mining: A contribution to reindustrializing the city, *Journal of Industrial Ecology*, 15 (3): 339–341.

Canada, S., Cohen, G., Cable, R., Brosseau, D. Price, H. 2005. Parabolic trough organic Rankine cycle solar power plant. Conference report NREL/CP-550–37077. Boulder, CO: National renewable Energy Laboratory.

Carson, R. 1962. *Silent Spring*. New York, NY: Houghton Mifflin.

Chang, I. C. and Sheppard, E. 2013. China's eco-cities as variegated urban sustainability: Dongtan eco-city and Chongming eco-island, *Journal of Urban Technology*, 20 (1): 57–75.

Charnovitz, S. and Fischer, C. 2015. *Canada – Renewable Energy*: Implications for WTO law on green and not-so-green subsidies, *World Trade Review*, 14 (2): 177–210.

Charnovitz, S. 2014. Green subsidies and the WTO, Policy Research Working Paper #7060. Washington, DC: World Bank.

Chaudhary, A., Krishna, C. and Sagar, A. 2015. Policy making for renewable energy in India: Lessons from wind and solar power sectors, *Climate Policy*, 15 (1): 58–67.

Cherp, A. and Jewell, J. 2011. The three perspectives on energy security: Intellectual history, disciplinary roots and the potential for integration, *Current Opinion in Environmental Sustainability*, 3: 202–212.

Chien, S. 2013. Chinese eco-cities: A perspective of land speculation-oriented local entrepreneurialism, *China Information*, 27 (2): 173–196.

Chien, S., Zhu, X. and Chen, T. 2015. Self-learning through teaching: Singapore's land development policy transfer experience in China, *Environment and Planning C: Government and Policy*, 33: 1639–1656.

Chufart-Finsterwald, S. 2014. Environmental technology transfer and dissemination under the UNFCCC: Achievements and new perspectives, *Environmental Claims Journal*, 26 (3): 238–260.

Cimino, C. and Hufbauer, G. 2014. Trade remedies: Targeting the renewable energy sector. Report on Green Economy and Trade, UNCTAD Ad hoc Expert Group 2: Trade remedies in green sectors: The case of renewables.

Cosbey, A. and Mavroidis, P. C. 2014. A turquoise mess: Green subsidies, blue industrial policy and renewable energy: The case for redrafting the subsidies agreement of the WTO, *Journal of International Economic Law*, 17, 11–47.

Crane, H., Kinderman, E. and Malhotra, R. 2010. *A Cubic Mile of Oil*. Oxford University Press USA.

Crutzen, P. J. 2002. Geology of mankind – the Anthropocene, *Nature*, 415: 23.

Cuvilas, C. A., Jirjis, R. and Lucas, C. 2010. Energy situation in Mozambique: A review, *Renewable and Sustainable Energy Reviews*, 14: 2139–2146.

Dai, Y. and Xue, L. 2015. China's policy initiatives for the development of wind energy technology, *Climate Policy*, 15 (1): 30–57.

De Connick, H. and Sagar, A. 2015. Making sense of policy for climate technology development and transfer, *Climate Policy*, 15 (1): 1–11.

Despommier, D. 2013. Farming up the city: The rise of urban vertical farms, *Trends in Biotechnology*, 31 (7): 388–389.

Desrochers, P. 2002a. Industrial ecology and the rediscovery of inter-firm recycling linkages: historical evidence and policy implications, *Industrial and Corporate Change*, 11 (5): 1031–1057.

Desrochers, P. 2002b. Cities and industrial symbiosis: Some historical perspectives and policy implications, *Journal of Industrial Ecology*, 5 (4): 29–44.

Desrochers, P. and Shimizu, H. 2012. *The Locavore's Dilemma: In Praise of the 10,000-Mile Diet*. New York: Public Affairs.

Dong, C., Shao, L., Fu, Y., Wang, M., Xie, B., Yu, J. and Liu, H. 2015. Evaluation of wheat growth, morphological characteristics, biomass yield and quality in Lunar Palace-1, plant factory, greenhouse and field systems, *Acta Astronautica*, 111 (May–June): 102–109.

Falconer, A. and Frisari, G. 2012. San Giorgio Group case study: Ouarzazate I CSP. Climate Policy Initiative, August 2012, Available at: http://climatepolicyinitiative. org/wp-content/uploads/2012/08/Ouarzazate-I-CSP.pdf.

Freeman, C. and Louça, F. 2001. *As Time Goes By: From the Industrial Revolutions to the Information Revolution*. Oxford: Oxford University Press.

Freeman, C. and Perez, C. 1988. Structural crises of adjustment: Business cycles and investment behaviour, in G. Dosi et al. (eds.), *Technical Change and Economic Theory*, pp. 38–61. London: Pinter Publishers.

Frey, C. 2016. Tackling climate change through the elimination of trade barriers for low-carbon goods: Multilateral, plurilateral and regional approaches. In V. Mauerhofer (ed.), *Legal Aspects of Sustainable Development*, Springer International, doi 10.1007/978-3-319-26021-1_22.

Frisari, G. and Falconer, A. 2013. San Giorgio Group case study: Ouarzazate I CSP Update. Climate Policy Initiative, available at: http://climatepolicyinitiative.org/ wp-content/uploads/2012/08/Ouarzazate-I-CSP-Update.pdf.

Fücks, R. 2015. *Green Growth, Smart Growth: A New Approach to Economics, Innovation and the Environment*. London: Anthem Press.

Gallagher, K. P. 2016. *The China Triangle: Latin America's China Boom and the Fate of the Washington Consensus*. New York: Oxford University Press.

Gerschenkron, A. 1962. *Economic Backwardness in Historical Perspective*. Chicago, IL: University of Chicago Press.

Goldstone, J. 2010. The new population bomb: The four megatrends that will change the world, *Foreign Affairs* (January–February).

Goldstone, J. A. 2002. Efflorescences and economic growth in world history: Rethinking the 'Rise of the West' and the Industrial Revolution, *Journal of World History*, 13 (2): 323–389.

Gottmann, J. 1961. *Megalopolis: The Urbanized Northeastern Seaboard of the United States*. New York: Twentieth Century Fund.

Green, F. and Stern, N. 2016. China's changing economy: Implications for its carbon dioxide emissions, *Climate Policy*, 16 March 2016, 1–21, at: http://www.tandfonline.com/doi/pdf/10.1080/14693062.2016.1156515.

Green, M. 2016. Revisiting the history books, *PV Magazine* (June): 96–101.

Grubb, M. with Hourcade, J,-C. and Neuhoff, K. 2014. *Planetary Economics: Energy, Climate Change and the Three Domains of Sustainable Development*. London: Routledge.

Grübler, A., Nakićenović, N. and Victor, D. 1999. Dynamics of energy technologies and global change, *Energy Policy*, 27: 247–280.

Guillén-Burrieza, E., Zaragoza, G., Miralles-Cuevas, S. and Blanco, J. 2012. Experimental evaluation of two pilot-scale membrane distillation modules used for solar desalination, *Journal of Membrane Science*, 409–410: 264–275.

Hall, P. 1996. *Cities of Tomorrow: An Intellectual History of Urban Planning and Design in the Twentieth Century* (updated edition). Oxford: Blackwell.

Harari, Y. N. 2014. *Sapiens: A Brief History of Humankind*. London: Vintage.

———— 2016. *Homo Deus: A Brief History of Tomorrow*. London: Vintage.

He, G., Avrin, A.-P., Nelson, J. H., Johnston, J., Mileva, A., Tian, J. and Kammen, D. M. 2016. SWITCH-China: A system approach to decarbonizing China's power system, *Environmental Science and Technology*, 50: 5467–5473.

Hodes, G. 2013. Perovskite-based solar cells, *Science*, 342 (6156): 317–318.

Hoornweg, D., Bhada-Tata, P., and Kennedy, C. 2013. Waste production must peak this century. *Nature* 502: 615–617.

Howse, R. 2010. Climate mitigation subsidies and the WTO legal framework: A policy analysis, Winnipeg, Manitoba: International Institute for Sustainable Development (2010).

Hu, M.-C. and Mathews, J. A. 2005. National innovative capacity in East Asia, *Research Policy*, 34 (9): 1322–1349.

Hu, M. C., Chen, Y. H. and Huang, L. C. 2014. A sustainable vegetable supply chain using plant factories in Taiwanese markets: A Nash-Cournot model, *International Journal of Production Economics*, 152 (June): 49–56.

Hu, M.-C., Wadin, J. L., Lo, H.-C. and Huang, J.-Y. 2016. Transformation toward an eco-city: lessons from three Asian cities, *Journal of Cleaner Production*, 123: 77–87.

Hughes, T. P. 1976. The science-technology interaction: The case of high-voltage power transmission systems, *Technology and Culture*, 17 (4): 646–662.

———— 1983. *Networks of Power: Electrification in Western Society, 1880–1930*. Baltimore, MD: Johns Hopkins University Press.

———— 1987. The evolution of large technological systems. In W. E. Bijker, T. P. Hughes and T. J. Pinch (eds), *The Social Construction of Technological Systems*, pp. 51–82. Cambridge, MA: MIT Press.

Huntington, S. P. 1993. The clash of civilizations? *Foreign Affairs*, 72 (3): 22–49.

ICTSD 2015. Climate change, trade, and sustainable energy: Post-2015 development agenda, Geneva: International Centre for Trade and Sustainable Development.

IEA 2007. *Contribution of Renewables to Energy Security*. Paris: International Energy Agency.

IPCC 2011. *Special Report on Renewable Energy Sources and Climate Change Mitigation*. UN: Intergovernmental Panel on Climate Change.

Jackson, T. 2009. *Prosperity without Growth: Economics for a Finite Planet*. London: Earthscan.

Jacobs, J. 1969. *The Economy of Cities*. New York: Random House.

Jacobson, M. Z. and Delucchi, M. A. 2011. Providing all global energy with wind, water and solar power, Pt 1: Technologies, energy resources, quantities and areas of infrastructure, and materials, *Energy Policy*, 39 (3): 1154–1169.

Jacobson, M. Z., Howarth, R. W., Delucchi, M. A., Scobie, S. R., Barth, J. M., Dvorak, M. J., Klevze, M., Katkhuda, H., Miranda, B., Chowdhury, N. A., Jones, R., Plano, L. and Ingraffea, A. R. 2013. Examining the feasibility of converting New York State's all-purpose energy infrastructure to one using wind, water and sunlight, *Energy Policy*, 57: 585–601.

Jänicke, M. 2008. Ecological modernisation: New perspectives, *Journal of Cleaner Production*, 16: 557–565.

———— 2012. 'Green growth': From a growing eco-industry to economic sustainability, *Energy Policy*, 48: 13–21.

Johnson, O. 2014. Promoting green industrial development through local content requirements: India's National Solar Mission, *Climate Policy*, doi: 10.1080/14693062.2014.992296.

Kaldor, N. 1970. The case for regional policies, *Scottish Journal of Political Economy*, 17: 337–348.

Kent, A. and Jha, V. 2014. Keeping up with the changing climate: The WTO's evolutive approach in response to the trade and climate conundrum, *The Journal of World Investment and Trade*, 15: 245–271.

Kim, S. Y. and Thurbon, E. 2015. Developmental environmentalism: Explaining South Korea's ambitious pursuit of green growth, *Politics and Society*, 43(2): 213–240.

Klare, M. T., 2012. *The Race for What's Left: The Global Scramble for the World's Last Resources*. New York: Metropolitan Books.

Korotayev, A., Goldstone, J. A. and Zinkina, J. 2015. Phases of global demographic transition correlate with phases of the Great Divergence and Great Convergence, *Technological Forecasting & Social Change*, 95: 163–169.

Korotayev, A. V. and Tsirel, S. V. 2010 A spectral analysis of world GDP dynamics: Kondratieff waves, Kuznets swings, Juglar and Kitchin cycles in global economic development, and the 2008–2009 economic crisis, *Structure and Dynamics*, 4 (1): http://escholarship.org/uc/item/9jv108xp.

Krook, J. and Baas, L. 2013. Getting serious about mining the technosphere: A review of recent landfill mining and urban mining research, *Journal of Cleaner Production*, 55: 1–9.

Kruyt, B., van Vuuren, D. P., de Vries, H. J. M. and Groenenberg, H. 2009. Indicators for energy security, *Energy Policy*, 37: 2166–2181.

Kumar, K. S., Tiwari, K. N. and Jha, M. K. 2009. Design and technology for greenhouse cooling in tropical and subtropical regions: A review, *Energy and Buildings*, 41: 1269–1275.

Kuntze, J.-C. and Moerenhout, T. 2013. Local content requirements and the renewable energy industry – a good match? Geneva: ICTSD.

——— 2014. Are feed-in tariff schemes with local content requirements consistent with WTO law? In F. Baetens and J. Caiado (eds), *Frontiers of International Economic Law: Legal Tools to Confront Interdisciplinary Challenges*. Nijhoff, The Netherlands: Brill (Society of International Economic Law).

Lam, D. 2011. How the world survived the Population Bomb: Lessons from 50 years of extraordinary demographic history, *Demography*, 48 (4): 1231–1262.

Leal-Arcas, R. and Filis, A. 2015. Renewable energy disputes in the World Trade Organization, *Oil, Gas and Energy Law Intelligence*, 13 (3): 1–51.

Lema, R. and Lema, A. 2012. Technology transfer? The rise of China and India in green technology sectors, *Innovation and Development*, 2 (1): 23–44.

Leung, G. C. K. 2011. China's energy security: Perception and reality, *Energy Policy*, 39: 1330–1337.

Lewis, N. S. 2016. Research opportunities to advance solar energy utilization, *Science*, 351 (6271) (22 January 2016): doi: 10.1126/science.aad1920.

Li, J. 2015. Wastes could be resources and cities could be mines, *Waste Management & Research*, 33 (4): 301–302.

Li, J., Zeng, X., Chen, M., Ogunsitan, O. A. and Stevels, A. 2015. 'Control-Alt-Delete': Rebooting solutions for the e-waste problem, *Environmental Science & Technology*, 49: 7095–7108.

Lin, Yifu 2003. Development strategy, viability, and economic convergence, *Economic Development and Cultural Change*, 53: 277–308.

Liu, Zhenya 2015. *Global Energy Interconnection*. Cambridge, MA: Academic Press.

Lovelock, J. 1995. *The Ages of Gaia: A Biography of Our Living Earth*. New York: W.W. Norton.

——— 2010. *The Vanishing Face of Gaia: A Final Warning*. New York: Basic Books.

——— 2015. *A Rough Ride to the Future*. New York: Overlook Press.

Lovelock, J. and Margulis, L. 1974. Atmospheric homeostasis by and for the biosphere: The Gaia hypothesis, *Tellus*, 26 (1/2): 1–10.

Lovins, A. 1976. Energy strategy: The road not taken, *Foreign Affairs*, 55 (1): 65–96.

Low, P., Marceau, G. and Reinaud, J. 2012. The interface between the trade and climate regimes: Scoping the issues, *Journal of World Trade*, 46, 485–544.

Mahmoudi, H., Abdul-Wahab, S. A., Goosen, M. F. A., Sablani, S. S., Perret, J., Ouagued, A. and Spahis, N. 2008. Weather data and analysis of hybrid photovoltaic-wind power generation systems adapted to a seawater greenhouse desalination unit designed for arid coastal countries, *Desalination*, 222: 119–127.

Mathews, F. 2011. Towards a deeper philosophy of biomimicry, *Organization & Environment*, 24 (4): 364–387.

Mathews, F. 2016. From biodiversity-based conservation to an ethic of bioproportionality, *Biological Conservation*, 200: 140–148.

Mathews, J. A. 2008a. Energizing industrial development, *Transnational Corporations*, 17 (3): 59–84.

———— 2008b. Towards a sustainably certifiable futures contract for biofuels, *Energy Policy*, 36 (5): 1577–1583.

———— 2009. China, India and Brazil: Tiger Technologies, Dragon Multinationals and the building of National Systems of Economic Learning, *Asian Business and Management*, 8 (1): 5–32.

———— 2010. Designing energy industries for the next industrial revolution, *Organizational Dynamics*, 39 (2): 155–164.

———— 2011. Naturalizing capitalism: The next Great Transformation, *Futures*, 43: 868–879.

———— 2012. Green growth strategies: Korea's initiatives, *Futures*, 44: 761–769.

———— 2013a. The renewable energies technology surge: A new techno-economic paradigm in the making? *Futures*, 46: 10–22.

———— 2013b. Greening of development strategies, *Seoul Journal of Economics*, 26 (2): 147–172.

———— 2015. *Greening of Capitalism: How Asia Is Driving the Next Great Transformation*. Redwood City: CA: Stanford University Press.

———— 2016a. Competing principles driving energy futures: Fossil fuel decarbonization vs. manufacturing learning curves, *Futures* (84): 1–11.

———— 2016b. Global trade and promotion of cleantech industry: A post-Paris agenda, *Climate Policy*, published online at: http://www.tandfonline.com/doi/full/10.1080/14693062.2016.1215286.

Mathews, J. A. and Kidney, S. 2012. Financing climate-friendly energy development through bonds, *Development Southern Africa*, 29 (2): 337–349.

Mathews, J. A. and Reinert, E. S. 2014. Renewables, manufacturing and green growth: Energy strategies based on capturing increasing returns, *Futures*, 61: 13–22.

Mathews, J. A. and Tan, H. 2011. Progress towards a Circular Economy in China: Drivers (and inhibitors) of eco-industrial initiative, *Journal of Industrial Ecology*: 15 (3): 435–457.

———— 2014. Manufacture renewables to build energy security, *Nature*, 513 (11 September): 166–168.

———— 2015. *China's Renewable Energy Revolution*, London: Palgrave Macmillan.

———— 2016. Circular Economy: Lessons from China, *Nature*, 331 (24 March): 440–442.

Mathews, J. A., Hu, M.-C. and Wu, C.-W. 2011. Fast-follower industrial dynamics: The case of Taiwan's Solar PV industry, *Industry and Innovation*, 18 (2): 177–202.

Mathews, J. A., Hu, M.-C. and Tan, H. 2016. Low-carbon cities: The Chinese experience. In Shobhakar Dhakal (ed.), *Low-Carbon Cities*. Heidelberg: Springer eBooks.

Mathews, J. A., Tang, Y. and Tan, H. 2011. China's move to a Circular Economy as a development strategy, *Asian Business & Management*, 10: 463–484.

Mattoo, A. and Subramanian, A. 2012. *Greenprint: A New Approach to Cooperation on Climate Change*. Washington, DC: Center for Global Development.

———— 2013. Four changes to trade rules to facilitate climate change action. CGD Policy paper 021. Washington, DC: Center for Global Development.

McCloskey, D. 2016. Explaining the Great Enrichment: A humanistic and social scientific account, *Scandinavian Economic History Review*, 64 (1): 6–18.

Mokyr, J. 1990. *The Lever of Riches: Technological Creativity and Economic Progress.* Oxford: Oxford University Press.

——— 2016. *A Culture of Growth: The Origins of the Modern Economy.* Princeton, NJ: Princeton University Press.

Mol, A. P. J. 2006. Environment and modernity in transitional China: Frontiers of ecological modernization, *Development and Change*, 37 (1): 29–56.

Mol, A. P. J. and Sonnenfeld, D. A. (eds) 2000. *Ecological Modernisation Around the World: Perspectives and Critical Debates.* London: Routledge.

Morris, I. 2015. *Foragers, Farmers and Fossil Fuels: How Human Values Evolve.* Princeton, NJ: Princeton University Press.

Morris, C. and Pehnt, M. 2012. *Energy Transition: The German* Energiewende. Berlin: Heinrich Boell Foundation.

Moser, M., Trieb, F. and Kern, J. 2010. Combined water and electricity production on industrial scale in the MENA countries with concentrating solar power. Paper presented at the 6th Euromed conference, 2010.

Mumford, L. 1961. *The City in History: Its Origins, Its Transformations, and Its Prospects.* New York: Harcourt, Brace & World.

Ng, S., Mabey, N. and Gaventa, J. 2016. Pulling ahead on clean technology: China's 13th Five Year Plan challenges Europe's low carbon competitiveness. London: E3G.

Nykvist, B. and Nilsson, M. 2015. Rapidly falling costs of battery packs for electric vehicles, *Nature Climate Change*, 5: 329–332.

Ortman, S. G., Cabaniss, A. H. F., Sturm, J. O. and Bettencourt, L. M. A. 2015. Settlement scaling and increasing returns in an ancient society, *Science Advances*, at: http://advances.sciencemag.org/content/1/1/e1400066.full.pdf+html.

Palenzuela, P., Zaragoza, G., Alarcón-Padilla, D., Guillén, E. and Ibarra, M. 2011. Assessment of different configurations for combined parabolic-trough (PT) solar power and desalination plants in arid regions, *Energy*, 36: 4950–4958.

Perez, C. 2010. Technological revolutions and techno-economic paradigms, *Cambridge Journal of Economics*, 34: 185–202.

Polanyi, K. 1944/1957/2001. *The Great Transformation: The Political and Economic Origins of Our Time* (Foreword Joseph E. Stiglitz; Introduction Fred Block). Boston, MA: Beacon Press.

Pomeranz, K. 2000. *The Great Divergence: China, Europe and the Making of the Modern World Economy.* Princeton, NJ: Princeton University Press.

Rachman, G. 2016. *Easternisation: War and Peace in the Asian Century.* London Bodley Head.

Register, R. 1987. *Ecocity Berkeley: Building Cities for a Healthy Future.* Berkeley, CA: North Atlantic Books.

——— 2006. *Ecocities: Rebuilding Cities in Balance with Nature.* Gabriola Island, BC: New Society Publishers.

Reinert, E. 2007. *How Rich Countries Got Rich … and Why Poor Countries Stay Poor.* London: Constable.

Renn, O. and Marshall, J. P. 2016. Coal, nuclear and renewable energy policies in Germany: From the 1950s to the 'Energiewende', *Energy Policy*, 99 (c): 224–232.

Rennkamp, B. and Boyd, A. 2015. Technological capability and transfer for achieving South Africa's development goals, *Climate Policy*, 15 (1): 12–29.

Resnick, D., Tarp, F. and Thurlow, J. 2012. The political economy of green growth: Cases from Southern Africa, *Public Administration and Development*, 32: 215–228.

Rifkin, J. 2013. *The Third Industrial Revolution: How Lateral Power Is Transforming Energy, the Economy, and the World*. New York: St. Martin's Griffin.

———— 2014. *The Zero Marginal Cost Society: The Internet of Things, the Collaborative Commons, and the Eclipse of Capitalism*. New York: St. Martin's Press.

Rippy, M. 1972. *Oil and the Mexican Revolution*. Leiden: Brill.

Rosenstein-Rodan, P. N. 1943. Problems of industrialisation in Eastern and South-Eastern Europe, *Economic Journal* 53 (210/211) (June–Sep.): 202–211.

Rubini, L. 2012. *Ain't wastin' time no more*: Subsidies for renewable energy, the SCM agreement, policy space, and law reform, *Journal of International Economic Law*, 15: 525–579.

Rutledge, I. 2006. *Addicted to Oil: America's Relentless Drive for Energy Security*. London: I. B. Tauris.

Sanderson, H. and Forsythe, M. 2013. *China's Superbank: Debt, Oil and Influence – How China Development Bank Is Rewriting the Rules of Finance*. New York: Bloomberg Press.

Scheer, H. 2011. *The Energy Imperative: 100 Percent Renewable Now*. Abingdon: Earthscan/Routledge.

Schumpeter, J. A. 1912/1934. *The Theory of Economic Development: An Inquiry into Profits, Capital, Credit, Interest and the Business Cycle*. Boston, MA: Harvard University Press.

———— 1928. The instability of capitalism, *The Economic Journal*, 38 (151): 361–386.

———— 1947. *Capitalism, Socialism and Democracy*. New York: Harper.

Schwab, K. 2015. *The Fourth Industrial Revolution*. Davos, Switzerland: World Economic Forum.

Scott, C. A., Kurian, M. and Westcoat, J. L. 2014. The water-energy-food nexus: Enhancing adaptive capacity to complex global challenges. In M. Kurian and R. Ardakanian (eds), *Governing the Nexus*, pp. 15–18. Dordrecht: Springer.

Shatat, M., Worall, M. and Riffat, S. 2013. Opportunities for solar water desalination worldwide: Review, *Sustainable Cities and Society*, 9: 67–80.

Shellenberger, M., Nordhaus, T., Navin, J., Norris, T. and Van Noppen, A. 2008. Fast, clean and cheap: Cutting global warming's Gordian Knot, *Harvard Law and Policy Review*, 2 (1): 93–118.

Sieferle, R.-P. 1982/2010. *The Subterranean Forest: Energy Systems and Industrial Revolution*. (Translated by Michael Osmann. Second paperback edition.) Isle of Harris, UK: White Horse Press.

Smalley, R. E. 2005. Future global energy prosperity: The terawatt challenge, *MRS Bulletin*, 30 (June): 412–417.

Smil, V. 2005. *Energy at the Crossroads: Global Perspectives and Uncertainties*. Cambridge, MA: MIT Press.

Sohn, Y. (ed.) 2004. *Japanese Industrial Governance: Protectionism and the Licensing State*. London: Routledge/Curzon.

Sonneveld, P. J., Swinkels, G. L. A. M., Bot, G. P. A. and Flamand, G. 2010. Feasibility study for combining cooling and high grade energy production in a solar greenhouse, *Biosystems Engineering*, 105: 51–58.

Sovacool, B. and Brown, M. A. 2010. Competing dimensions of energy security: An international perspective, *Annual Review of Environment and Resources*, 35: 77–108.

Sovacool, B. and Bulan, L. C. 2012. Energy security and hydropower development in Malaysia: The drivers and challenges facing the Sarawak Corridor of Renewable Energy (SCORE), *Energy Policy*, 40: 113–129.

Spaargaren, G. and Mol, A. P. J. 1992. Sociology, environment, and modernity: Ecological modernization as a theory of social change, *Society & Natural Resources: An International Journal*, 5 (4): 323–344.

Spence, M. 2011a. *The Next Convergence: The Future of Economic Growth in a Multispeed World*. New York, NY: Farrar, Straus and Giroux.

Spence, M. 2011b. Asia's new growth model, Project Syndicate (1 June 2011), available at: http://www.project-syndicate.org/commentary/spence23/English (accessed 18 June 2011).

Stadelmann, M., Frisari, G. and Rosenberg, A. 2014. The role of public finance in CSP: Lessons learned. San Giorgio Group Policy brief. Climate Policy Initiative, available at: http://climatepolicyinitiative.org/wp-content/uploads/2014/06/The-Role-of-Public-Finance-in-CSP-Lessons-Learned.pdf.

Steffen, W., Broadgate, W., Deutsch, L., Gaffney, O. and Ludwig, C. 2015. The trajectory of the Anthropocene: The Great Acceleration, *The Anthropocene Review*, 2 (1): 81–98.

Steffen, W., Crutzen, P. and McNeill, J. R. 2007. The Anthropocene: Are humans now overwhelming the great forces of Nature? *Ambio*, 36 (8): 614–621.

Sun, Z.-C., Yu, Q.-L. and Han, L. 2015. The environmental prospects of cultured meat in China, *Journal of Integrative Agriculture*, 14 (2): 234–240.

Sze, J. 2015. *Fantasy Islands: Chinese Dreams and Ecological Fears in an Age of Climate Crisis*. Oakland: University of California Press.

Thurbon, E. 2016. *Developmental Mindset: The Revival of Financial Activism in South Korea*. Ithaca, NY: Cornell University Press.

Toner, P. 2001. 'History versus equilibrium' and the theory of economic growth, by Mark Setterfield: A comment, *Cambridge Journal of Economics*, 25 (1): 97–102.

Trieb, F., Mueller-Steinhagen, H., Kern, J., Scharfe, J., Kabariti, M. and Al Taher, A. 2009. Technologies for large-scale seawater desalination using concentrated solar radiation, *Desalination*, 235: 33–43.

Tuomisto, H. L. and Texeira Mattos, M. J. 2011. Environmental impacts of cultured meat production, *Environmental Science & Technology*, 45: 6117–6123.

Unruh, G. C. 2002. Escaping carbon lock-in, *Energy Policy*, 30 (4): 317–325.

Voituriez, T. and Wang, X. 2015. Real challenges behind the EU-China PV trade dispute settlement, *Climate Policy*, 15 (5): 670–677.

Weiss, L. 2014. *America, Inc? Innovation and Enterprise in the National Security State*. Ithaca, NY: Cornell University Press.

Wilson, E. O. 2016. *Half-Earth: Our Planet's Fight for Life*. New York: Liveright (W. W. Norton).

World Bank 2012. *Renewable Energy Desalination: An Emerging Solution to Close the Water Gap in the Middle East and North Africa*. Washington, DC: The World Bank.

Wrigley, E. A. 2013. Energy and the English Industrial Revolution, *Philosophical Transactions of the Royal Society A*, 371: 201106568 (pp. 1–10).

WTO 2011. *Harnessing Trade for Sustainable Development and a Green Economy*. Geneva: World Trade Organization.

——— 2014. Canada: Measures relating to the Feed-in Tariff program, Implementation notified by respondent, 15 June 2014. Geneva, World Trade Organization. See text at: https://www.wto.org/english/tratop_e/dispu_e/cases_e/ds426_e.htm.

——— 2016. Dispute DS456, India – Certain Measures Relating to Solar Cells and Solar Modules. Geneva: WTO, at: https://www.wto.org/english/tratop_e/dispu_e/cases_e/ds456_e.htm.

Wu, M. and Salzman, J. 2014. The next generation of trade and environment conflicts: The rise of green industrial policy, *Northwestern University Law Review*, 108 (2): 401–474.

Yergin, D. 1988. Energy security in the 1990s. *Foreign Affairs*, 67 (1): 110–132.

——— 2006. Ensuring energy security, *Foreign Affairs*, 85 (2): 69–82.

Youn, H., Bettencourt, L. M. A., Lobo, J., Strumsky, D., Samaniego, H. and West, G. B. 2016. Scaling and universality in urban diversification, *Interface (Journal of the Royal Society)*, 13: 1–7, 20150937. http://dx.doi.org/ 10.1098/rsif.2015.0937.

Young, A. 1928. Increasing returns and economic progress, *The Economic Journal*, 38 (152): 527–542.

Zaragoza, G., Bucholz, M., Jochum, P. and Pérez-Parra, J. 2007. Watergy project: Towards a rational use of water in greenhouse agriculture and sustainable architecture, *Desalination*, 211: 296–303.

Zenghelis, D. 2012. A strategy for restoring confidence and economic growth through green investment and innovation. Policy brief. Grantham Research Institute, London School of Economics; Centre for Climate Change Economics and Policy, University of Leeds.

Zhang, W. and White, S. 2016. Overcoming the liability of newness: Entrepreneurial action and the emergence of China's private solar photovoltaic firms, *Research Policy*, 45 (3): 604–617.

Zysman, J. and Huberty, M. 2011. *Green Growth: From Religion to Reality*. Berkeley, CA: Berkeley Roundtable on the International Economy.

——— 2013. *Can Green Sustain Growth? From the Religion to the Reality of Sustainable Prosperity*. Stanford, CA: Stanford University Press.

INDEX

Lightning Source UK Ltd.
Milton Keynes UK
UKHW011321280819
348692UK00001B/176/P

9 781783 086412